You Are There *teleplays*
The Critical Edition

The Center for Telecommunication Studies
Film as Literature Series

You Are There *teleplays*
The Critical Edition

by
Abraham Polonsky

Critical Commentary by
John Schultheiss

Edited by
John Schultheiss
and
Mark Schaubert

The Center for Telecommunication Studies
California State University, Northridge

DEDICATION

This book is dedicated to Charles W. Russell, the creative producer of *You Are There*, who provided a world of rational life in a time of hysterical nonsense, danger, and personal timidity.

—Abraham Polonsky

YOU ARE THERE teleplays are printed with the permission of Abraham Polonsky and CBS News, a division of CBS Inc.

PRINTED IN THE USA
REVISED EDITION
1997
previous edition 0-9635823-0-5

Published by
The Center for Telecommunication Studies
California State University, Northridge
18111 Nordhoff Street
Northridge, CA 91330
with assistance from
Sadanlaur Publications
Los Angeles, California

ISBN 0-9635823-2-1
Library of Congress Catalog Card Number 97-067547

Contents

Introduction

Back in the early fifties, if you were young, bookish and inclined toward the arts, history or politics and if your parents or next-door neighbors could afford a television set, you probably devoted yourself to CBS between the hours of 5:00 and 7:30 p.m. on Sunday. *Omnibus, You Are There* and *See It Now* (1952-53) or *Quiz Kids* (1953-54) drew many of us from the playground and kept others of us from the dinner table. We quickly developed viewing habits bordering on the slavish.

For me, the show of shows in those long-ago days was *You Are There*. Sunday after Sunday I thrilled to the voice of Walter Cronkite asking, "What sort of a day was it?" And answering, "A day like all days, filled with those events that alter and illuminate our times. And you were there!" And I was! I was there when Troy fell, when Socrates drank the cup of hemlock, when Caesar was assassinated, when Joan was burned at the stake, when Lee surrendered to Grant.

Sunday evenings became a magic carpet, wafting me through the screen of our Motorola console and into the time warp of dramatic historical events.

—Larry Ceplair
"Great Shows: *You Are There*"

Larry Ceplair expresses the pleasurable feelings of many about this marvelous show. But while the nostalgia level is indeed high, for the editors of this volume (as for Ceplair), a deeper analytical interest resides in the political irony that this show which depicted historical events was written by men—Walter Bernstein, Arnold Manoff, and Abraham Polonsky—who had been denied their livelihood (blacklisted) as screen and television writers because their values, ideologies and interpretations of political events had been deemed a threat to the American way of life. The presence of these writers on the show had profound artistic and political influence. As Walter Bernstein puts it (*Inside Out: A Memoir of the Blacklist*, 1996), "We wanted to tell the truth about history so far as we could learn it through research, to show the reasons behind the event. Our agenda was to pick subjects that, if possible, had some bearing on what was happening in the world today."

The focus of this volume is on Abraham Polonsky's work for the series. Ten of his most provocative teleplays are printed here to elucidate those noted political ironies. These scripts provide an extraordinary opportunity for textual analysis, as this blacklisted writer has imbued each historical reconstruction with contemporary significance.

This work for television is remarkably congruent with the thematic and philosophical concerns of Polonsky's distinguished literary and film accomplishments. Through each of his novels and feature films, Polonsky has always conducted a campaign against social and political intolerance. In *You Are There* he and his colleagues were able to fight "a kind of guerrilla war against McCarthyism." Accordingly, the critical commentaries and the prefaces place the television work within the context of Polonsky's entire career.

You Are There was, in Ceplair's words, "a crucible in which were forged several illustrious careers." In addition to the three blacklisted writers, these artists include: producer Charles W. Russell, who went on to produce *The Untouchables* and *Naked City*; designer Bob Markell, who subsequently produced *The Defenders* and *NYPD*; assistant director John Frankenheimer, who has directed over 29 movies; and director Sidney Lumet, a consummate professional of "awe-inspiring vitality, one of the most productive and respected directors in film and television."

Here is Sidney Lumet's perspective, written specifically for this volume:

One could always tell when a script arrived from Abe. There was a flow to the dialogue and a beauty in the language that was completely rare in most American scripts. In addition, he was one of the few writers who could write believable European period dialogue without it sounding silly.

At the beginning of the blacklist, when Charlie Russell hinted that we might be getting scripts from "other" sources, I thought he meant only Walter Bernstein. At the time, I didn't know of the triumvirate of Bernstein, Polonsky, and Manoff (it sounds like a law firm). But when the amount of scripts reached the level it did, I asked Charlie how Walter could keep up with such a schedule. It was then he told me about the other two. There was no concern about using the three blacklisted writers except there would have been a real danger if any word had gotten out. One of our sponsors was "America's Electric Light & Power Companies." I never knew who they were, but by their name, it seemed to me they must have been a powerful Washington lobby group who would not have been thrilled at the news. In addition, many of the subjects were, by their nature, political—"Cortez Conquers Mexico" was clearly about imperialism, "The Crisis of Galileo" about recanting, "The Vindication of Savonarola" about the suppression of art— and if word got out, all sorts of idiotic charges of red propaganda would have been leveled at the show. I remember we did "The Crisis of Galileo" much around the time that Ed Murrow did his explosive show about Joe McCarthy. As far as I know, these were the first shows to speak out against the madness that was overrunning the country.

One of the sadnesses was that I couldn't meet with any of the writers. Contact was kept at an absolute minimum so that Charlie Russell was the connection. I had known Walter Bernstein and of course saw him socially during this period. But I had never met Polonsky. The level of sheer writing was so high that to some degree the shows almost directed themselves. Good words were not to be found easily in television scripts.

One reading of Polonsky's work will not only tell you what we missed when this marvelous writer was caged but also what we gained, and why that time is still referred to as the Golden Age of Television.

—Sidney Lumet
1997

Viewed today, the show's quality is unmistakable and enduring. The ideas were well selected, the stories and locales were exhaustively researched, and the scripts were exceptionally written, using, whenever available, the actual words of the characters. While it lasted, it stood as a monument to the vision and courage of Charles Russell—to whom this book is dedicated—and the talents of an extraordinary crew. "It was," says Russell, "a happy coincidence of friends, good writers, a new show and my desire not to participate in the climate of fear."

Abraham Lincoln Polonsky

A Season of Fear:
Abraham Polonsky, *You Are There*, and the Blacklist

by
John Schultheiss

What sort of a day was it? A day like all days, filled with those events that alter and illuminate our time . . . and YOU WERE THERE.
> —Tag line for each *You Are There* episode, written by Abraham Polonsky

You Are There was a television version (1953-1957) of a successful radio series (1947-1950) created by Goodman Ace. It attempted to faithfully reconstruct history, drawing on authentic primary sources and actual quotations, by employing the device of cameras and television journalists reporting on significant past events as currently breaking stories. Important historical figures like Galileo or Sigmund Freud were interviewed by CBS reporters as though the event were happening now. "Each program was to be a dramatic recreation of a specific personal moment in history. Authentic and specific, no speculation. Any political statements had to be relevant to the time."[1]

The shows utilized reporters from the CBS News Department to provide coverage and interviews. To the great advantage of the program, the following top-level newsmen were regularly featured: Harry Marble, Don Hollenbeck, Edward P. Morgan, Winston Burdett, Ned Calmer, Lou Cioffi, Charles Collingwood, Allan Jackson, Bill Leonard (later to become the head of CBS News), Mike Wallace, and Walter Cronkite, the anchor who provided opening and closing commentaries.

Sidney Lumet (*12 Angry Men, The Pawnbroker*) directed the shows (presented live during 1953-1954, on film from 1955 on), with John Frankenheimer (*The Manchurian Candidate, Seven Days in May*) as assistant director for many episodes. The list of distinguished actors who appeared on the show included: Paul Newman, James Dean, Rod Steiger, Kim Stanley, E.G. Marshall, Richard Kiley, John Cassavetes, Beatrice Straight, Lorne Greene, Robert Culp, Leslie Nielsen, Joseph Wiseman, James Gregory, Philip Borneuf, Barry Jones, Robert Middleton, William Prince, Mildred Dunnock.

Perhaps the most indispensable protagonist was Charles W. Russell. Russell (a film actor in *The Purple Heart* and *The Late George Apley*, a radio actor in *Yours Truly, Johnny Dollar*) was the producer and something of a hero of what would turn out to be the extraordinarily daring cultural adventure of *You Are There*. He had always considered himself apolitical, but he now became involved in events that had tangible social and political reverberations.

Russell really had begun it all by employing three blacklisted writers to provide teleplays, under the cover of fronts, for another television series he was producing called *Danger* (1951-1954; see Appendix I). These writers were: Walter Bernstein *(The Front, Fail Safe, The Molly Maguires)*, Arnold Manoff (a novelist, *Telegram from Heaven*, and noted short story writer, "All You Need Is One Good Break"), and Abraham Polonsky. The programs were very successful, and CBS offered Russell and Lumet the *You Are There* series to produce and direct.

Russell's relationship with the blacklisted writers continued over into the new series, with the full knowledge that his own career would be in jeopardy if his association with them were to be revealed. And, in spite of his apolitical self-characterization, Russell admits, in his autobiographical retelling of the *You Are There* story ("In the Worst of Times It Was the Best of Times"), to having asked the Polonsky-Manoff-Bernstein trio, "Listen, I don't want to know what your private political beliefs are. All I want to know is, do you want to overthrow the government, the country?"

"No," was the reply. "We just want to overthrow CBS."[2]

As a *metaphoric* response to the blacklist era they did just that. Polonsky, Bernstein, and Manoff became the chief writers of *You Are There*, which premiered on CBS-TV in 1953. Most of the scripts that they wrote, with Russell's acquiescence, made the show, according to Polonsky, "probably the only place where any guerrilla warfare was conducted against McCarthy in a public medium."[3]

Walter Bernstein, in *Inside Out: A Memoir of the Blacklist*, underscores this notion:

History served us well. We had no need to invent conflicts to serve our purpose. They were there for the taking and we happily and conscientiously took them. In that shameful time of McCarthyite terror, of know-nothing attempts to deform and defile history, to kill any kind of dissent, we were able to do shows about civil liberties, civil rights, artistic freedom, the Bill of Rights. . . . We wrote and Russell produced and Lumet directed a dramatic program in which we tried our best to celebrate the human spirit, to show the forces that throughout history tried to stunt and oppress that spirit, to explain as clearly as we could its victories and its defeats. We never tried to shape history to prove a political point. What was important was the subject matter.[4]

These three men selected historical events to be dramatized which could serve to illuminate what was going on in Cold-War America. In Abraham Polonsky's words:

We were making history comprehensible in terms of what we thought was significant at that time--without distorting history to do it! We said that history, if it's treated with accuracy as best as we could research it and find it, would achieve whatever aim history should achieve; that is, to tell the reasons for what happened in history. The show was deliberately political--but it was not political propaganda. And there's a difference in that. In propaganda you deliberately and consciously have a message that you want people to understand and for which you find illustrations. What we did was political interpretation. And in the interpretation you try to make it dramatically flow out of the natural historical conflict that existed. You can decide for yourself, in terms of what your aims in life are, whether lessons can be drawn from that. But I can't make it strong enough that we really tried to make these things as accurate as we could insofar as the research demonstrated what happened in history.[5]

Thus, there is a level of ironic fascination surrounding the fact that shows with such redolent historical themes were being authored by men who had been denied their livelihood as screen and television writers, "because their values and ideologies and interpretations of political events had been deemed subversive of the American ethos."[6]

To Illuminate Our Time:
Abraham Polonsky's Existential Response

A Season of Fear is Abraham Polonsky's metaphor for political repression. It is the title of his 1956 blacklist novel, which crystallizes the existential attitude that pervades his significant writings:

> In today's world every man has the expectation of becoming a refugee. You can even be a refugee in your own country, or should I say especially in your own country? Well, a refugee can retain his dignity only by becoming an exile, a man who passionately struggles to return home, to overturn the government which has banished him or pursued him. A man must love his native land and refuse to give it up.[7]

The author of these words, which were written from the perspective of an outcast during the Cold War, is the same Polonsky who is openly acknowledged as the creator of two cinema classics: *Body and Soul* (1947), which essentially defined the Hollywood boxing movie, and *Force of Evil* (1948), a film noir/social problem film/cult phenomenon of enduring celebrity. This is the same writer-director of *Tell Them Willie Boy Is Here* (1969), a post-blacklisting story with rich autobiographical resonances, which deals with a renegade American Indian's struggle against the white man's oppressive authority.[8]

It is known that Polonsky was blacklisted for seventeen years—from *I Can Get It for You Wholesale* (1951), the last screen credit under his own name, until *Madigan* (1968). What is not so openly acknowledged is the work which he created during this period utilizing pseudonyms or "fronts." Most noteworthy of the produced writings are:

- A feature-length screenplay for *Odds Against Tomorrow* (1959, directed by Robert Wise). The original writing credit was "signed" by John O. Killens and Nelson Gidding, but in August 1996 Polonsky's author credit was restored to him by the Writers Guild.
- The teleplays under discussion for *You Are There*. Here the writing credits were attributed to fronts "Jeremy Daniel," "Leo Davis," or "Dunn Barrie."

This is work which has acquired a critical cachet of its own: *Odds Against Tomorrow* was embraced by the *Cahiers du Cinema* critics—one of the three all-time favorite films, along with *The Best Years of Our Lives* and *The Asphalt Jungle*, of the great French film maker, Jean-Pierre Melville; while the *You Are There* series enjoys classic standing from the television "Golden Age," with two Emmy Awards and a Peabody Award for Outstanding Achievement in Education.[9]

He was called "the most dangerous man in America" by Congressman Harold H. Velde during Polonsky's appearance before the House Un-American Activities Committee (HUAC) on 25 April 1951, a characterization prompted by his awareness of Polonsky's "Black Radio" activities for the Office of Strategic Services (OSS—now the CIA) during WWII. And yet here is Polonsky in the 1950's writing the screenplay text for a United Artists feature film on racial intolerance, and providing regular commentaries (via the *You Are There* teleplays) on intellectual and political freedom in a dominant electronic medium for major capitalist sponsors—the CBS Television Network, the Prudential Insurance Company of America, and America's Electric Light and Power Companies. The exile strikes back.

Chapter One. The Polonsky-Bernstein-Manoff-Russell unit worked on *You Are There* from the premiere episode, "The Landing of the Hindenburg" (air date: 1 February 1953) to "The Triumph of Alexander the Great" (air date: 27 March 1955), the last filmed New York show. (Both were Polonsky scripts; front name for both: "Jeremy Daniel"). During the residency of this artistic group, topics for the shows were chosen from historical events which seemed to provide the greatest potential for the exploration of the themes of political and religious intolerance and censorship—challenges to moral and intellectual freedom—the very challenges which the writers themselves felt they were confronting from their situation as blacklisted artists. Abraham Polonsky:

> *You Are There* is based on historical incidents and famous people in general. But the minute we three start to work on it, they get to be *certain kinds of famous people* whose historical significance depends on the kind of events that were then [in the 1950s] dominating American society and life. The reinterpretation of history in terms of the present is the role of all historians: what does it mean, what does it signify today.
>
> (Polonsky, Interview with Author, 15 July 1989)

This multilayered approach to the selection of symbolically rich themes is quite evident from even a brief sketch of some of the shows written by the blacklisted trio:

"The Execution of Joan of Arc" by Abraham Polonsky
    (front: Jeremy Daniel), air date: 1 March 1953
"The Witch Trial at Salem" by Arnold Manoff
    (front: Kate Nickerson), air date: 29 March 1953
"The Impeachment of Andrew Johnson" by Walter Bernstein
    (front: Leslie Slote), air date: 12 April 1953
"The Crisis of Galileo" by Abraham Polonsky
    (Jeremy Daniel), air date: 19 April 1953
"The Death of Socrates" by Arnold Manoff
    (Kate Nickerson), air date: 3 May 1953
"The Dreyfus Case" by Walter Bernstein
    (Leslie Slote), air date: 31 May 1953
"The Vindication of Savonarola" by Abraham Polonsky
    (Jeremy Daniel), air date: 13 December 1953
"The Trial of Peter Zenger" by Arnold Manoff
    (Kate Nickerson), air date: 7 March 1954
"The Scopes Trial" by Abraham Polonsky
    (Jeremy Daniel), air date: 16 May 1954
"The Passage of the Bill of Rights" by Arnold Manoff
    (Kate Nickerson), air date: 26 December 1954
"The Trial of Susan B. Anthony" by Arnold Manoff
    (Kate Nickerson), air date: 23 January 1955
"The Tragedy of John Milton" by Abraham Polonsky
    (Jeremy Daniel), air date: 30 January 1955

Chapter Two This might be dubbed the William Dozier period. Dozier was the executive producer of the show and administratively Russell's boss. The transition from the first (Charles Russell) phase began when film production was scheduled to move to Hollywood, a shift Dozier favored. (The first episode of the Dozier era would be "The Completion of the First Transcontinental Railroad," air date: 3 April 1955).

The demarcation between the two phases of the series is easy to pinpoint. Charles Russell, in his manuscript "In the Worst of Times It Was the Best of Times," relates that Dozier had been quite aware very early on that blacklisted writers were writing the key shows. But Dozier desired greater creative influence and more personal recognition for the program's production accomplishments. He found it expedient, therefore, to expunge Russell and his creative unit. Accordingly, when the Hollywood move had been decided, he informed on Russell and the blacklisted writers to CBS. In Russell's words:

> Dozier told CBS that he had *recently* [emphasis added] learned about Russell's subversive activities including using blacklisted writers on the program—which could mean only one thing—and if that information were revealed it would seriously jeopardize the image of The Prudential Insurance Company . . . . We all knew that Bill Dozier didn't care who wrote the shows as long as they were good and he gained the recognition. He reminded me of the man who sells his soul to the devil in exchange for knowledge and power—but Bill wanted it both ways: he didn't want to make the actual deal. Eternal damnation made him uncomfortable." (pp. 150, 152)

The Polonsky era ended with CBS's firing of Charles Russell.

Thematic Analysis. The significance of the Polonsky group to the series is *implicitly* acknowledged by Rutgers University historian, Robert F. Horowitz, in his "History Comes to Life and *You Are There*." While Horowitz does not reveal any awareness of the authorship of the earlier shows by blacklisted writers using fronts—indeed, no mention of writers by name is made at all—his analysis of the content of the shows is perceptive enough to detect the differences in orientation of those written by the Polonsky group from those scripted by others.

Horowitz in his study distinguishes between Progressive and Consensus schools of historiography. The *Progressive* camp stresses economic, class, political, and sectional conflict as its interpretive structure for explaining history: class conflicts between "the haves and the have nots" (see "The Trial of Susan B. Anthony," "The Emergence of Jazz"), ideological disputes between conservatives and liberals (see "The Signing of the Magna Carta," "The Sailing of the Mayflower," "The Crisis of Galileo," "The Scopes Trial"), sectional and geographical differences among peoples (see "The Execution of Joan of Arc," "The Conquest of Mexico by Cortes," "The Hatfield-McCoy Feud"). *Consensus* interpretation emphasizes continuity and lack of conflict, a persistence—especially in American history—of particular unifying and enduring traditions and themes: all Americans of whatever ethnic backgrounds or station share an underlying common outlook, common goals, and a common ideology.

Recall that the New York-based Polonsky group was in residence from February 1953 to March 1955. With commendable perception, Horowitz astutely *contrasts* the "earlier shows which evoked elements of the old Progressive view" *to* those of the late-1955 to 1957 period (the William Dozier Hollywood regime), when "the emerging Consensus interpretation was influencing more of the broadcasts."[10] By delineating these chronological periods, Horowitz is identifying, without being explicitly aware of it, the Polonsky group's (pseudonymous) influence in shaping the intellectual orientation of the show's first phase. (The orientation is usually expressed through a structure of *progressive thematic oppositions*, discussed below).

The chronological breakdown underscores the philosophical shift in the second (Dozier) phase of Consensus, which reflected an interpretive approach which the historian John Higham calls "a massive grading operation to smooth over America's social convulsions."[11] Horowitz's perception calls our attention to the remarkable phenomenon that, given the climate of opinion in the early 1950s that sought harmony and continuity in public discourse, the shows by the Polonsky group did have a heightened social and political sub-text—an intellectual provocation and elan—which the programs of subsequent phases lacked.[12]

Primary source material (Russell's records of actual authorship of the scripts) provides a statistical impact: of the 95 episodes produced under the aegis of producer Charles W. Russell, 56 (verifiable) teleplays were written by the Walter Bernstein-Arnold Manoff-Abraham Polonsky combination. Polonsky wrote 24. (See Appendix II.)

> I am not eager, sir, that my tombstone should read: "Here lies a man who survived despite all." He who dies after his principles have died, sir, has died too late.
> —"The Tragedy of John Milton"

The difficulties of dealing with the ambiguities and subtleties of the sweep of complex historical movements within the framework of a 25-minute dramatized episode are self-evident. The approach developed, therefore, by Polonsky, Bernstein, Manoff, and Russell for the series—illustrated by the individualized nature of the shows' titles—involved focusing on a single protagonist or incident in a specific place that would provide a sufficiently fertile context in which the relevant historical, philosophical, and ethical issues could be presented and debated. Historical documents (letters, speeches, published sources) of the original events always formed the basis of each dramatized show. End credits of each episode included the following statement: "All the events reported and seen are based on historic fact and quotation."[13]

The artistic strategy for the most personal of the *You Are There* episodes is perhaps best illustrated by a deconstruction of an individual teleplay. One of Polonsky's most resonant scripts, "The Tragedy of John Milton" (air date: 30 January 1955), could function as a paradigm by which an investigator could trace the social, political, intellectual subtext of an era. The "John Milton" script shares with the other major Polonsky teleplays a similar intellectual and ethical vision, a structure built on recurring *thematic oppositions:*

INDIVIDUALISM v. CONFORMITY

INVENTION v. CONVENTION
(Innovation, Creativity)   (Formulaic Repetition)

FREEDOM v. CONSTRAINT
(Artistic, Religious, Political)   (Censorship)

Here is the opening exposition:

WALTER CRONKITE
Walter Cronkite reporting. August 13, 1660. The restoration of Charles II to the throne of England continues smoothly as royalist politicians replace republican ones in all public offices, and former high church officials once again dominate the spiritual councils of the nation. In general the people seem happy and attend in great numbers the fêtes and festivals which have been arranged to mark the end of the 12-year-old Commonwealth founded by the Puritan army under the leadership of Oliver Cromwell. Nevertheless, there have been a number of anxious inquiries from abroad about the fate of some distinguished republican Roundheads, notably the blind poet, John Milton.

Each day as Parliament adds and subtracts names from the official list of those to be punished by death, imprisonment or other civil disabilities, new Puritan leaders have been arrested. The most notable of these are being held in the Tower of London. Others are being sought for throughout the land. Among the latter is John Milton who disappeared from his home three months ago and has not been seen or heard of since. The fact that Milton is blind makes it difficult for him to travel and it is believed he is in hiding in London. We take you to London where Parliament is in session . . .

All things are as they were then except . . . YOU ARE THERE.

Subtext: if we were to read this clash of historical oppositions through the prism of Polonsky's early 1950s perspective, we could reformulate this 1660 discussion in terms of a post-WWII artist in collision with the unsalutary climate of the 1950's Cold War—a moral and political crisis with which Polonsky and his blacklisted colleagues could intimately identify.

Polonsky uses the Puritan, William Prynne (played in the telecast by Philip Borneuf), as an example of the opportunist who calculates his physical survival by conforming to the current social and political orthodoxy.

REPORTER

What is your reason [for your constant addition of new names of those who are to be executed]?

PRYNNE

Because while the house cannot punish all of these Roundheads, I can draw attention to these vermin and keep their names and crimes before the members and the people. In this way they will suffer the pains of notoriety and the punishment of their neighbors until such time as the anger and hate of all the people rise and they force this house and the king to go beyond this small list of regicides.

Subtext: blacklisted persons of the post WWII era were victims of ultra-right members of Congress (HUAC), red-baiting journalists (George Sokolsky, Victor Riesel, Walter Winchell, Jack O'Brien, Hedda Hopper), conservative organizations (The Motion Picture Alliance for the Preservation of American Ideals, The American Business Consultants, Aware, Inc., The American Legion, The Catholic War Veterans) and their publications (Red Channels, Counterattack, The American Legion Magazine, Firing Line)—all of which could function as counterparts to William Prynne.

Polonsky's contempt for the survival-at-the-expense-of-honor expediency is palpable. The investigations by the government of America's intellectual life in the 1950s produced many persons who were prepared to cooperate with HUAC, to inform on friends and colleagues in order to protect their own careers.[14] An understanding of this background gives power to the following:

REPORTER
Do you realize the grave risk you run, sir, in opposing these popular measures for revenge?

ANDREW MARVELL
[A poet of great intellectual merit; played in the telecast by Richard Kiley.]
I am not like those in the land who having shared the life of the republic, would now find safety by being first to cry down their own companions. I am not eager, sir, that my tombstone should read: "Here lies a man who survived despite all." He who dies after his principles have died, sir, has died too late.

(This conviction is clearly one that Polonsky feels needs repeating, and in another teleplay he has Nathan Hale proclaim: "I know I'm quite young. Nevertheless, I am too old to betray what I believe is just.")

It is to John Milton (played in the telecast by Barry Jones) that Polonsky, quite logically, gives the expanded forum to engage the elements of intellectual freedom. For example, a sense of historical irony is surely suggested in the following comments by Milton, now given a 1950s thematic update, which signify the displeasure of Polonsky and other artists who fought in WWII--that their loyalty, patriotism, and political involvements would be questioned and/or condemned by the very country for which they risked their lives.

MILTON
How strange it is, sir, how passing strange, that this parliament which owes its freedom and power to the very men it hunts and kills, forgets that its independence was won by those it condemns. Men do not easily learn from history but must, like sad dogs, be beaten more than once to learn the simplest rule of liberty.

REPORTER
What is that rule, sir?

MILTON
Not to forsake it!

And it is, ultimately, John Milton who recapitulates a universal theme of man's life and art, a theme as relevant to the 20th century as to the 17th.

MILTON
When a king forbids books and free thought, it is his nature; but when a free government does so, that teaches men to hate such governments as if they were hating tyrants . . . . Tell me, any of you, do you know of one honest government that has fallen because its people were free to write, to speak, to think, to worship as their consciences bade them? . . . Who kills a man kills a reasonable creature, God's image; but he who destroys a good book kills reason itself. Many a man lives a burden to the earth, but a good book is the precious lifeblood of a master spirit embalmed and treasured upon a purpose to a life beyond life.

The salient aspect about the "Progressive Period"-*You Are There* scripts is their *contemporaneity*. Certain themes and social issues never die, and it does not require a tortured process of deconstruction to see in these historical tapestries a remarkable prescience for the postmodern world implications of Jesse Helms, Robert Mapplethorpe, multi-culturalism, Salman Rushdie, Sister Souljah, Two-Live Crew, "Cop Killer," gangsta rap, political correctness . . . ad nauseam—all provocations toward intolerance and censorship, possessing kaleidoscopic moral and political coloration.

Over the last decade the United States has become a more divided and diverse society, anxious over deep-rooted social ills, and fearful that the American Dream is slipping out of reach. There has been an increase in art with social and political content—art that reflects and comments on the ills of our society, including AIDS, homelessness, misogyny, homophobia, and racism. Provocative content with a radical social or political subtext has always had the potential to disturb: this was a cultural reality for the 1950s as well as for the 1990s. The contemporary scene, for example, finds Anne Imelda Radice, the National Endowment for the Arts acting chairman, stating before

Congress in May 1992, that the endowment would not fund art that deals with "difficult subject matter."[15]

For difficult subject matter try: Girolamo Savonarola.

"The Vindication of Savonarola" (air date: 13 December 1953) contains Polonsky's profile of Savonarola (1452-1498), a character who reflects disturbing historical complexity and contradiction. Savonarola (played in the telecast by Joseph Wiseman) was a Dominican friar of great reputation for his learning and asceticism. His city of destiny was Florence, where he fought boldly against the tyrannical abuses of Medici rule. He introduced a democratic government, and, from a positive interpretation of his role, was not ambitious or an intriguer— but one who wanted to found Florence, heart of Italy, as a well-organized Christian republic that might initiate the reform of Italy and of the Church. However, his is also a paradoxical association with the so-called "bonfire of the vanities," the destruction of items as various as personal ornaments, lewd pictures, cards, as well as books, manuscripts, and works of art: aspects of what he considered a humanistic paganism that corrupted manners, art, poetry, and religion itself.

> Savonarola was an ambiguous character in the history of Florence. Savonarola wanted the people to have more power against the aristocracy; at the same time he had the feeling that so much that was produced should be burnt and destroyed because it led to obnoxious anti-church points of view. There was a combination of a genuine sort of democratic leadership, a people's leadership which he tried to represent, and his anti-intellectual attitude towards art which made him burn books and other elements which gave him offense. So I used that ambiguity in writing the piece.

> This is a problem you always have in history: that because the received tradition of art seems far above the heads of the ordinary people, the masses, the person fighting for the economic and social aims of the masses finds himself attacking works of artistic merit—because they're aristocratic in origin! And I used that in my story.[16]
> (Polonsky, Interview with Editor, 15 July 1989)

The strikingly current relevance of this ambiguity is captured by Polonsky in the following debate. It is a passage which reiterates the thematic oppositions of *Convention (Past) v. Invention (Present)* and *Individualism v. Conformity.*

REPORTER
Some very honest men question your right to burn works of art that you just happen not to like. These men say that you are hostile to learning, to art, and would reduce all men to simple obedient creatures.

SAVONAROLA
I am not hostile to art. When the great library of codices and miniatures, the books and manuscripts collected by the Medici were offered up for sale to be dispersed through the world, we monks at San Marco sold our lands, we beggared ourselves, we paid the money. We brought the library here, and here in all Italy is the one place where anyone can come and read and study without bending a knee to a prince or merchant or priest. Is this to be hostile to art?

REPORTER
Well, no, Father, but those books are books of the past, and it's the artists of the present that you condemn.

SAVONAROLA
I do not condemn artists, only those knaves who prostitute their art and their skill. All the world knows that the most eminent artists and poets of our city are my friends, and, in the sense that I follow God, my followers. Does not Fra Bartholomeo love me as I love his paintings? And della Robbia, whose sculptures the world acclaims, acclaim my teachings? I have led the two of them into the monastic order. And Lorenzo di Credi, Cronaca, Botticelli! And even the young Michelangelo Buonarotti came from the Medici palace to hear my sermons when I upbraided his master.

REPORTER
Yes, I know, Father. But those great artists are your followers. What of the others who are not?

SAVONAROLA
I know whom you mean—*these men who are bought and sold in the marketplace like sheep and goats. They work for evil*

princes whose courts and palaces are the refuge of all the beasts and monsters on the earth. Yes, they flock to their halls, these wretches, because it is there that they find ways and means to satisfy their evil passions and lusts. These are the false councillors who continuously devise new taxes and burdens to drain the blood of the people. *These are the flattering philosophers and poets who by force of a thousand lies praise the destroyers and with a million arguments justify, gild, and make palatable the evil that is corrupting the citizens. Such artists, I must condemn.*[17]

Like all good writing, this raises more questions than it answers. Consider: Savonarola's attitudes are rendered with such a rhetorical dignity and an authoritative citation of artistic references that his position approaches eloquence. His advocacy of the selective suppression of artists and philosophers with whom he disagrees actually takes on a certain cogency.

However, by raising the Liberty/Censorship theme (through the commentator's questions), Polonsky's script forces a debate on the intellectual freedom issue and widens the arena to include the opportunity for contemporary (1950s/1990s) cross-references. The possible meanings of the ideas result in a stimulating ambiguity. On one level, the italicized sentences in the above passage invite recognition of those complex individuals who, at the time of the show's original broadcast, were possibly receiving Polonsky's condemnation—the cooperative witnesses who gave names to HUAC. Those informers' actions are colored and complicated by their strident attempts at self-justification (Elia Kazan), philosophical epiphany (Edward Dmytryk), devastating guilt (Larry Parks), profound remorse (Sterling Hayden), or all of the above (Budd Schulberg, David Raksin).[18]

But, as an indication of an enduring topicality, those same sentences have the capacity to reflect the 1990's debate on cultural freedom, when some supporters of the NEA, for example, believe that some compromise of artistic freedom is necessary to save the endowment. The compromisers appear willing to trade artistic creativity for the continued subsidization of "safe" art, such as orchestras, operas, and large, established museums. From such a perspective, Savonarola's words take on a chilling contemporaneity.

The "Progressive" scripts tended to reiterate the idea that American history has at times been driven by class conflict and ethnic and racial tension. Polonsky's script for "The Emergence of Jazz" (air date: 5 September 1954), for example, acknowledges that these adversities were the context for the development of jazz music. Here is a scene in which jazz pianist and composer Jelly Roll Morton (played in the telecast by Billy Taylor) explains how this "new music" comes about:

MORTON

It comes from hearing your mother's voice when you're on her knee and hearing there the voice of Africa and the drums and the people crying when they were dragged out of their homes and brought here to be slaves . . . and it comes from working in the fields and talking up and singing against the hot sun and the pain and not letting on to the master what you were saying . . . and the river boat whistles and the locomotive trains . . . and the marching songs and funerals, and always the blues, always the slow drag, always searching for home and not finding it but not stopping, always looking . . .

And to famous cornet player King Oliver (played in the telecast by Louis Armstrong), Polonsky gives these lines:

OLIVER

Funny, how you get to like something that's really rotten, but you get to like it cause it feeds you. You like what you need to like and you do what you need to do. I remember when they used to make the colored players sit with their faces to the wall and their backs to the folks outside and play that way, and now the black and white are side by side sometimes.

Producer Charles Russell explains that for a time during the show's early phase the Prudential Insurance Company was the only sponsor. Given the politically redolent nature of many of the scripts by the blacklisted writers, Russell quite consciously scheduled "material that might be considered controversial or unacceptable—on the unsponsored weeks." But the shows elicited very little negative reaction from conspiratorially-minded viewers, as Bernstein writes: "Surprisingly there was little backlash, possibly because we were scrupulous in our research and Russell had taken the precaution of having distinguished history professors go over relevant scripts to confirm their accuracy."[19] And here is an explanation from Polonsky:

If the show had been attacked by McCarthy, or if Arthur Schlesinger, who was part of the cold war, had written a letter to the *New York Times* saying that this was a lot of communist propaganda, the show would have been in big trouble. But it was cloaked in history, and we were very careful in the presentation of the material not to give way to obvious propaganda.[20]

But the politically charged subtexts of the scripts were quite evident to perspicacious viewers. Producer Russell, who knowingly was putting his neck on the line every time an episode like "The Crisis of Galileo" or "The Scopes Trial" was aired, recounts in his memoir an encounter with one such astute observer—the famed journalist, Edward R. Murrow.

Edward R. Murrow's program *See It Now* originated in the studio next to ours at Grand Central and followed *You Are There* on the air. We would frequently meet early Sunday mornings at the Pentagon restaurant directly across the street. We'd sit at the bar and he'd order his Scotch with a dash of water but no ice and I'd have a Bloody Mary or coffee, depending on the show for that day. One morning he said, "You know, Charles, I watch your program on the control room monitor, whenever possible, before going to air. It's a damn good program. I admire it." He finished his drink and before leaving he looked at me from under his eyebrows and asked, "How do you get away with it?"

This was after the Rosenberg executions and prior to the Army-McCarthy hearings.

It was after this that Murrow did his memorable program where he confronted McCarthy. The image of a self-serving politician was exposed. Murrow did this program despite the network's strong objections. Perhaps *You Are There* might have been of some help in his decision. I'd like to think so.[21]

The "progressive" tension in the teleplays is further clarified by noting Polonsky's position on the role of the artist, intellectual freedom, and social commitment:

The role of the artist is not to worry about political sensitivities of people, but to stimulate them into new areas of experiment and expression. A real work of art is a very great discovery made through a complex process of creation. It is a process in which one kind of reality is transformed into another and so the product always contains more than the artist can conceive at any stage therein . . . . The tendency in social commitment is conformity, as in the United States and in the Soviet Union. Yet if people are offended because their cherished illusions are shaken or their covering faiths outraged, well, that is the very point of literature, that is the very motion of a truthful life, to be shaken up, to be disturbed, to be awakened, even from a dream of the American or Soviet Paradise. There is no idea, no theory, no way of life that cannot be reshaped, illuminated and made more human by being subject to the imagination and criticism of the artist.[22]

In the cinema of Abraham Polonsky, each protagonist struggles to find meaning—logic, order, moral values, self-definition—in an incomprehensible, hostile world. Every work by Polonsky contains a moment when the hero recognizes the necessity to create meaningful existential values.

Tell Them Willie Boy Is Here (1969):

LOLA
They're white. They'll chase you forever.

WILLIE
How long is that? Less than you think.

LOLA
It's crazy, Willie. You can't beat them. You can't win. Never.

WILLIE
Maybe, but they'll know I was here.

Force of Evil (1948):

A flawed hero moves toward self-recognition by facing the truth about himself and the corrupt values by which he has lived: "If a man's life can be lived so long and come out this way, like rubbish, then something was horrible and had to be ended one way or another and I decided to help."

Body and Soul (1947):

A boxer regains his integrity by winning a match which the criminals had pressured him to throw. The film contains the classic line of existential defiance: "Whatta you going to do, kill me? Everybody dies."

"The Fate of Nathan Hale":

"In this profound action we can say that he did not die in vain or too soon, for he died fulfilling the purpose which *in his own mind* was the ideal of his own life, and the nation to come."

The films present a cohesive vision of the relationship between individual behavior and political values. They express the need to assert humanity—a sense of personal identity—against the urban, economic corruption of the present. Always there is elevated literary style, sardonic wit, an existential cynicism which continually remind us of the world's perverse ironies:

"The Emergence of Jazz":

The war [WWI] is something thrown on us by the failure of the old, the generations of our fathers before us. It is the proof that their culture and civilization amount to nothing but one grand zero. So people here [in Paris], the young, the intellectuals, the artists, they seize upon jazz as a message from the future. Goodbye to big orchestras, the harmonies, the terrible banality of musical past, and welcome to that cocktail of sound and color, improvised, polyphonic, American jazz. The Americans don't want to hear it because it is the free creation of the Negro people whom they don't recognize as free and equal. That is an irony, isn't it, that from the slaves and the oppressed comes the only original contribution to art made by the American nation. Jazz is a liberation of music from the chains of convention and snobbery. It comes from the human heart, not from the academies. It is free. It is honest. It is art the way art should be. All the rest, as our great poet Verlaine has said, is merely literature.

All the rest, as a character in *Body and Soul* has said, is conversation.

"I always write about the same thing," Polonsky says, "how people seek to fulfill themselves and what society suppresses in them through convention and force. To keep suppressing what's powerfully present in your character is to deny your existence as a human being. Not to fulfill yourself is not to live."[23]

Polonsky has declared in his best novels and screenplays that people can, within limits, control their lives, their environments. Even though individuals are continually snared in the webs of other people's plans, they paradoxically remain free to choose and to act. Polonsky's heroes are, as we have observed them during literal and metaphorical "seasons of fear," dialectical people: "liberated captives."[24]

NOTES

1. Charles W. Russell, "In the Worst of Times It Was the Best of Times," (Unpublished Manuscript, 1982), p. 60. Russell's manuscript, his production notes, and his annotated listings of all of the *You Are There* episodes on which he was producer represent primary research materials for this study. They, along with all of the teleplays written by Abraham Polonsky for the series, are contained in the Polonsky Collection, Radio-TV-Film Department, California State University, Northridge.

The original *radio* series premiered on 7 July 1947 as *CBS Is There*, and was produced and directed by Robert Lewis Shayon. The episodes were written by Irve Tunick, Michael Sklar, and Joseph Liss; real-life CBS newsmen and announcers were used, such as: Don Hollenbeck (used later on the television version, until *he* was blacklisted), John Daly, Richard C. Hottelet, Ken Roberts, Harry Marble, Jackson Beck. Guy Sorel was the signature voice, and the only permanent actor in the cast; he played such roles as William the Conqueror, Napoleon, etc. In 1948, in an attempt to create even greater listener involvement, the name was changed to *You Are There*. The show was a Sunday sustainer (non-sponsored, financed by CBS) from the fall of 1947 through its demise in 1950. [See John Dunning, *Tune in Yesterday: The Ultimate Encyclopedia of Old-Time Radio 1925-1976* (Prentice-Hall, 1976), pp. 665-656; Frank Buxton & Bill Owen, *The Big Broadcast 1920-1950* (Viking , 1972), pp. 334-335.]

2. Russell, "In the Worst of Times," pp. 25A-25AA.

The beginning of a special "guerrilla" unit is described by Russell: "Arnie had gotten together with Abe and Walter to discuss their survival. As blacklisted writers they knew they couldn't make it individually but they could collectively. The only question was, what show could they take over? Abe and Arnie had been based in Hollywood and were out of touch with people in New York. However, Walter had a friend at CBS named Russell. They survived and enjoyed a satisfying working association—under the worst of circumstances. It was silly, deadly serious, absurd but fun. A unique relationship developed." ("In the Worst of Times," p. 74.)

CBS newsman Mike Wallace was regularly employed on the *You Are There* telecasts (in episodes "Cortes Conquers Mexico" and "The Crisis of Galileo" in this volume). In a 9 October 1996 letter to the editors, Wallace writes: "I remember just about all the CBS News correspondents who served as location reporters on *You Are There*--and that included most of the veterans of CBS News' glory days, from Cronkite to Sevareid to Collingwood et al--as well as us lesser lights who looked on that broadcast series as a pleasant and engrossing respite from our day to day chores.

"Oh, there were some who cavilled that we were performing as mere 'actors' reading phony scripts, but it was difficult to resist the guileless enthusiasm that Sidney Lumet brought to his job as director.

"I don't think that many of us even knew or were especially aware of Abraham Polonsky, for it was Charlie Russell, the producer who enlisted us. The show was part of early television's voyage of discovery and we were pleased to be aboard!"

In *Inside Out: A Memoir of the Blacklist* (New York: Alfred A. Knopf, 1996), p. 217, Walter Bernstein discusses Charles Russell: "We liked and admired Russell, liked him for his unpretentious generosity, admired him for his courage. He found us exotic. We included him in our insults, which he took accurately as a sign of affection. He came to lunch with us and took us to dinner in expensive restaurants. We appreciated his taste in all things, from scripts to clothes. Clothes looked good on Russell; he could have been an ad for the Ivy League. When we talked politics, he listened with polite disinterest, waiting patiently for the topic to change. He had no interests apart from his work. . . . We grew very fond of him very fast."

3. Polonsky, "How the Blacklist Worked in Hollywood," *Film Culture* (Fall/Winter, 1970), p. 47.

Producer Charles Russell, in his memoir, describes a conversation he had with director Sidney Lumet about the blacklist and "the cruelty and injustice and the fear and terror created by McCarthyism. In his hyperactive way, Sidney was trying to educate me and fill me in on what was going on. 'Listen, when I was a kid I used to hang around with a bunch of guys who were involved in all sorts of radical groups. Maybe today they could be called subversive.'

"I interrupted him, 'I'm using some blacklisted writers on the program, Sidney. If it is revealed, it will come as a complete surprise to you. Understand.'

"I understand,' Sidney said, 'and I don't want to know what other writers are doing scripts.' Then he asked quietly, 'You got Bernstein working, haven't you?' I nodded and he said, 'Great.'

"I don't think this revelation came as a surprise to Sidney, since he hadn't seen a writer in the office, rehearsal hall, or studio in months. It was a protective measure for me. I also didn't want the script rewritten during rehearsals or on air day. Whenever a new writer's name appeared on the cover of a script, if I were asked where the person came from, I always had a good story. I hadn't been in acting for nothing." ("In the Worst of Times," p. 40).

4. Bernstein, *Inside Out*, p. 222.

The skein of memoirs extends to Walter Cronkite's *A Reporter's Life* (New York: Alfred A. Knopf, 1996). Here is a bit of Cronkite's reminiscence: "*You Are There* was an exciting show to do. It was presented on Sunday evenings, when most Broadway theaters were dark, and it gave a chance for older actors and ingenues alike to try their hand at this new thing called television. E.G. Marshall, Shepperd Strudwick, Lorne Greene, Ray Walston, Kim Stanley, Paul Newman and Joanne Woodward were all part of what we came to know as Sidney Lumet's Players.

"Sidney was our director, and he was to go vaulting to Hollywood to become one of the industry's most talented and successful moviemakers. He and our producer, Charles Russell, would become Hollywood heroes when, long after the fact and when it was again safe to speak out, it was revealed that throughout the long run of *You Are There* they had employed several of the screenwriters who had been blacklisted in the fifties' anti-Communist hysteria." (pp. 309-310) [A reading of this last paragraph should consider the precision of such wording as "throughout the long run," which implies that blacklisted writers were utilized for the complete span of the show (1 Feb 53--13 Oct 57), when Polonsky's script for "The Triumph of Alexander the Great," which aired 27 Mar 55, was the last episode written by a blacklisted writer. Equally imprecise are the words, "long after the fact and when it was again safe to speak out," since Charles Russell--and, by extension, the blacklisted trio of writers--was fired only two years into the series purportedly because of his association with the writers. It was hardly a "safe" environment. See the Preface to "The Tragedy of John Milton."]

5. Abraham Polonsky, Interview with Author, July 15, 1989.

Robert F. Horowitz, "History Comes to Life," *American History/American Television: Interpreting the Video Past*, edited by John E. O'Connor (New York: Frederick Ungar Publishing Co., 1983), pp. 79, 93, writes: "During its four-year run [1953-1957], the award-winning show maintained a high standard of programming and was consistently entertaining, informative, and instructive . . . . All in all, *You Are There* was an effective attempt at presenting history on television. After each show was over, if one had listened and watched carefully, one could explain how a particular event happened, why it happened, and what effects it had in the immediate future. It was an impressive and creative method of handling historical material. The *You Are There* programs were dramatically sound, informative, and accurate portrayals of historical events, and although the production techniques of television have now moved way beyond the sedentary stage-piece version of action that was presented, for their time they were extremely fine television broadcasts. As an interpreter of American history, *You Are There* was an accurate mirror of the intellectual climate of opinion in the 1950s, and the degree of intelligence and sophistication that came through was a definite achievement for mass-audience television."

6. Larry Ceplair, "Great Shows: *You Are There*," *Emmy Magazine* (January/February, 1982), p. 44.

7. Polonsky, *A Season of Fear* (New York: Cameron Associates, 1956), p. 52. This was also Polonsky's proposed title for the project which recently lured him out of retirement: the screenplay for a film to be directed by Bertrand Tavernier, produced by Irwin Winkler, on the Hollywood blacklist era. The purity of the political and civil liberties concepts, as envisioned by Polonsky, became hopelessly compromised when Tavernier withdrew and Winkler decided to direct the picture himself. When Winkler chose to alter the character, played by Robert DeNiro, *from* a former member of the Communist party who opposed HUAC on the grounds of First Amendment freedoms *to* innocent victim, Polonsky took his name off the film. The resulting work, *Guilty by Suspicion* (1991, for which Winkler takes sole screenwriting credit though much of Polonsky's material remains), is another textbook example of Hollywood's traditional pusillanimous approach to divisive moral and political issues. The usual decision is to simplify the moral complexities and eliminate ideological ambiguities. [See "Ceremonies of Innocence," in Michael Wood's *America in the Movies* (New York: Columbia University Press, 1989): "Why must the victims always be innocent?"]. For a fuller discussion of the Polonsky/*Guilty by Suspicion* episode, see Victor Navasky, "Has *Guilty by Suspicion* Missed the Point?" *The New York Times*, 31 March 1991.

8. *Body and Soul* and *Force of Evil* are routinely characterized as "a pair of movie classics" (*The New York Times Book Review*, 7 June 1992); *Force of Evil* "stands up under repeated viewings as one of the great films of the modern American cinema" (Andrew Sarris, *The American Cinema*, 1968); both receive treatment as *Cult Movies* (Delta, 1981) by Danny Peary.

Polonsky: "What attracted me to the Willie Boy story was the similarity to what happened to me during the blacklist period. In a fundamental way everybody who got blacklisted was on the run, a fugitive from then on, trying in some way to survive in a society where his profession or her occupation were forbidden to them. You were a fugitive in your own country." (Transcript of a filmed interview of Polonsky, Walter Bernstein, and Charles W. Russell, by Allan Warren, housed in the Abraham Polonsky Collection, Radio-TV-Film Department, California State University, Northridge.)

9. Michael Wilmington, "*Odds Against Tomorrow*," *The Los Angeles Times*, 10 April 1988; Larry Ceplair, "Great Shows: *You Are There*," *Emmy Magazine* (January/February, 1982), pp. 43-47. This critical commentary to the present volume of Polonsky's *You Are There* scripts has been published in slightly different form as "A Season of Fear: The Blacklisted Teleplays of Abraham Polonsky," *Literature/Film Quarterly*, Vol. 24, No. 2, 1996, pp. 148-164. *Force of Evil: The Critical Edition* (The Center for Telecommunication Studies, California State University, Northridge, 1996) contains Polonsky's screenplay, with annotations and critical commentary by John Schultheiss; edited by Schultheiss and Mark Schaubert.

10. Horowitz utilizes the episodes of "Grant and Lee at Appomattox" (air date: 30 October 1955) and "Daniel Webster's Sacrifice to Save the Union" (air date: 28 October 1956) as examples of Consensus historiography. This demonstrates, on the basis of explicit chronological evidence, that the shift in the philosophical orientation of the program occurs during the Dozier-dominated

post-March, 1955 period. It also, therefore, tacitly recognizes the link of the earlier Progressive period to the presence of the blacklisted writers and Charles Russell's stewardship. See Horowitz, "History Comes to Life," pp. 85-91.

When contacted in early 1991 regarding the *You Are There* series, William Dozier said that "he was too weak and ill to be interviewed." (Letter from David Culbert, senior associate editor, *Historical Journal of Film, Radio, and Television*, 23 March 1991.) Dozier died on 23 April 1991.

Dozier, a film and television executive of divergent background, was once described by *Los Angeles Times* columnist Art Seidenbaum as "having more titles than a silent movie." In his capacity as production supervisor at RKO, Dozier's name has been associated with such distinguished pictures as *Notorious, The Spiral Staircase,* and *Crossfire.* But, in a career shift which is coincidental with the change of regime within the discussed *You Are There* creative unit, he became the West Coast chief of CBS and later the production head of Screen Gems. And, significantly, he also formed his own Greenway Productions at 20th Century Fox, which produced *Batman,* a series that he ruefully admitted brought him the most recognition and money. In a moment of insight, he had no illusion where his true fame lay. "If I got hit by a truck, the *New York Daily News* would say '*Batman* Producer Killed' while the *New York Times* would refer to me as the 'Ex-Husband of Joan Fontaine [his second wife].'" (*Los Angeles Times,* 25 April 1991.)

11. John Higham, "The Cult of 'The American Consensus': Homogenizing of Our History," *Commentary* (February, 1959), p. 94; quoted in Horowitz, p. 91.

12. Walter Bernstein, whose screenplay for *The Front* (1976) was inspired by his *Danger/You Are There* experiences, has some thoughts about the program's later phases: "When CBS revived *You Are There* [in the 1970s], the producer of it knew that I had written for it under another name during the blacklist period and asked me to write some. I wrote two or three of them——and the shows were no good. I mean it wasn't that mine were good and the rest weren't. The producers were scared. In a funny kind of way, they were very timid on the subject matter. The whole idea that we built the shows on——What was the historical conflict at the time that produced the drama of the show?——they were frightened at the very idea that you might deal with conflict. The show was unsuccessful because of that. The irony was that during this supposedly liberated time when they could have been more daring—they weren't. They were scared to death." (Filmed Warren Interview)

13. "Almost Nothing But the Truth: How 'You Are There' Gets There With the Facts," *TV Guide,* 28 May 1954, pp. 10-11.

14. This concern with oppressive regimes and the censoring of individual thought is understandably a solemn theme for Polonsky. Two additional texts which allow Polonsky to make direct connections to contemporary American life in this regard are "The Crisis of Galileo" and "The Execution of Joan of Arc."

Polonsky's script for "The Crisis of Galileo" (air date: 19 April 1953) has perhaps the most pointed cross-reference to conformist America of the 1950s, due to the program's historical context of the Inquisition (the seventeenth century edition). Galileo is made to recant his beliefs by the Holy Office in Rome, an action described in the script as "a repudiation of his whole life."

Galileo's submission to the authority of the Church is analogous to the cooperation required by HUAC of those who appeared before it. The recantation is spiked by a promise to inform on others.

GALILEO

I swear that I will never more in the future say, or assert anything, verbally or in writing, which may give rise to a similar suspicion of me; but that if I shall know any heretic, or anyone suspected of heresy, *I will denounce him to the Holy Office, or to the Inquisitor and Ordinary of any place where I may be.*

The Galileo crisis has traditionally functioned as a useful shorthand for the conflict between weakness and integrity, and has acquired a certain ironic poignance from the version (especially the first English-language production in Los Angeles in 1947) of *Galileo* (*Leben des Galilei*) by Bertolt Brecht. (Brecht's Marxist leanings led to his examination by HUAC in 1947.)

Polonsky's convictions regarding such acts of ethical compromise are voiced, in his "Galileo" script, by the scientist William Harvey: "I reject the action of Galileo Galilei as a betrayal of the work of his life and the truth about Nature and the Universe which we scientists must defend no matter what the personal consequences."

"The Execution of Joan of Arc" (air date: 1 Mar 53) deals with both political and religious freedom. To the English, Joan "disaffects, distorts and leads into sin *the minds of the common people* of France. She hoodwinks them with cheap miracles which any fraud can invent. We do not object to the soldier, but to the charlatan, the traitor, and the witch."

Polonsky's teleplay also confronts the issue of individual conscience in the context of Joan's greater allegiance to what she assumed to be the direct commands of God to those of the church. The question ultimately becomes one of her submission to the church. And note well: *obedience to the court that was trying her would inevitably be made the test of such submission!* (HUAC, anyone?) And, just as inevitably, the price is recantation and informing:

CAUCHON
[Bishop of Beauvais, in whose diocese Joan had
been captured]
You must declare that you have committed treason against the Lord and the rightful king of France, Henry VI of England, and throw yourself on the mercy of the court and the Church, and *you must tell who aided and abetted you in this crime of treason and heresy, and renounce all you have done and all you have said,* and make yourself small and nothing and the miserable wretch and sinner that you are.

15. Archibald L. Gillies, "Art Is Supposed to be 'Difficult,'" *The Los Angeles Times*, 5 August 1992.

The problems of fundraising for "difficult subject matter" are exemplified in the "Exiles and Emigres: The Flight of European Artists from Hitler" exhibition, which opened in February 1997 at the Los Angeles County Museum. This project is a sequel to "Degenerate Art: The Fate of the Avant-Garde in Nazi Germany," which was an enormously successful exhibition at LACMA in 1991. Both exhibitions were organized by Stephanie Barron. According to *The Los Angeles Times*, "when appeals for funds went out, not a single American corporation agreed to contribute. Apparently the subject matter is too tough for the business sector, which typically avoids any association with arts that have political overtones.

"Fortunately for the museum, necessary funds were secured from other sources: agencies of the United States and German governments, individual donors and foundations established by two prominent Hollywood personalities, filmmaker Steven Spielberg and actress Sharon Stone." (Suzanne Muchnic, "Starry Support for 'Exiles and Emigres,'" 24 February 1997.)

16. Polonsky Interview, July 15, 1989.

17. A similar exchange can be found in Polonsky's "The First Command Performance of *Romeo and Juliet*" (air date: 21 February 1954). It is an dramatization of the *Elizabethan* debate between artistic vision and social responsibility. Here the discussion is about the moral implications of theatre. The spokesperson for the state is Sir Richard Martin, master of the mint and Lord

Mayor of London (a sort of sixteenth-century Jesse Helms), "who is giving the opinions of the Common Council of the city about the new theatrical rage."

REPORTER

Sir Richard, do you object to the players companies and their plays?

RICHARD

As to the devil and his works.

REPORTER

Why do you object to these plays? Everyone likes them.

RICHARD

Everyone likes sin, must we therefore pamper and love it? These plays are a special cause of corrupting the youth, containing nothing but unchaste matters, lascivious devices, shifts of cozenage, and other lewd and ungodly matters. Such as frequent them are of a rude and refuse sort of young gentlemen as have small regard of credit or conscience. They are drawn into imitation and not of avoiding that which these vicious plays represent.

REPORTER

But, Sir Richard, the new playhouses afford a popular place for meeting and amusement for all the city.

RICHARD

I have written the Lord Chamberlain not to grant any license for the erection of any playhouse. They are the ordinary places for vagrant persons, masterless men, thieves, horsestealers, cozeners, coney catchers, contrivers of treason, and other idle and dangerous persons to meet together and make their matches to the great displeasure of almighty God and the hurt and annoyance of her majesty's people.

REPORTER

Aren't you looking on the very worst side of the theatre?

RICHARD

I am seeing it from the side of a governor of this city, and I see that plays maintain idleness in such persons as have no vocation and draw apprentices and other servants from their ordinary works and all sorts of people from the resort into sermons and other Christian exercises to the great hindrance of trades.

REPORTER

But the queen favors it?

RICHARD

The queen is a queen. I am speaking of the mob in the city who gather at playhouses and spread the plague to each other as lovers spread kisses.

REPORTER

Would you forbid plays altogether?

                              RICHARD
I would and I will. I am not ignorant of what is alleged by some for the
defense of these plays that the people must have some kind of
recreation and that policy requires to divert idle heads and others ill
disposed from worse practices by this kind of exercise. I say let them
go to church and work hard.

                              REPORTER
And leave the plays for the court?

                              RICHARD
There are those in the court who are also corrupt, but they harm
themselves and not the kingdom.

     "The Emergence of Jazz" (air date: 5 September 1954)—same censorship
theme, updated idiom:

     Jazz music is the indecent story syncopated and counterpointed. Like the
     improper anecdote, also, in its youth, it is listened to blushingly behind
     closed doors and drawn curtains, but like vice, it grows bolder until it
     dares decent surroundings. On certain natures, loud and meaningless
     sound has an exciting, almost intoxicating effect, like crude colors and
     strong perfumes, like the sight of flesh or the pleasure in blood. It is a
     point of civic honor to suppress it.

     18.   The single best study of the Hollywood blacklist period is Victor S.
Navasky, *Naming Names* (New York: The Viking Press, 1980). See, especially, the
chapter "Stars, Stripes, and Stigmas," pp. 197-313.
     19. Russell, "In the Worst of Times," p. 74; Bernstein, *Inside Out*, p. 222.
     20. Polonsky, Filmed Warren Interview.
     21. Russell, "In the Worst of Times," p. 82.
     Director Sidney Lumet has expressed a similar gratification in speculating on
You Are There's contribution to McCarthy's demise: "We always took pride in
"The Witch Trial at Salem" [written by Arnold Manoff, fronted by "Kate
Nickerson"] because we did it the same week that Ed Murrow did his McCarthy
show, so we like to think we were slight contributors to the general attack on
him." [Frank R. Cunningham, *Sidney Lumet: Film and Literary Vision* (The
University Press of Kentucky, 1991), p. 19.] In his comments in the current *You
Are There Teleplays* volume, Lumet cites "The Crisis of Galileo" as an influence. In
fact, "The Witch Trial at Salem" was broadcast on 29 March 1953, "The Crisis of
Galileo" on 19 April 1953, while Murrow's "A Report on Senator Joseph R.
McCarthy" aired on 9 March 1954. The actual *You Are There* episode that was
broadcast the Sunday before Murrow's Tuesday McCarthy report was "The Trial
of John Peter Zenger" (also directed by Lumet and written by Arnold Manoff,
fronted by "Kate Nickerson"), which--given the show's theme of freedom of the
press--could certainly serve to support Lumet's anecdote. Faulty memories aside,
there seems to be some justification to the claim that *You Are There*--not in a single
episode, but as a nuanced component in a process of erosion--helped in the general
attack on McCarthy.
     22.   Polonsky [signed "Timon"], "The Troubled Mandarins," *Masses &
Mainstream*, Vol. 9, No. 7, August, 1959, p. 45.
     23.   Lawrence Christon, "Polonsky Staging First Play," *The Los Angeles
Times*, 2 October 1981.
     24.   Larry Ceplair coined the oxymoronic phrase, "liberated captives," in
"Creative Forgetting," *Nation*, 14 June 1980.

Walter Bernstein. A staff writer for *The New Yorker* and a war correspondent for *Yank* during World War II (a collection of wartime writings was published as *Keep Your Head Down*, 1946), Walter Bernstein is one of the triumvirate of writers (along with Arnold Manoff and Abraham Polonsky) who wrote the most thematically compelling teleplays for *You Are There* during the blacklist era. His screenplay of *The Front* (1976, directed by formerly blacklisted Martin Ritt, starring Woody Allen) is based on the experiences of these three men as fronted writers on the early television series *Danger* and *You Are There*. Bernstein's primary fronts or pseudonyms for these shows were "Paul Bauman," "Leo Davis," "Eliot Asinof," "Alex Furth," "Howard Rodman," and "Leslie Slote." His valuable biographical history of the blacklist is *Inside Out: A Memoir of the Blacklist* (Alfred A. Knopf, 1996). Bernstein is a distinguished screenwriter of such works as: *That Kind of Woman* (1959, a film notable for its polished, sardonic dialogue) and *Fail Safe* (1964, a terrifying and convincing anti-war melodrama, the deadly earnest flip side of *Dr. Strangelove*)—both directed by *You Are There's* Sidney Lumet; *The Money Trap* (1966, a marvelously structured, underrated film noir); *Semi-Tough* (1977, a provocative and genre-wrenching chapter, according to scholar Brian Henderson, in the evolution of the romantic comedy); *The Molly Maguires* (1970, another collaboration with *The Front's* Martin Ritt)—a further eloquent illustration of the subtextual use of blacklist era conceits, one of the most powerful narratives employing the "informer theme" in American cinema.

Arnold Manoff. A writer of screenplays, such as *Casbah* and *No Minor Vices* (both 1948), Arnold Manoff is the author of a celebrated short story, "All You Need Is One Good Break," adapted for Broadway (1950); a novel, *Telegram from Heaven* (1942), adapted by daughter Dinah Manoff for the stage (1992). After he was blacklisted, Manoff joined Polonsky and Bernstein on *Danger* and *You Are There*. His fronts for these programs were "Joel Carpenter" and "Kate Nickerson." His teleplay of "The Death of Socrates" (air date: 3 May 1953), fronted by Nickerson, may very well be the single most prestigious episode of the *You Are There* series. The historical Socrates narrative, with its conflict of individual conscience versus the state, embodied the dominant metaphorical issues that energized the three writers' "guerrilla warfare." The contemporary implications of Manoff's teleplay were unmistakable: "They could not but grieve for the loss of this stubborn old man, simple and gentle of soul and sharp and clear of mind, who would never let them rest in their comfort and vanity and ignorance. And they were forced to think better and deeper of the true dignity and noble aspirations of man beyond his strivings for luxury, wealth and power. The cup of poison then became in their minds a test and symbol of high principles and purity. And all who would live by such goals were bound for centuries after to taste again in some way this bitter brew." The program won an award from The Museum of Modern Art (1962), but Manoff was unable, even at that late date, to officially accept the writer's credit. Fittingly, the award's citation is a validation not only of Manoff's individual talent, but of the artistry of the entire series: "*You Are There* was one of radio's most original concepts. Transferred to television it lost none of its excitement, and gained enormously in its ability to re-create history with respect to authenticity, and for educating and entertaining equally well. This particular episode ["Socrates"] illustrates its power to dramatize material that in another form might be academic or dry."

Note on the Texts

The principal source for the texts reprinted here is the material found in producer Charles Russell's private collection, the quality of which ranges from complete, neatly typed shooting scripts to fragmented, carbon copy drafts. Two of the anthologized scripts ("The Torment of Beethoven" and "The Tragedy of John Milton") were filmed; kinescopes of the live broadcasts of "The Crisis of Galileo," "The Vindication of Savonarola," and "Mallory's Tragedy on Mr. Everest" exist in the UCLA Television Study Center; and The Museum of Broadcasting in New York contains a kine of "The Emergence of Jazz." Thus, the content of six of the ten published teleplays can be verified by these records of the broadcasts, and the texts for these in the present volume therefore have been made to conform, except where noted, to the actual performances. In the case of "The Secret of Sigmund Freud" and "The Recognition of Michelangelo," only the Russell material is currently extant—and both episodes are missing Cronkite's opening expositions.

Sections which occurred in Polonsky's original scripts but which were either not shot or cut out in the editing are indicated by bold square brackets [ ].

CORTES CONQUERS MEXICO

Hernan (or Hernando) Cortes (b. 1485, Medellin, Spain—d. 2 December 1547, near Seville), the Spaniard who conquered Mexico in the 16th century, was—with Francisco Pizarro, conqueror of Peru—the greatest of the Spanish conquistadors. Cortes was 33 years old when he set out in February 1519 to colonize the mainland of America. On the mainland he did what no other expedition leader had done: he exercised and disciplined his army, welding it into a cohesive force. But the ultimate expression of his determination to deal with disaffection was when he burned his ships. By that single action Cortes committed himself and his entire force to survival only through conquest.

By 1521 the Aztec Empire in Mexico had been destroyed; the Aztec priest-king Montezuma was dead; the Aztec capital of Tenochtitlan was in ruins; and Cortes had founded New Spain, the first of the great Spanish American possessions. His conquest, achieved initially with barely 400 Spanish soldiers, represented the peak of his extraordinary career. It set the pattern for Pizarro's later conquest of the Incas of Peru and remains to this day one of the most fascinating and colorful campaigns in history.

The key to that conquest lay in the political crisis within the Aztec Empire. Cortes was fortunate in being presented at the outset with a captured princess who spoke Nahuatl, the language of the Aztecs. She became his "tongue," his adviser on Indian affairs, and, later, his mistress. It was she who worked on the complicated enigmatic mind of Montezuma so subtly that he became the voluntary prisoner of Cortes. Historians agree that any assessment of Cortes's two campaigns against the Aztecs must take account of his ability to attract and retain the loyalty of this extraordinary woman. She was given the title Dona Marina by the Spaniards, but, to the Aztecs, Cortes and his "tongue" were one—"Malinche."

❖❖❖

As an illustration of the sophistication of theme and characterization, note the scene (p. 56-57) between Cortes and his mistress-interpreter, Marina (played in the episode by Eartha Kitt). She asks Cortes whether she has been a good servant. Cortes answers, "Yes." Has she been a faithful tongue to the Indians? Yes. A friend? Yes. And a wife? (Cortes doesn't answer. He stands stiffly, a little coldly.) Finally: "I have a wife across the seas." Marina: "What soldier does not have a wife somewhere across some sea?"

Robert Horowitz writes: "Such a sophisticated conversation, which hints at interracial sex, would clearly not appear on a television program directed at children. That this dialogue was spoken on an *adult* show broadcast in 1953 was remarkable in itself." ("History Comes to Life and *You Are There*," p. 81.) (Language of even more astounding candor for the period is to be found in "The Secret of Sigmund Freud.")

It will be noted that all of Polonsky's teleplays for *You Are There* (and those by Bernstein and Manoff as well) respect the intelligence, sophistication, and maturity of a viewing audience that was considered to be sufficiently educated to recognize or to connect with the historical framework of a given episode. There was at least the assumption made at that time (these episodes were written in the early 1950s) that the audience of the day was likely to seek elucidation of complex or unknown aspects of a dramatization by additional reading and research of its own. (The broadcasts were directed at an age range from high school students on up; kinescopes—16mm prints photographed from the video screen—and directly filmed versions of the shows were made available by CBS News and the Prudential Insurance Company of America to schools for study.)

As for the trio of writers—Abraham Polonsky, Walter Bernstein, Arnold Manoff—which was creating these scripts, a remarkable working protocol developed. As Bernstein explains: "We had established in fact what we had always extolled in theory, a kind of commune. . . . We found that we were operating on the subversive principle of 'From each according to his ability, to each according to his need.' Since we were each of similar ability, at least as far as television was concerned, that took care of itself. So did the question of need. No one took more than one job for himself. That became automatic, taken for granted, an unconscious basis for the group. If one of us had a job and found another, the second job was offered to the group as a matter of course and taken by whoever needed it the most at that moment, to pay rent or a doctor's bill or even alimony. The need was never questioned; we all were in need. . . . There was no sense of charity or even obligation. We had simply discovered we were together not just to help ourselves but one another. It was what gave the group its moral and emotional base. It defined who we were." (*Inside Out*, pp. 215-216.)

CORTES CONQUERS MEXICO
by Abraham Polonsky
(signed by Jeremy Daniel)

Air Date:
April 5, 1953

YOU ARE THERE
November 11, 1519

FADE IN:

INT. CBS STUDIOS

> CRONKITE

November 11, 1519, Walter Cronkite reporting. Today, the uneasy armed truce in Europe was shattered. War between Spain and France seems inevitable.

We have just learned that Charles V, King of Spain, has made a secret pact with the Papal League of Italy. The object: the destruction of French power on the Continent. The plan of Charles V to wipe out the new national states and create a unified Europe under his throne depends in the main on his economic ability to support the vast military operations to which he is committed.

Proof of the imminence of war can be found in the rise in taxes and increased demands for shipment of gold and silver from the Spanish Indies. Whether this bullion, without which the war cannot be waged, will arrive in time, or at all, is one of the key questions in the minds of those who still hope and pray for peace. For a further report on this situation we take you to Santiago de Cuba, capital of the island of Cuba, in the Spanish Indies, and Bill Leonard. All things are as they were then, except . . . YOU ARE THERE.

INT. SANITAGO DE CUBA — THE GOVERNOR'S PALACE

DIEGO VELASQUEZ sits at a table reading from a document, addressing as in TV broadcasts, an invisible audience. A candle stands on either side of the document. Beside him, an armed soldier. Behind him, the outspread banner with the arms of Spain. He reads, audio off, as the reporter speaks. Diego is a fat man, usually merry, but now vindictive and hurt.

LEONARD
(very hurried to get governor on)

This is Bill Leonard in the governor's palace in Santiago de Cuba. For ten minutes now, Governor Diego Velasquez of Cuba has been reading the charges which he will bring against Hernan Cortes before the Royal Audencia, the tribunal sent from Spain. As you know, Cortes left Cuba about eighteen months ago in command of an expedition to Mexico. The first eleven charges of the accusation related to Cortes' refusal to ship any of the vast treasures which he has been reported to have seized from the natives. His Excellency, Don Diego de Velasquez, Governor of Cuba . . .

Cross fade, REPORTER out, GOVERNOR in.

DIEGO

. . . and other grave crimes of treason against His Majesty, Charles V of Spain.

Twelve: My express written orders to Hernan Cortes were to barter with the natives and explore the coast, but he, defying me, has founded cities and set himself up as feudal lord of New Spain, known to the barbarians there as Mexico.

Thirteen: After I revoked his command as Alcade of Santiago and leader of the Armada, having learned on good authority of his rebellious disposition and treasonable ambitions, he did secretly set sail against my express orders by bribing my representatives and the officers of the crown.

Fourteen: He committed an act of piracy against eleven ships, 100 sailors, 553 soldiers, 32 cross-bowmen, 13 arbusquiers, 200

(MORE)

DIEGO (CON'T)
Indian slaves and a few menial Indian women; and also 10
heavy guns, 4 falconnets and 10 horses. All these he did
appropriate to his own uses, and further to prevent the loyal
captains from returning to Cuba, he did burn the ships and
destroy them utterly till they lay broken like dead whales on
the beach, marooning His Majesty's ministers and soldiers.

Fifteen: The said Hernan Cortes, in direct contravention of his
orders and the faith of a good Christian, has permitted the
barbarians to continue with their abominable practices of
human sacrifice and cannibalism, and has entered into
relations with an Indian slave woman, known as Dona Marina
or Malinche; all this to consolidate his private claims against
the rights of the King-Emperor of God's Holy Roman Empire
and Spain. For all these reasons and others too numerous to
mention, I, Diego Velasquez, governor of Cuba, have decided
to send a vast Armada of sixteen ships to seize Hernan Cortes
and set up in New Spain a rightful representative of His
Majesty, in order to expedite the shipments of bullion which
have been requested for the Holy Wars against France. If
Hernan Cortes resists, my orders are that he be killed. If he
returns in chains, he will be tried for treason and heathenish
practices and other abominations too vile to be mentioned . . .

Cross fade to REPORTER.

LEONARD
These formalities of charges and countercharges will continue
for some time as the friends of the accused man take up his
defense. Meanwhile, we take you to the capital of the Aztec
empire in Mexico and the headquarters of Captain Cortes
where we will get a report on the situation there and the
attitude of the commander, from Harry Marble.

INT. PALACE OF AXAYACATL

A long corridor. At the farthest end much military activity. A cannon
being dragged past. Coming down corridor into camera, a soldier on
guard, in full armor.

MARBLE

This is Harry Marble in the palace of Axayacatl, the
headquarters assigned to the expeditionary force of Captain-
General Cortes by the Aztec emperor, Montezuma II.

While relations between the Spaniards and Aztecs have
remained friendly on the surface, tensions continue to build,
and for the past six days all military personnel have been
under a continuous alert. The small force of 400 Spaniards and
their 200 Indian allies from Tlaxcala are surrounded by three
hundred thousand Aztec inhabitants of this great city and the
garrison of fifty thousand crack palace troops of Montezuma.

The soldier has passed the camera which pans with him to reveal the
council chamber and the Spanish captains meeting within.

MARBLE (CON'T)

You are looking directly into the council chamber and at the
leading Spanish captains. This is an emergency meeting called
to decide on the next move to be made, in this great adventure
which has opened a new world of matchless wealth and
civilization to Spanish ambitions.

As the soldier turns back to the corridor and marches down it, the
camera pans back with him. CORTES is coming in the opposite
direction. The soldier stands stiffly to one side as his general passes him.

MARBLE (CON'T)

Here comes Captain-General Cortes now on his way to the
conference.
          (as Cortes comes closer to the camera)
Captain Cortes . . .

Cortes faces into the camera. The soldier walks guard in the rear.

MARBLE (CON'T)

Are you familiar with the charges placed against you by the
governor of Cuba?

Cortes is a decisive man, with a bold eloquent voice. he is a mixture of
shrewdness and force, of real religious conviction and very material
ambition.

CORTES

I am familiar with these false charges. They began before I left
Cuba and they will continue until this great country is added
to the Spanish empire.

MARBLE

How do you expect to meet these charges?

CORTES

By actions. From now on I shall ignore the governor of Cuba
and communicate directly with the King of Spain.

MARBLE

There were certain specific charges against you with relation to
Dona Marina.

CORTES

She is a slave, given to me by my Indian allies and has been of
great value as an interpreter. The Indians call her "the tongue
of Cortes."

MARBLE

I believe there were other charges of a religious nature, raised
by Governor Velasquez?

CORTES

My mission is to take this land for Charles V, my emperor, and
to convert these barbarians to our holy faith. The mission is
not yet accomplished. Nevertheless, as a symbol of my
intentions, I have ordered a troop of soldiers under Captain
Pedro de Albarado to raise the cross right in the main temple
of the Aztecs and to cast down their murderous idols. This is
now being done.

MARBLE

Do you think it's wise at this moment to antagonize the
emperor Montezuma and the entire priesthood and people of
the Aztecs?

CORTES

It is unwise. But I can no longer bear the sight of the victims
(MORE)

CORTES (CON'T)
sacrificed daily outside the very doors of this palace. I did
what I had to do and will bear what has to come. It is a
philosophy I recommend to all men.

He turns abruptly on his heel and enters the council room. The guard
then poses himself in front.

MARBLE
That was Captain-General Hernan Cortes, Commander of the
Spanish expedition into the interior of Yucatan and Mexico.
This direct attack by the Spaniards on the religious
superstitions of the Aztecs may lead to serious repercussions.
We now take you to the main temple of the Aztecs directly
outside here. Come in, Mike Wallace.

EXT. TEMPLE — MEXICO

Temple of the war god, steps and summit. A Spanish soldier, fully
armored and bearing the pennant with the king's arms mounts into view.
He plants the pennant.

WALLACE
Mike Wallace reporting. We are in the central market square
on top of the main Aztec temple. The Spanish soldier you see
there is Captain Pedro de Albarado, whom the Indians call
Tonatio which means the sun. He is second in command to
Hernan Cortes.

Within the chapel is the Aztec God of War. The Spanish
soldiers call him Old Witchywolves, but this affectionate
description hardly suggests what goes on here. Each day a
few human beings, and on grand holidays as much as twelve
thousand men, women and children, are sacrificed here, their
hearts cut out by obsidian knives and their bodies flung down
the 124 steps that lead to the paved courtyard below. The still-
beating hearts are burned in braziers to the greater glory of
Montezuma and the God of War.

A soldier or two enter the temple and carry out ceremonial objects which
they unceremoniously drop down into the square below.

WALLACE

Within the temple is the great drum made of serpent skins
which can be heard all over the city when it is struck to
summon the people . The walls of the temple are stained with
human blood.

A priest ascends now bearing his sacred sacramental objects for blessing
the cross. They carry out the idol.

WALLACE

That is Father Olmeda. Today, by command of Hernan Cortes,
the idol is to be cast down, and in its place a cross erected and
consecrated.

Soldiers ascend with the cross.

WALLACE

Earlier the Aztec priests were hustled away by armed Spanish
troops, and one Aztec priest who resisted was killed. As yet
there have been no reactions from the populace or the Aztec
garrison.

The cross is erected.

WALLACE

The raising of the cross right here in the heart of Mexico City in
the very temple of the chief Aztec god is an act of unparalleled
daring, of religious faith, but of folly, too. For we are here in
the heart of this dark and golden continent . . .

Services to bless the cross begin and carry through to the end. Flowers
are placed at the foot of the cross, etc.

WALLACE (CON'T)

. . . surrounded by unimaginable dangers, strange men,
stranger customs and even stranger beasts . . .

Below us, on one side of the temple is the palace of
Montezuma, and on the other side the headquarters of Cortes.
We now take you back to the headquarters of the Spanish
expeditionary force . . . and Harry Marble . . .

INT. PALACE OF AXAYACATL — COUNCIL ROOM OF CORTES

> MARBLE
>
> This is Harry Marble in the council room of the Spanish
> expeditionary forces. No agreement has been reached on what
> the next step should be in the present campaign. Cortes has
> met strong disapproval on his orders to violate the Aztec gods.
> The feeling of most of the leaders is that the Spaniards should
> take what treasure they have and escape back to the coast.
> Cortes is opposed to this. At the moment he is preparing to
> dictate a dispatch to the King of Spain.

Cortes is alert to the profound danger of the situation which he never
underestimates.

> CORTES
> (dictating)
>
> Write as I speak. To his most high, mighty and Catholic
> Prince, Invincible Emperor and our sovereign liege: I am
> desirous that Your Majesty should know of matters concerning
> this land, which is so great and marvelous . . .

Camera in on OLID, a gloomy, irascible captain.

> MARBLE
> (hushed on mic)
>
> Captain Cristobal de Olid . . .

> CORTES
> (over)
>
> . . . that, as I wrote in my former letter and dispatch, Your
> Majesty may well call himself emperor of it with no less reason
> and title than he now does of Germany, which by grace of God
> Your Majesty now possesses.

> OLID
> (gulping wine, ironically)
>
> He may call himself emperor of the world also, which he holds
> as lightly as we hold Mexico.

CORTES
(frowning)
Well, Captain, having discovered Mexico, we must conquer it
before it conquers us.
(to scribe again as the camera moves)
In my former letter, most excellent prince, I informed Your
Majesty of all the towns and villages which up to that time I
held as subject and conquered. And I also mentioned news . . .

Camera on DE LEON, a suspicious man, always looking for an angle.

MARBLE
(in and out fast)
Captain Juan Velasquez de Leon, nephew of the governor of
Cuba who is seeking to replace Cortes.

CORTES
. . . of a great ruler named Montezuma and that I intended to
advance and see him wherever he might be found. We have
sought him here in Tenochtitlan, beyond the high mountains
and snows and floods, and we have found him out.

DE LEON
Or has he enticed us, like a spider in his web.

CORTES
(softly)
Where else do you find the spider, if not in his web?
(to scribe again)
The great city of Tenochtitlan is built in the midst of a salt lake,
and it is two leagues from the heart of the city to any point on
the mainland, hence the hazard of our position. Four
causeways lead to it, all made by hand. The city itself is as
large as Seville or Cordova.

SANDOVAL
But more beautiful by far.

Camera on SANDOVAL.

MARBLE
(under him)
Captain Gonzalo de Sandoval, personal friend and townsman
of Cortes.

SANDOVAL
(a tough, honest, very sensitive man)
Tell him how it is, Hernan, and how we thought we were
enchanted when first we saw it from the high mountains, the
snows up there and the sun below.

CORTES
(affectionately smiling)
I will . . . .

As Cortes describes the city, the camera will discover DONA MARINA
sitting in the shadows, impassive, her eyes always on Cortes, resplendent
in full Indian costume.

CORTES
Tenochtitlan stands in the waters and many other towns and
cities stand around the lakes, one of which is salt and the other
sweet. In the center is the huge and cursed . . .

Somewhere here the camera pauses on Dona Marina.

MARBLE
(quickly)
Dona Marina, slave, interpreter to Cortes for the last fourteen
months.

CORTES
. . . temple where you can smell the dried blood of the men and
women they sacrifice there, and all around are the floating
gardens and the red and white flowers, white walls and walls
that are pale and pink. There is an aqueduct that brings fresh
water from Chapultepec, and on the lakes a multitude of
canoes, and in the cities temples and oratories like towers and
fortresses and all gleaming white, and it is a wonderful thing
to behold . . . three thousand barbarians and we but four
hundred men.

OLID

If we die like rats in the trap of Montezuma, our souls will go
and the treasure will still be here in the oratories and temples.

At this moment PEDRO DE ALBARADO enters. He is gay and wears a
flower in his helmet.

PEDRO
(shouting and interrupting)
Rejoice! The War God is down and the cross of the Prince of
Peace is risen.

The men shake their heads despondently. Marina rises and goes to the
window and looks out on the temple and street. Cortes crosses himself.

CORTES
Was there trouble, Pedro?

PEDRO
Nothing.
(taking some wine)
The smell of blood in the temple is like a place where they
slaughter animals.

CORTES
(to scribe with much emotion)
Most Catholic Majesty, I forbade these Indians to make human
sacrifice to the idols as was their wont, because, besides being
an abomination in the sight of God, it is prohibited by Your
Majesty's laws which declare that he who kills shall be killed.

OLID
(gloomily)
And so all of us will die, for God knows, we have killed.

DE LEON
The question is, what do we do now, not in heaven, but here?

PEDRO
(the quarreling starts to mount)
We have the gold, at least enough for each man. Let's go back
to Spain and enjoy it.

OLID
(quite hastily)
And if the Indians raise the drawbridges?

PEDRO
(shouting)
We will lower them.

SANDOVAL
(soberly)
I think, Hernan, we had best depart with our men to the coast,
for here we are too few.

Cortes hammers on the table for order.

CORTES
(shouting)
And what are we *there* if the governor of Cuba should send an
armada to pick up the prizes of all the works we have done,
and the deaths we have died? And hang us besides! Captains,
what do we do? I must have your advice on this matter. We
are like visitors in the world of dreams. We see everything,
but nothing can we touch, or bring back.

PEDRO
For my part, I say, let us do something, no matter how
dangerous so long as it is something, and we either win or
lose.

They are all talking at once. Their fear makes them quarrel.

DE LEON
You call that reason? Let us escape while we can, and if we
have to, abandon the treasure. What good is the treasure if
we're dead?

OLID
Can we make a treaty with Montezuma?

CORTES
We can make it, but since he is stronger, he can break it.

ALL TOGETHER

We have gone too far . . . A wise general knows when to
retreat, etc.

Suddenly the great drum in the temple sounds, a great hollow boom
from outside. The voices die down. In silence they look at each other.
Marina, who is at the window, turns to them.

MARINA

It is the temple drum, my lords, and the priests of Montezuma
are calling the people and the soldiers.

OLID
(angrily)

Couldn't the cross wait another day?

The drum sound again.

CORTES
(in his great voice)

The cross is our strength, and if the devil beats a drum, do we
fly? Go to your posts. I have to decide, and when I decide we
will do it. And whatever happens, in God's name it will be
done.

The captains go out quickly. Their voices call outside to the men. Cortes
goes to the window and looks out. The drum sounds again.

Cortes stands and listens. He is now, as we can see, terribly depressed,
almost lost.

CORTES

Marina?

MARINA
(submissively)

My lord.

CORTES

What will happen to us here?

The drum sounds again.

MARINA
(indicating the temple outside and the
drum with a gesture)
We will all die, some in battle and some on the altar.

CORTES
The altar is torn down.

MARINA
What is torn down can be raised.

In her voice, her manner, she is making love to him, although her words
are those of the slave.

MARINA (CON'T)
I am the tongue of Cortes and speak for him and to him. The
Indians call me Malinche and now they call you Malinche, for
we are as one in their minds, and I am as powerful in this
whole realm as you are. Now when you are cast down, I will
fall, and when you die, I will die.

CORTES
(with sudden despair)
If I only knew which danger was the most practical, I would
practice it.

MARINA
(with triumph, for she has the answer)
O Hernan Cortes, the Indians are men as I am a woman, and
they live as you do by what they believe. And you are going
to die here in Tenochtitlan unless you listen to their thoughts.

CORTES
I do, and I say the trouble is they no longer think we are gods.
Our magic is gone.

MARINA
I knew that secret long ago. But Montezuma is their king and
their god, and his flesh is sacred, and his feet must not touch
the ground, and kings from the south and north have died on
his altars because he is the King of Kings, and the people do
not even dare raise their eyes to look at him, he is so high.

CORTES

But you do.

MARINA

I was a slave sold by his kind and my eyes are free. And I can
see what Montezuma cannot see and you cannot see. If you
kill Montezuma, another will become king. If you bewitched
Montezuma and spoke through his mouth, this empire would
be yours and the land and the people, and you would be safe.

CORTES

I cannot bewitch anyone.

MARINA

You can take him hostage and hold him and speak through
him, if you dare. If you dare you can hold him, and the land
will listen to you, if he proclaims that you are an emissary of
the gods.

CORTES

And if he will not?

MARINA

You will die. But if you do not dare, we will all die anyway.
                    (looking out the window as the drum
                    strikes)
Perhaps on that altar.
                    (kneeling at his feet)
That is my advice, my lord. You cannot defeat the hundred
thousand soldiers of Montezuma, but you can defeat him, and
through him, the empire.

CORTES
                    (looking down at her with a rising spirit,
                    his daring flooding upon him as it
                    always does when action comes)
Then we will take him. We will try. And if he falls, then a
slave they gave me will have struck him down, and with it, the
great empire.
                    (raising her tenderly, joyfully)
I give you your freedom, Marina, for you have given me mine
back again.

MARINA

What freedom, my lord?

CORTES
(buoyant)
To go as you will, as I go. To be free.

She shakes her head.

CORTES

What can I give you?

MARINA

Have I been a good servant?

CORTES

Yes.

MARINA

And been your faithful tongue to the Indians?

CORTES

Yes.

MARINA

And a friend?

CORTES

Yes.

MARINA
(softly)
And a wife?

Cortes doesn't answer. He stands stiffly, a little coldly.

CORTES

I have a wife across the seas.

MARINA
(bitterly)
What soldier does not have a wife somewhere across some
sea?

She turns from him to the wall, facing away. He looks for a moment and
strides out. At the door he starts to shout.

CORTES
De Sandoval, de Olid, de Albarado, de Leon . . . here!

The captains join him in the corridor and they all speak furiously. Each
runs on a task.

MARBLE
We will now take you back to the temple and Mike Wallace
where we hear troops from the Aztec garrison have
surrounded the grounds and the cross is being destroyed. The
city is stirring with excitement over what they regard as
sacrilege, and on the causeway a gang of Aztec youth attacked
two Spanish soldiers. Come in, Mike Wallace.

EXT. TEMPLE — STEPS AND SUMMIT

Aztecs are pulling down the cross.

WALLACE
(very excited)
They are pulling down the cross. Below the square is filled
with Aztec soldiers, and the people are coming into the side
streets and the lagoons are filling with canoes. The men are all
armed.
(as the cross falls)
There goes the cross.

The cross is flung down the steps.

WALLACE (CON'T)
That's the way they fling the bodies of the sacrificed victims
down the steps after the ceremony of tearing out the heart.

The idol of the war god is borne back up the stairs and ceremoniously carried into the temple. The bearers follow with the fire to relight the sacred vessels.

> WALLACE (CON'T)
> And here is the War God himself being carried in to be set up, and the ceremonial fire in which the smoking hearts are burned is being rekindled.

An Indian priest comes to the parapet and looks down.

> WALLACE (CON'T)
> Below the Spaniards are bringing their heavy field guns out and covering the square and side streets with them. There goes a patrol of about fifty men, the musketeers in front, and here come the horses. As usual, the Indians fall back from the horses.

The priest calls over others who stand and look down.

> WALLACE (CON'T)
> The Spaniards are clearing the road between their palace and the palace of Montezuma. Come in now, Winston Burdett.

INT. PALACE OF MONTEZUMA — A CORRIDOR

Indians are slowly backing down to camera as armed and armored Spaniards advance into the corridor. Men peel off and halt in front of doorways, etc. The effect should be of a plan in which troops are being placed at strategic places.

> BURDETT
> Winston Burdett here. We are in the anterooms of Montezuma's palace, and for the last few minutes, groups of Spanish soldiers have been infiltrating and taking strategic positions covering all entrances and exits. The Tlaxcalan allies of the Spaniards have been disposed, almost two thousand strong, down the back lane that leads from behind the patio of Montezuma's palace to the palace where Cortes has his headquarters. Here is Captain-General Cortes now.

Cortes comes down the corridor with his captains and Dona Marina. Pan them into an anteroom. The Spaniards talk. Albarado draws his sword but Cortes makes him resheathe it. An Indian enters. He carries one of the heavy Indian swords, edged with obsidian. He approaches the group.

> BURDETT (CON'T)
> The Aztec you see there is chamberlain to Montezuma. The Spaniards have requested an audience with Montezuma, but the chamberlain is insisting that the Spaniards disarm before they enter the presence of the Emperor.

Suddenly the Indian raises his sword in a threatening way. Albarado draws and runs him through. The Indian falls to the ground. The Spaniards walk off leaving him lying there. Two Spanish soldiers with crossbows enter and stand guard in the room. The Indian lies there.

INT. MONTEZUMA'S CHAMBER

Cortes, his captains and Marina enter.

The Spaniards pause at the threshold. A slow pan down a long room. At the other end, magnificent, melancholy, sits Montezuma on a wooden backless chair on which is draped a feather-robe, etc. By him stands an Indian noble, armed. Cortes advances to within ten or fifteen feet of Montezuma, removes his helmet and kneels on one knee.

> CORTES
> Your Majesty.

There is no sign of recognition or anything from Montezuma. Cortes rises.

> CORTES (CON'T)
> (polite)
> Sir, I have certain complaints which I wish to place before you for your consideration.

> MONTEZUMA
> Malinche, I sent my chamberlain to tell you that soldiers do not wear arms in the presence of Montezuma.

CORTES
(with a smile)
We carry our arms the better to defend Your Imperial
Highness against whatever dangers may be abroad.

MONTEZUMA
(dryly)
I know of no dangers except from abroad.

CORTES
Your Majesty is badly informed.

As they talk the captains spread out and place themselves strategically.
Montezuma watches them uneasily.

CORTES
However, there is, sir, a matter of great import to speak of. I
cannot understand how so great a lord and as wise a man as
you are, has not yet thought it out that the idols you keep in
the temples are not gods, but very bad things known as devils.
I raised in their place the true cross, and I learn that your
priests have torn down this cross and put in its stead the Satan
that eats human hearts and flesh. Was this on your command?

MONTEZUMA
(a little sharply)
My priests placed their gods in the temple built and raised for
their gods. If you wish to raise a cross, raise it in your own
temple . . . which is in your own land.

CORTES
(with great earnestness)
It seems to me, my lord, that we should speak more of these
grave matters, and at our leisure. It would be well for you to
come with us to our palace, and rest awhile with us there,
surrounded and protected by my soldiers who love and
respect Your Majesty and would do all his commands.

MONTEZUMA
(rises, his voice trembling with anger)
My person is not such as to be in prison, and even if I were
willing, my people would not tolerate it.

Marina has gone to the balcony and looks down on the crowd and excitement gathering there.

CORTES
(silkily)
You would not be a prisoner but my guest, as I am your guest in your land and not your prisoner. You may be sure that I and my men will serve you faithfully.

MONTEZUMA
I am faithfully served by my own.

Crowd noises up outside. The temple drum sounds again.

CORTES
I beseech Your Majesty to come freely with me. No harm will come to you.

MONTEZUMA
(slowly sitting down as the drum sounds)
I will not come.

CORTES
(listening to the gathering storm, but remaining calm)
Give it your true consideration, sir. I would speak to you of the safety of your eternal soul, and of the matters of this land and its people, and of your allegiance to the great king across the seas whose vassal I am and whose vassal you must be, since he is of the East and you did tell me of the tale of Quetzalcoatl who would one day come himself or send emissaries to lead the Aztec peoples.

MONTEZUMA
(rising, in a burst of fury)
If you had come to save our souls and our souls alone, I could have understood it, for men preach what gods they believe in . . . and if you had come only to steal our treasure and our lands, I could have understood it, for men steal what they can take . . . but you would steal both our souls and our lands and treasures. What does that leave us? It leaves us slaves,
(MORE)

MONTEZUMA (CON'T)

without our gods and without our fortunes. If you attempt this, Malinche, you will all die. They will tear our your hearts on the altars and eat your flesh at the temple steps.

Albarado draws his sword.

ALBARADO
(yelling)
Why waste words? Let him come or we will run him through the body.

MARINA
(appearing behind Montezuma, close, quickly)
I advise you to move without noise, for then they will honor you.

Suddenly Montezuma is surrounded by armored men and drawn swords and stands in the net of steel. The swords and the death are around him. Outside, the great temple drum is struck, again and again.

MARINA
(at Montezuma's ear, talking rapidly)
I know their powers, for you gave me in slavery to them and I have been with them from the day they landed on our shores. Their boats came across the wide seas, and they have powers you have not seen yet. Truly they are what you thought they were, emissaries from that other kingdom to which some day we will all go. And behind them are others, numberless.

The king is upset, frightened, confused. A cannon goes off outside. Crowd noises up.

MARINA (CON'T)
You are the king and you must save this city and all cities from their wrath, for they kill like giants.

CORTES
Speak to your people and calm them, Montezuma. Say that you are coming with us of your own will, as you are, for you must come, and you will come.

MARINA
(swiftly, softly, eagerly in the
king's ear)
This is the moment of your destiny, as was predicted and as
was said in our history, and these strangers are here. If you do
not listen, the peoples and the cities will die.

CORTES
(more loudly)
Speak to the people and tell them we are come here from the
east and the prophecy is come to life.

As Montezuma hesitates, Cortes approaches him, sword in hand, and
suddenly explodes.

CORTES
(raging)
Go to that balcony and speak to your people. Speak or you
will see such blood in your streets that even you who have
slaughtered in your temples by the thousands will hang back
in horror and amazement. And you will not die until it is all
done and all are dead but you. You will be the last.

He grabs Montezuma and pulls him to the balcony.

CORTES (CON'T)
I will put this city to fire and sword and no one will move or
walk or breathe here until eternity.

He puts the sword to Montezuma's back and pushes him out on the
balcony. As Montezuma hesitates, Cortes presses against him.

CORTES (CON'T)
I speak for a greater king and God than any you have known.
Tell them. Tell them and we will be brothers and we will love
and protect each other. Tell them, or else you and all of them
will die. Now speak.

Montezuma speaks, and with hesitation and infinite sadness, as behind
him the Spaniards realize that their daring gesture has won the day and
the empire.

MONTEZUMA

Brothers and friends, you know that for a long time you and
your forefathers have been subjects and vassals of my
ancestors and mine, and have always been well treated by
them and by me. You must know from your ancestors that we
and ours are not native to this land, but came from a far off
country under a lord whom we know as Quetzalcoatl, who left
us and said that one day he would return or send someone
with power and force to attract us to his sway again. And you
know how we have always been expecting him, and his
emissary is here in the person of the Great Captain who has
told us of his Emperor who commands us to return to his
service across the seas. We have waited for him a long time
and now he is here. I beg you to obey him as you would me,
and render him what he wills as your lord and in this way you
will do me great pleasure.

In the silence now, Montezuma returns. As he faces into the room Cortes
motions to one of the captains who suddenly produces a set of chains for
Montezuma. The king shrinks back in horror as he sees them.

MONTEZUMA
(in a defeated voice, utterly broken)
I said I would go with you.

CORTES
Then come. I bear you great love, my king, and you have our
services forever.

The captain with the chains walks in front, then Montezuma guarded,
and then Cortes. Marina remains alone in the room, bends down and
picks up one of Montezuma's feathers that has fallen to the floor and
carries it out.

Superimpose over the room the top of the temple, as Spanish soldiers
once again raise the immense cross, and the services and blessings begin.

CRONKITE
(voice over)
And the cross was raised again. In his dispatches to Charles V
of Spain, Cortes finished his report.

CORTES
(voice over)
And Your Majesty, having passed six days there in the great
city of Tenochtitlan, and having seen something of its marvels,
though little in comparison with what is to be seen and
examined, I considered it essential both from my observation
of the city and the rest of the land, that its ruler should be in
my power and no longer entirely free . . . *and this is now done.*

From Your Sacred Majesty's very humble slave and vassal who
kisses the royal hands and feet of Your Highness, Hernan
Cortes, Captain-General and Lord Justiciar of Yucatan.

INT. CBS STUDIOS

CRONKITE
With the seizure of Montezuma, the conquest of Mexico was
assured, although the Indians did rebel, and Montezuma was
killed, and Cortes did ravage that great city in the plain of
Mexico. As for Marina, Cortes gave her away to a friend. And
the Indians passed into slavery from which they emerged
some four hundred years later into a new nation. While in the
great ruin, archaeologists still dig and marvel at the civilization
which Cortes found there, the land of Eldorado. Strangely
enough there is no statue of Cortes in all of Mexico, and the
Indian word for traitor is the name of the slave who was the
tongue of Cortes.

What sort of a day was it? A day like all days, filled with those
events that alter and illuminate our time . . . and YOU WERE
THERE.

FADE OUT.

THE CRISIS OF GALILEO

Galileo Galilei (b. 15 February 1564, Pisa, Italy—d. 8 January 1642, Arcetri, near Florence), Italian mathematician, astronomer, and physicist, made several significant contributions to modern scientific thought. As the first man to use the telescope to study the skies, he amassed evidence that proved the Copernican theory that the Earth revolves around the Sun and is not the center of the universe, as had been believed. His position represented a radical departure from accepted thought in that Copernican theory contradicted the Scriptures on significant points. He reminded Church authorities of its standing practice of interpreting Scripture allegorically whenever it came into conflict with scientific truth.

Unfortunately, Cardinal Robert Bellarmine, the chief theologian of the Church, was unable to appreciate the importance of the new theories and clung to the time-honored belief that mathematical hypotheses have nothing to do with physical reality. He only saw the danger of a scandal, which might undermine Catholicism in its fight with Protestantism. He accordingly decided to check the whole issue by having Copernicanism declared "false and erroneous" and the book of Copernicus placed on the Index (*Index Librorum Prohibitorum*—the list of forbidden or otherwise restricted material deemed morally harmful by the Roman Catholic Church). The decree came out on 5 March 1616.

In 1624 Galileo obtained permission from Pope Urban VIII to write about "the systems of the world," both Ptolemaic and Copernican, as long as he discussed them noncommittally and came to the conclusion dictated to him in advance by the pontiff—that is, that man cannot presume to know how the world is really made because God could have brought about the same effects in ways unimagined by him, and he must not restrict God's omnipotence. Thus, in 1632, Galileo produced his great book, *Dialogue Concerning the Two Chief World Systems—Ptolemaic and Copernican.*

It was pointed out to the Pope that despite its noncommittal title, the work was a compelling and unabashed plea for the Copernican system. The strength of the argument made the prescribed conclusion look anticlimactic and pointless. The Pope, in anger, ordered a prosecution. Galileo was covered by license. Therefore, the only legal measures would be to disavow the licensers and prohibit the book. But at that point a document was "discovered" in the file, to the effect that during his audience with Bellarmine on 26 February 1616, Galileo had been specifically enjoined from "teaching or discussing Copernicanism in any way," under the penalties of the Holy Office. (The consensus of historians, based on evidence made available when the file was published in 1877, has been that the document had been planted and Galileo was never so enjoined.) The Church authorities, on the strength of the "new" document, were able to prosecute him for "vehement suspicion of heresy."

He was found guilty of having "held and taught" the Copernican doctrine and was ordered to recant. Galileo recited a formula in which he "abjured, cursed and detested" his past errors. The sentence carried imprisonment, but this portion of the penalty was immediately commuted by the Pope into house arrest and seclusion on his little estate at Arcetri near Florence, where he returned in December 1633. The sentence of house arrest remained in effect throughout the last eight years of his life.

In 1634 he completed *Discorsi e dimostrazioni mathematiche intorno a due nuove scienze attenti alla meccanica (Dialogue Concerning Two New Sciences . . .)*, in which he recapitulated the results of his early experiments and his mature meditations on the principles of mechanics. This, in many respects his most valuable work, was printed in 1638.

❖❖❖

Galileo's recantation before the Inquisition is, of course, the thematic cynosure of this parable—as it is viewed within the contemporary context of HUAC's inquisition in Hollywood. It may be interesting to place Polonsky's teleplay of the Galileo tale (1953) in a line following the most famous treatment of this story, Bertolt Brecht's *Galileo*. (This theatrical production opened in Hollywood on 30 July 1947, ironically just two months before the first session of HUAC hearings opened in Washington, D.C. The play starred Charles Laughton, was directed by Joseph Losey, and was produced by John Houseman, T. Edward Hambleton, and Norman Lloyd.)

The Galileo case underscores the ambiguity which surrounds the phenomenon of political, religious, and intellectual censorship by established authorities—and the possible motivations of individuals in (qualifiedly) acceding to it. Theatre critic Eric Bentley, for example, in his essay "The Science Fiction of Bertolt Brecht," virtually excuses Galileo for his weakness in giving in to the Church, and stresses instead his "slyness and cunning" in writing his *Discorsi* and smuggling them out for publication. Indeed, a sympathetic interpretation of these events, of great appeal to many who rationalized their own cooperation with HUAC, supposes that Galileo had given in because he knew that it was more important for him to continue his work than to die in defense of it. [This is precisely the argument that Dr. Paget makes to the exiled John Milton, in Polonsky's "The Tragedy of John Milton" (p. 305). If you seek a specific indication of how Polonsky reacts to this motive for recantation, note Milton's response.] Or, at the very least, he might have recanted out of fear, knowing all the while that he was right; then, after a period of years, have decided that, even though there was a risk involved, he had to set down the principles of his new physics on paper and get them published.

But, in spite of the sympathetic and positive interpretations of the Galileo character in Brecht's play which have persisted over the years, there is evidence that Brecht himself did not intend this, that he could not find it in his heart to forgive Galileo his cowardice. For example, the Danish physicist Professor C. Mooler, with whom Brecht discussed the subject, said that "Brecht was of the opinion that Galileo's recantation represented defeat, which was in years to come to lead to a serious schism between science and human society." (Quoted in Frederic Ewen, *Bertolt Brecht: His Life, His Art, and His Times*, p 332.)

Passages from the play tend to support the contention that Brecht means to indict Galileo for his cowardice and betrayal. Note this exchange between Galileo, who enters "changed, almost unrecognizable," from his ordeal with the Inquisition, and Andrea, his student and disciple, who looks at him in dismay, knowing that he has recanted:

ANDREA
Unhappy is the land that breeds no hero.

GALILEO
No, Andrea: Unhappy is that land that needs a hero.

There is speculation that Brecht raises the argument that the writing of the *Discorsi* completely justified the recantation—simply so that the argument could be demolished. After many years Andrea is asked by Galileo to take the manuscript to Holland. Andrea is overcome. "Everything is changed!" he [Andrea] cries. Galileo asks why.

ANDREA
We lost our heads. With the crowd at the street corners we
said: "He will die, he will never surrender!" You came back: "I

surrendered but I am alive." We cried: "Your hands are stained!" You say: "Better stained than empty."

Andrea, in other words, sees his mentor's surrender to authority simply as a sly tactic by which he may gain the time he needs to continue his important work. But Galileo denies this:

GALILEO

I recanted because I was afraid of physical pain.

ANDREA

No!

GALILEO

They showed me the instruments.

ANDREA

It was not a plan?

GALILEO

It was not.

In a following tirade of self-loathing, Galileo declares that if he had held his ground his scientific knowledge could have freed the people from their tormentors. In fact, he concludes: "As a scientist I had an almost unique opportunity. In my day astronomy emerged into the marketplace. At that particular time, had one man put up a fight, it could have had wide repercussions. I have come to believe that I was never in real danger, for some years I was as strong as the authorities, and I surrendered my knowledge to the powers-that-be, to use it, no, not *use* it, *abuse* it, as it suits their ends. I have betrayed my profession. Any man who does what I have done must not be tolerated in the ranks of science." [An indispensable reference for this entire issue is Bruce Cook's *Brecht in Exile* (Holt, Rinehart and Winston, 1982), especially "Galileo in Hollywood," pp. 165-181.]

In spite of Brecht's intractable language, the more benign interpretation of the historical Galileo and the character created by Brecht persists; and, in the context of the blacklist period, is available to be coopted by informers who seek amelioration for their actions. Typical is composer David Raksin, who named eleven names to the Committee (20 September 1951). He said to Victor Navasky in *Naming Names*: [It was] "like the Spanish Inquisition, so maybe the best I can do is to come out of it alive. I didn't want people to think that this particular brand of progressive ideology was something I was ready to destroy myself over.

(You know, at the end of Brecht's *Galileo* there's a monumental confusion. The student says, 'Now I understand—you capitulated to write your book.') It may have been that at that moment we were required to rise to a stature we just didn't have." (pp. 251-252)

The problem with invoking Galileo as a role model is the failure to make the distinction between betraying your own conscience and betraying other human beings. Polonsky's position on this matter seems to be articulated in his teleplay, in the words of physiologist William Harvey: "I reject the action of Galileo Galilei as a betrayal of the work of his life and the truth about Nature and the Universe which we scientists must defend no matter what the personal consequences." (p. 95) It can also be found in Polonsky's tragic image of Galileo, contained in a poignantly rendered stage direction. (p. 96) :

> Galileo starts to drink, and then suddenly he puts the glass down and covers his face with his hands and begins to weep silently.

❖❖❖

Charles Russell, producer of *You Are There*, writes that "when I got Abe's script and read it, I put it in the bottom drawer of my desk, without sending it to mimeo and the normal distribution. I knew this might be going too far—a show about civil liberties in the most oppressive times. It wasn't historical accuracy that concerned me, it was the point of view and the timing.

"After reading the script [executive producer] William Dozier came out of his office, looking upset, and told me to wait, that he would be right back. I knew he was taking the script down to the Catholic Archdiocese in the Random House building, two blocks south on Madison Avenue [in New York; CBS was at 485 Madison]. I also knew his visit was not for a blessing but for clearance.

"He returned and issued the edict. 'I have marked the lines in the script that Jeremy [Polonsky] must change. And all references to the Church's torture of Galileo must be eliminated or this show will not go on the air.'

"I met with Abe at his apartment to try to get around the restrictions and not ruin the show. We went over the script, carefully eliminating or substituting words the church considered offensive and cutting any reference to the Church's torture of Galileo, softening the Holy Office figures and their efforts to force the scientist to recant. [As an example of the revisions: a line like "They will test your intention on your flesh, here in this chamber" was changed to "I will not shame you with my threats."] However, a key scene (p. 82-86), where Cardinal

Barberini [played in the episode by William Prince] urges Galileo [Philip Bourneuf] to submit, was played in a bare dungeon with some torture instruments hanging on the walls.

"The reaction to the show was universally positive. It was a very daring show." (Russell, "In the Worst of Times," pp. 74-76.)

❖❖❖

Historical Update. Three hundred and fifty-nine years after formally condemning Galileo Galilei for entertaining scientific truths it long denounced as against-the-Scriptures heresy, the Roman Catholic Church admitted its error. On 31 October 1992 the Pontifical Academy of Sciences, a commission of historic, scientific, and theological inquiry which Pope John Paul II appointed himself, brought a "not guilty" finding for Galileo. The commission found that Galileo's clerical judges acted in good faith but rejected theories because they were "incapable of dissociating faith from an age-old cosmology"—the biblical vision of the Earth as the center of the universe.

"This subjective error in judgment, so clear to us today, led them to a disciplinary measure from which Galileo 'had much to suffer.' These mistakes must be frankly recognized, as you, Holy Father, have requested," Cardinal Paul Poupard, the commission chairman, told the Pope.

The case was important to him, John Paul said, because over the centuries it had become "the symbol of the Church's supposed rejection of scientific progress, or of 'dogmatic' obscurantism opposed to the free search for truth." Galileo's condemnation, John Paul lamented, had led may scientists to conclude that there was "an incompatibility between the spirit of science and its rules of research on the one hand, and the Christian faith on the other."

"A tragic mutual incomprehension has been interpreted as the reflection of a fundamental opposition between science and faith. The clarifications furnished by recent historical studies enable us to state that this sad misunderstanding now belongs to the past," the Pope said.

(William Montalbano, "Earth Moves for Vatican in Galileo Case," *Los Angeles Times*, 1 November 1992, p. 1.)

THE CRISIS OF GALILEO
by Abraham Polonsky
(signed by Jeremy Daniel)

Air Date:
April 19, 1953

YOU ARE THERE
April 30, 1633

FADE IN:

INT. CBS STUDIOS

CRONKITE

Walter Cronkite reporting. CBS Television today takes you
back to Rome, Italy, on April 30, 1633, to witness the final steps
in the crisis of Galileo Galilei, a leading astronomer of Europe.
At the moment he is detained under examination by the Holy
Office of the Inquisition, in Rome, having been summoned
there to answer questions about the publication of his book of
dialogues on the motion of the earth around the sun . . . the
publication of this work having been forbidden by the Holy
Office on the basis that it is opposed to the beliefs of certain
members of that body. CBS Television newsmen are standing
by to bring you an on-the-spot report. We are going to take
you first to Arcetri, Italy for an interview with Galileo's
daughter. All things are as they were then, except . . . YOU
ARE THERE.

*CONVENT OF ST. MATTHEW, ARCETRI — THE PHARMACY OR
STILL ROOM*

A window, a row of flowering plants in pots, some bottles, vials,
sunlight, calm, peace. A nun, SISTER MARCIA CELESTE, is watering
the plants. She is dressed in the habit of the order of St. Francis, a
woman filled with much sweetness and piety, naive, devoted to her

father and her church. She has been in this convent for eighteen years, and the world has gone by like a rude storm outside.

LEONARD
(low voiced, respectful)
This is Bill Leonard. We are inside the pharmacy of the convent of St. Matthew in Arcetri. That is Sister Maria Celeste, the older of Galileo's two daughters, both of whom are attached to this convent. The nuns here . . .
(convent bells ring)
. . . belong to the order of St. Francis of Assisi, and live according to their vows of extreme poverty. The cells are small, simple, bare; the life, one of discipline and faith.
(the bells stop . . . A dog barks off)
It is spring here in Florence and the hills are full of flowers and nightingales. Yet between the Arno and Rome, the black plague kills as it runs, and springtime is also deathtime in Italy. In this simple pharmacy Sister Marie Celeste prepares the medicines and philtres used against all diseases, and we hear that she prepared two special ones for her father when he set out for Rome.

While Leonard is speaking, Sister Maria finishes with the flowers, arranges a few things. The bell rings again twice. She faces a small crucifix on the wall, crosses herself and turns into the camera. An expectant and pleasant smile on her face.

There is no break hardly between Leonard's last words and his first question.

[LEONARD
Thank you, Sister. There's so much plague around . . . . I wonder, could you tell me what remedies you gave your father when he set out for Rome?

SISTER MARIA
(a little professional smile, the doctor
to the patient)
I can. Two pots of electuary. One consists of dried figs, walnuts, rue, and salt, mixed together with honey. A piece the size of a walnut is to be taken in the morning, fasting, with a
(MORE)

SISTER MARIA (CON'T)
little Greek wine, or any other good wine. The other pot is
somewhat more tart, but equally efficacious.

As the bell rings, the sister kneels, says a short prayer, and then rises to
face into camera.]

LEONARD
Thank you, Sister. Have you heard from your father?

SISTER MARIA
(a sweet, disciplined voice)
I have.

LEONARD
What does he write?

SISTER MARIA
That the . . .
(she hesitates)
. . . *affair* in Rome is going well and that he has many friends
and his health is good.
(she smiles soberly)
Naturally, at first I was greatly troubled when I learned he was
detained by the Holy Office. I was anxious and uneasy.

LEONARD
We hear that he's been treated extremely well.

SISTER MARIA
So my lord and dear father writes to me, and since I am
convinced of the righteousness of his cause and his innocence
in this particular matter . . .

LEONARD
(interrupting)
Did he say what the exact charges were?

SISTER MARIA
(upset)
No one is supposed to say.

LEONARD

It has to do with his book of dialogues on the two principal systems of the world. He was originally forbidden to publish them.

SISTER MARIA

(with utter simplicity, but wisely)

I know of only one system, sir, that of God, and this I know my lord and father cherishes as I do.

LEONARD

He asserts that the earth moves around the sun.

SISTER MARIA

What he is accused of, I do not know, but what he is, I do know. He has been a friend and benefactor of this convent, and given and lent money to us. He even moved here to Arcetri to be close to me.

LEONARD

In Rome and in Pisa they say he is an enemy of the Church.

SISTER MARIA

(with great earnestness)

No more than I who have devoted my whole life to God. I know he is no enemy for he writes to me to have faith and trust the Lord and all will be well with him now in his great ordeal and trial. Tribulation is the touchstone whereon is proved the genuineness of our love for God.

LEONARD

Thank you, Sister Maria Celeste.

SISTER MARIA

(With a sudden swell of emotion)

I love my lord and father very much, even though I know we are but pilgrims and strangers here on this earth whether it moves or stands still in the firmament.

She moves suddenly away from him, and faces a crucifix on the wall. She prays to herself.

LEONARD
That was Sister Maria Celeste, the daughter of Galileo Galilei.
It is now time for the opening of the session of Holy Office of
the Inquisition in Rome, and the third examination of Galileo.
Come in, Harry Marble.

*INT. ANTEROOM AND CORRIDOR — HOLY OFFICE OF THE
INQUISITION*

Doors leading to an inner council or examination chamber are closed.
Down the corridor to antechamber come NICCOLINI and GALILEO.

Galileo should look as much like his picture as possible, powerful,
bearded. Obviously in his seventies, his body no longer obeys him as it
used to. He is even more acerb than as a young man.

Niccolini is in his late fifties, an ambassador, polished, diplomatic, very
intelligent, and a devoted follower of Galileo. He escorts Galileo down
the corridor. He finds him a chair in the anteroom. He helps him sit
down.

MARBLE
(as the above goes on)
This is Harry Marble outside the council chamber of Father
Firenzuola, Commissary General of the Inquisition. We are in
the buildings of the Holy Office. Approaching now for his
third scheduled examination is Galileo Galilei, the famous
astronomer from Florence, First Mathematician and
Philosopher to the Grand Duke of Tuscany, Cosimo II. With
Galileo is Francesco Niccolini, ambassador to Rome from
Tuscany, whose diplomatic dealings with the Holy Office and
the Papal Court have done much to avert the usual strict
imprisonment in such cases.

Galileo is sitting now, and Niccolini whispers intensely to him. Galileo
shakes his head irritably.

MARBLE (CON'T)
Naturally, while the proceedings here have been in secret,
rumors do fly and we understand that Galileo has steadfastly
denied any attempt to defy the Church or its teachings. He has
so to speak submitted himself to the discipline but made his
explanations. Just what they are we don't know.

Behind the two men, the doors to the chamber open and a young CARDINAL comes out.

> MARBLE (CON'T)
> That is Cardinal Francesco Barberini just coming out of the chambers.

Within the door we can see the scene, the two examiners, and someone testifying before them. The door is closed.

> MARBLE (CON'T)
> Cardinal Barberini is the nephew of the Pope, Urban VIII, who as Cardinal was himself a close friend and admirer of Galileo.

The cardinal comes up behind Niccolini, taps him on the shoulder. Ambassador and scientist are up in a moment, attentive to the dignitary. The cardinal is handsome and charming.

> MARBLE (CON'T)
> Cardinal Barberini is a follower of the Galilean experiments and has done everything to bring this affair to a quick and happy ending. The cardinal is admired everywhere for the breadth of his knowledge in the new sciences and his courage in defending the old mathematician.

There is a conversation in whispers, and then the cardinal takes Niccolini into the chamber, leaving Galileo alone in the anteroom where he sits down again. Close shot on Galileo.

> MARBLE (CON'T)
> Sir?
> (Galileo looks into camera)
> Do you think this will be your last examination by the Holy Office?

> GALILEO
> (bitterly)
> If they have the same patience with me as I have with the stars, I will be here forever.

> MARBLE
> And how are they treating you?

GALILEO

I'm just an old philosopher so they've given me the private
chambers of the examiner himself, my own servant, and the
ambassador sends in my meals twice a day . . . partridge, larks.
(ironically)
Isn't that fine? It's supposed to improve my voice.

MARBLE

I see you're in good health.

GALILEO

In bad health. I'm more than seventy. The deprivation of
exercise for the last forty days is very prejudicial for my health.
My digestion especially is troubled. Viscous matters
accumulate, and for the last three days painful twitchings in
the limbs have prevented my sleeping.

Galileo moves irritably away, followed by the camera.

MARBLE

Would you like to say anything about the accusations against
you?

GALILEO

It's forbidden to speak of that.

MARBLE

Do you feel that you'll be acquitted?

GALILEO

I can only hope so because I want to get back to my work.

MARBLE

If you are found guilty what will be the effect on the teaching
of the doctrines of Copernicus?

GALILEO

I'm more interested in what the effect will be on me.
(sudden spurt of anger)
The whole thing is just a scandal and invention of my scientific
enemies. His Holiness himself, Urban VIII, when he was
Cardinal wrote sonnets to me praising my genius and my
inventions. Am I less of a genius now? Have my discoveries

(MORE)

GALILEO (CON'T)

been disproved? Or have lies been spread about me and misrepresentations made. Those professorial idiots who daily darken the minds of the young even went so far as to complain that the design engraved on the title page of my book was heretical, that the type in some places was different, and that no matter what I said, I actually meant the opposite. The result is that no matter what I say, I'm wrong, and when I right myself I'm doubly wrong. Were I an angel from above, I would be found guilty under such circumstances.

MARBLE

But don't the Copernican doctrines contradict the Bible, violate its teachings, and don't you, by supporting them and advancing the theory of the double motion of the earth, do the same?

GALILEO

The Holy Spirit intended to teach us in the Bible how to go to heaven, not how the heavens go.

Irritated altogether now, Galileo turns away with his last word just as the doors to the chamber open and a dignified man of fifty comes out hastily. The man is smiling with self satisfaction. He is PROFESSOR CHIARAMONTI from Pisa. As Galileo heads back for his chair he sees Chiaramonti, stops dead, grows livid with rage. Chiaramonti smiles with great superiority and makes a little bow.

MARBLE
(quickly, low voiced)

Professor Chiaramonti, from the University of Pisa. He's the author of a book attacking Galileo and his theories as being both anti-scientific and anti-Church. Chiaramonti represents the vast majority of teachers and scholars and their opinions. Professor Chiaramonti . . .
(close shot of Professor, Galileo in
background listening)
Is there any comment you would now like to make on Galileo?

CHIARAMONTI

Let Galileo keep his opinions and welcome. I hold to mine.

MARBLE

Just exactly what is your opinion, Professor?

CHIARAMONTI

I will never concede his four new planets to this heretical
Florentine, though I die for it.

GALILEO
(sarcastically)

Why don't you look through my telescope?

CHIARAMONTI
(with only a half turn)

Because the so-called planets must be in the heavens and not in
a telescope.

GALILEO
(laughing contemptuously)

And if you put on your spectacles to pluck a chicken, are the
feathers in the spectacles or on the fowl?

MARBLE

Will you tell us specifically, Professor Chiaramonti, what
scientific evidence you have against the theory of the motion of
the earth?

CHIARAMONTI

The evidence is so plain that even he who runs may read.
Listen carefully. Animals that are capable of motion have
joints and limbs. The earth has neither joints or limbs.
Therefore it does not move. The planets, the sun, and the fixed
stars are all of one substance, that is to say, of the substance of
the stars; therefore they either move together or stand still
together. It is to the last degree unseemly to place among the
celestial bodies, which are divine and pure, the earth, which is
a sewer of filth.

GALILEO
(coming forward)

And what about the sunspots, and the mountains on the
moon?

CHIARAMONTI

They are in your heretical mind. Besides, since these so-called
satellites are invisible to the naked eye, they therefore exercise
no influence on the earth, and hence are useless and what is
useless does not exist.

GALILEO

Except when what is useless is a lying professor of astronomy,
and these exist by the thousands as thick as carrion flies.

As they argue, the door to the council opens and BARBERINI comes out.
He walks between the men and takes Galileo's arm, and leads him down
the corridor, while Chiaramonti stands and fumes.

MARBLE

It looks like Galileo is not to be examined just yet, and while
we have time, we'll take you to London, England, and an
interview with William Harvey, the distinguished English
physiologist and formerly a pupil of Galileo's. Come in,
Edward P. Morgan.

INT. THE LABORATORY OF WILLIAM HARVEY — LONDON,
ENGLAND

HARVEY is a man of fifty-five, with a very straight-on English
personality. He is looking straight into the camera, waiting to speak.

MORGAN

This is the laboratory of William Harvey, London, England.
Dr. Harvey is the author of the world famous work *De Motu
Cordis* which demonstrated the circulation of the blood. Dr.
Harvey, is there any comment you would like to make on the
case of Galileo Galilei?

HARVEY

I don't know all the facts. However, I do know Galileo.
Studied under him at Padua for awhile, and also under the
great physiologist Cosalpino.

MORGAN

You know Galileo is being examined by the Holy Office of the
Inquisition?

HARVEY

So I've heard.

MORGAN

What do you think of Galileo's work?

HARVEY

Most important since Copernicus and Kepler. You see, Galileo is an experimenter. He looks for facts and he goes where the ·facts lead him. All those others who oppose him are metaphysicians. They use words, not facts. And science is facts.

MORGAN

If Galileo recants before the Inquisition and denies his work, what do you think the effect will be?

HARVEY

It will make him look like a fool and a coward. What he has written and proved is the truth. And I tell you, there can be no progress in the world and no advance in science without freedom of the mind, freedom of thought and of work. If Galileo had been wise he would've come to England to work.

MORGAN

Thank you, Dr. Harvey. We return you to Rome, Italy.

INT. CELL

Cardinal Barberini stands and watches as Galileo walks around, looking first at one object and then at another.

HOLLENBECK

This is Don Hollenbeck back in Rome. We are down below the level of the square in one of the [torture] chambers of the Holy Office. [In extreme cases, the examination of heretics is carried on here.] Cardinal Barberini and Galileo entered a few minutes ago.

Galileo turns to Barberini.

GALILEO

Well?

BARBERINI

I bring you down here, Galileo, in a purely unofficial capacity.

GALILEO

I wish I may never see it in any other way.

BARBERINI

It is just to remind you, because you are a captious and
difficult old man who always wants his own way, that we are
dealing here with matters of life and death, your own and that
of God's Holy Church on earth.

Galileo looks around and shudders.

GALILEO

I would not like to face life and death down here.

BARBERINI

We live in terrible times, Galileo. The world shakes with guilt,
and heresy has gathered millions to itself in the countries of
England, and the Low Countries, in the German states. The
authority of the true Church has been weakened by wicked
men, and that means God's will on earth has been weakened
and men rush like crazy beasts from Paradise as Adam did
with Eve.
(pause)
Tell me truly, Galileo, do you believe in God?

GALILEO
(looking around)
Indeed I do.

BARBERINI

And the Catholic Church Universal on this earth?

GALILEO

I do. I'm no heretic.

BARBERINI

And do you have the interests of God and men in your heart?

GALILEO

What other interests are there but God in heaven and men on
earth?

BARBERINI

Then you must understand that whatever you do to weaken
the faith of men, no matter how sincerely or innocently, is
nevertheless an evil and to be rooted out. The preaching of
your doctrine weakens the faith of the common man.

GALILEO
(with spirit)

I have no doctrine. I tell what facts I see, and what they mean,
and never since I first looked out on the world with the eyes of
truth has one single common man come to me to protest that I
weakened his faith in God. Who protests? A Chiaramonti, a
Caccini, a Schiener, little men who have built themselves into
their little shops where they sell cheap falsehoods dear and
make boobies of the minds of the young! Cowards,
prevaricators, who will not even let a little light in for fear that
it disagrees with the superstitions of the past.

BARBERINI
(very solemn)

I warn you, Galileo, that this is serious, and it is of great
moment in the mind of His Holiness who loves you. For he
thinks not of his old friend who broke bread at his table, but of
the souls of mankind and their voices crying out to eternity
from the wilderness of earth. If you persist in this error and
defy the discipline of your Church, then the Pope will abandon
you. And if the Church abandons you . . .

GALILEO
(somberly)

I was in Venice thirty-three years ago, and saw Bruno
abandoned by the Church. And the republic burnt him like
tinder at the stake. Could that be the work of God, I asked
myself?
(with utter cold horror)
For he screamed . . .

He looks around the room again, touches one of the instruments.

BARBERINI
(energetically)

That was man's work and the arm of the state.

GALILEO

So it was, but Bruno was abandoned by the Church.

BARBERINI

Because he abandoned the Church. Would he recant? Did he repent? Did he return to the fold, or did he yell and harangue and curse God and its ministers on this earth? There is infinite care and mercy for those within the bosom of the Church, but not for those who persist in destroying it.

(coming close to Galileo, embracing
him)

You know, dear friend, dear master, how I follow your works as if they were oracles. But I believe in Jesus Christ, my king, and in the Church Triumphant on earth, and I believe with all my soul, so that I would die for it, and so must you. And it is more than a form of speech that you must make. For the Holy Office will test the inner intention of your mind if you do not convince them of your willingness to submit and make your admission in full faith. [They will test your intention on your flesh, here in this chamber.] I bring you here, dear master, as a pupil, a friend, in kindness and in hope.

GALILEO

(with a kind of passionate despair)

I want to live, old as I am, and worthless as this painful flesh is. These eyes of mine have seen more than any man since Adam. And there is more to be seen. For the motions of the earth and sun are nothing to the motions I have before me to discover.

(rolling an object along the table)

The motion of this, a ball, anything, any little thing you push or drop, contains within itself the laws of all the earth and all the planets and all of the sun, and there are other suns. I can see the universe in a grain of sand, and I see it march in time and in space, beautiful and precise, its laws universal, and everyone to be proven by machines we make, so that all the magic is gone, and what we have is true knowledge which a child can understand and a man can use. And I will write this book of knowledge if I have time, I hope, if I live, and there is some peace in my old age.

BARBERINI

If you believe with all your heart that you are right and the
Church is wrong, I do not wish to threaten you. Take what
must come as your truth seems to you. But in the light of
present knowledge as most men know it, one hypothesis is no
more absolute than another. I will weep for you and I will
pray for you, but I will not shame you with my threats. Sit
here and think, Galileo. Think of the rest of your life on earth,
which is a mere second in time, and the rest of your life in
eternity which is farther and longer than the most distant
flicker of light you saw in your telescope. Think earnestly and
well, and God be with you and bless you.

He makes the sign of a cross, and goes out leaving Galileo behind. As he
closes the door on him, he closes us out into the passageway.

HOLLENBECK

As Cardinal Barberini leaves Galileo behind here, we take you
to the Tuscan Embassy where Ambassador Niccolini has just
arrived. He may have some information on the examination of
Galileo which will take place shortly. Come in, Mike Wallace.

EXT. PATIO OF THE TUSCAN EMBASSY

A telescope is set up. Two of Galileo's pupils . . . ALLESANDRO, a boy
of about 17, and an older pupil in his twenties, FILLIPO. The patio is
planted and very pleasant. The telescope, instead of pointing to the
heavens, is pointing directly over the wall, straightaway. Filippo is
looking through it and the young pupil watches anxiously.

WALLACE

This is Mike Wallace in the patio of the Tuscan Embassy in
Rome. Ambassador Niccolini is on his way here, and those
two young men you see are pupils of Galileo, who are living
here at the embassy with him and serving as his secretaries.

Niccolini enters. The young men don't see him. He comes up behind
them.

WALLACE (CON'T)

That's Ambassador Niccolini now and from his expression he
doesn't seem to have any particularly cheerful news.

NICCOLINI
What are you looking for?

The young men spring up, bow.

PUPILS
Your Excellency.

They exchange looks. Allessandro tilts the telescope up toward the sky.

FILLIPO
The boy was worried about master Galileo so I trained the tube
on the Holy Office.

ALLESSANDRO
We saw the lock on the door as big as a moon, and a soldier
spit out of the window.

FILLIPO
What's the news, Your Excellency?

NICCOLINI
Mostly the same and a little worse.

He falls down wearily on a chair next to a table loaded with fruit. He
picks an orange and begins to peel it.

FILLIPO
Is he examined yet?

NICCOLINI
Not yet, but shortly. But this morning I saw his Holiness the
Pope, and I gave him the request of the Duke. His Holiness
gave me to understand that he is not concerned with matters
of scientific hypothesis, but only with things of faith and
morals.

FILLIPO
Did you ask him, Your Excellency, what would happen if a full
and free admission were to be made by the master?

NICCOLINI
He said, "The hand of God falls lightly on those He loves."

ALLESSANDRO

[If they love him so much why did they threaten him with
chains in Florence and make him go through all the lands of
the plague to come here to Rome . . . an old man, sick, weary.
Is that love?

FILLIPO
(giving him a push)
You'll learn soon enough about the ways of love.]
(to the ambassador)
Your Excellency. Will he recant?

NICCOLINI

It is not a question of recantation, but of full submission, on all
points, including the teaching of the theories of the earth's
motions and his agreement for the withdrawal of all his works.

FILLIPO
(passionately)
If that happens I leave Italy. I will not work here like a slave in
a land of slaves.

ALLESSANDRO

Do you want him to die?

FILLIPO

No, no. But I do not want the minds of the Italians to die
either, and not mine. How will it seem, all over Italy, in Pisa,
in Padua, in Venice, in Florence, in Milan, if he who founded
our astronomy and the new sciences, should publicly say he
was wrong, and all those fools and idiots who believe that
there are seven planets because we have seven sense orifices in
the head and there are seven metals, are declared right? How
will it seem if we all go about and say that what we see is false,
but that a book written by an ancient Greek two thousand
years ago is right? How will it seem if we must admit that the
universe revolves about the earth, when we know the earth is
but a speck in the vastness of time and space? The world will
laugh at the Italians if they do not live and die for their truths.

Niccolini gets up and takes his arm.

NICCOLINI
The walls have ears in Rome, and such talk makes trouble,
Fillipo.

he takes his arm and walks him out. The young man, Allessandro,
moves back to the telescope, tilts it down and looks again at the holy
office.

WALLACE
We take you back to the Holy Office of the Inquisition.

INT. COUNCIL ROOM

The examination is in session. Galileo, in penitential robes, stands below
the three EXAMINERS who are consulting, examining documents, a few
folios, etc.

Galileo waits. He looks very disturbed, haggard. The room is otherwise
empty, and the isolation of this old man there is both impressive and
frightening.

HOLLENBECK
This is Don Hollenbeck. The examination of Galileo is already
in session. They have been questioning him about the
particulars of his previous admonition from the Holy Office,
seventeen years before. The examiner on the left is the
Procurator Fiscal, Father Sincero, the one in the center, the
Commissary General of the Inquisition, Father Firenzuola, and
the third member is an official whose name we have not been
able to get.

The examiners turn back to their places. FIRENZUOLA holds a
document in his hand.

FIRENZUOLA
Galileo, I have here to hand a letter that you wrote on the 21st
of December 1613 to a friend and disciple Father Benedetto
Castelli. I quote:
          (reads)
I am inclined to think that Holy Scripture is intended to
convince men of those truths which are necessary for their
salvation, and which being far above man's understanding
                                                    (MORE)

FIRENZUOLA (CON'T)

cannot be made credible by any learning, or by any other means than revelation. But that the same God who has endowed us with senses, reason, and understanding, does not permit us to use them . . . that it seems I am not bound to believe.

(he lowers the paper)

I should like to remind you, Galileo, that you were admonished by the Church against such opinions and gladly accepted the warning at that time. The question is: have you returned to such opinions in the interim?

Galileo looks from one to another with a certain harassment. He wets his lips. He breaks out passionately.

GALILEO

It is impossible to think without bitterness that the fruits of my labors and studies for so many years (which gave to my name in the scientific world a certain splendor) should now be branded as criminal. All this depresses me to such an extent as to make me curse the time I have devoted to these labors. Yes, I regret having given to the world so much of my results. I even feel the desire to suppress, to destroy forever, to commit to the flames all I have done and what I have left. Thus, I should satisfy the burning hate of my academic enemies.

FIRENZUOLA

(coolly)

But you haven't answered the question.

GALILEO

(in a low, almost inaudible voice)

What I wrote then is not my opinion.

Firenzuola selects another document, checks it with his assistants.

FIRENZUOLA

I have here a still earlier letter of yours, written to Kepler on August 4, 1597, in which you say . . . "many years ago I became a convert to the opinions of Copernicus . . ." You say there a convert, and yet you pretend here to say that your use of the Copernican doctrines are a mere hypothesis.

GALILEO

The letter was very long ago.

FIRENZUOLA

The question is, what was in your mind when you disobeyed the admonition of this Holy Office and published your dialogues, saying there what was forbidden to be said, and by you agreed to be forgotten?

GALILEO

I did not mean to teach and defend those notions which the Holy Office by its injunctions had condemned.

FIRENZUOLA

Have you perused your dialogues anew?

GALILEO

I have.

FIRENZUOLA

And have you reflected on them?

GALILEO

I have. I had not seen them for three years and I read them to note carefully whether, contrary to my sincere intention, something had inadvertently fallen from my pen which might show the taint of disobedience on my part.

FIRENZUOLA

And what did you find?

GALILEO
(with great difficulty)

I freely confess that in some places, the argument is so made as to be stronger on the false side than I intended. I see I was misled by the natural complacency which every man feels with regard to his own subtleties.

FIRENZUOLA

So you admit you were in error?

GALILEO

My error then has been, and I confess it, one of vain glorious
(MORE)

GALILEO (CON'T)
ambition and of pure ignorance . . .
>   (he is choking on his own words)
. . . and inadvertence.

FIRENZUOLA
And you no longer hold those opinions on the mobility of the
earth and its motion about the sun?

Galileo shakes his head.

FIRENZUOLA
You must speak.

GALILEO
I do not, and I could add several dialogues to confute that
opinion more strongly.

FIRENZUOLA
You no longer hold the opinion then?

GALILEO
I am here to obey. I have not held the opinion since the
command was given to me to abandon it.

The examiners confer now very busily. Galileo watches them with
growing fright as one of them keeps shaking his head, this the
unidentified examiner.

GALILEO (CON'T)
Reverend Fathers . . .
>   (they turn and look at him)
It remains for me to pray you to take into consideration my
pitiable state of bodily indisposition, and my age of seventy
years.

The examiners confer again. They return to their places and Firenzuola
hands Galileo a document.

FIRENZUOLA
Read that, Galileo.

He does, and he grows pale and trembling.

GALILEO
(after he is finished)
And what of my books?

FIRENZUOLA
They will be forbidden.
GALILEO
And my person?

FIRENZUOLA
We are all your friends, and feel that you are honorable with
us, and we do not wish to bring you before the full assemblage
of Cardinals without urging extreme mercy for your
transgressions.

GALILEO
Thank you, Father.

FIRENZUOLA
What I say to you, and what I ask you to do, is said and done
in utter sincerity. I speak for the Holy Office of the Inquisition
here.
(pause)
Do you wish to read the document aloud?

GALILEO
(a murmur)
Yes.

FIRENZUOLA
Then kneel.

Galileo kneels and begins to read what in effect is a repudiation of his
whole life.

GALILEO
I, Galileo Galilei, son of the late Vincenzio Galilei of Florence,
aged seventy years, being brought personally to judgment,
having before me the Holy Gospels which I touch with my
hands, swear that I will always believe . . .

Fade him out as he continues to read.

HOLLENBECK

Galileo is recanting completely. We are going to try to get reactions on this from leading scientists here and abroad. The news of this will come as a severe blow to the thousands of followers of the new science, and yet will comfort Galileo's friends who have worried all these ten months about his health and his ability to sustain this severe crisis at his advanced age.

Fade out Hollenbeck and Galileo in.

GALILEO

. . . and I swear that I will never more in the future say, or assert anything, verbally or in writing, which may give rise to a similar suspicion of me; but, that if I shall know any heretic, or anyone suspected of heresy, I will denounce him to the Holy Office, or the Inquisitor and Ordinary of any place where I may be . . .

Fade out Galileo as he continues.

HOLLENBECK

We are ready with our interviews. Come in, Harry Marble.

INT. ANTEROOM TO COUNCIL CHAMBER

Professor Chiaramonti is smiling.

MARBLE

This is Professor Chiaramonti who has consistently represented the point of view opposed by Galileo. Professor Chiaramonti, is there anything you would like to say about the news of Galileo's recantation?

CHIARAMONTI

I am very pleased. It showed that he has finally come to see the vicious foolishness of his preposterous scientific theories, and, when the head of the whole Copernican school in the world denies them, the rest will follow. It justifies my work.

MARBLE

Thank you, Professor Chiaramonti. We now take you to London, England.

*INT. THE LABORATORY OF WILLIAM HARVEY — LONDON,
ENGLAND*

MORGAN
This is Edward P. Morgan again in the laboratory of William
Harvey, London, England. Dr. Harvey has been informed of
the news and has some comments to make.

Harvey who has been waiting with a paper in his hand, looks into
camera.

HARVEY
I don't believe it. But if it is true, if Galileo has gone back on
his work, then he cannot be considered responsible for his
words. Men cannot change facts with words.
(he looks at paper and starts to read)
I reject the action of Galileo Galilei as a betrayal of the work of
his life and the truth about nature and the universe which we
scientists must defend no matter what the personal
consequences.

He looks up.

MORGAN
Thank you, Dr. Harvey. We take you back to Rome, Italy.

EXT. THE PATIO OF THE TUSCAN EMBASSY

The stars are out, the night is mild. Niccolini is absent, but the boys are
waiting, and as they watch Galileo comes in, dressed in his regular
clothes again. He leans on the arm of the ambassador, they seat him, and
one pours him wine, and another hands him bread and they make him
comfortable. No one speaks. Allessandro is weeping. Fillipo is dark and
angry. Niccolini is relieved.

WALLACE
This is Mike Wallace in the Tuscan Embassy where Galileo has
just returned. He is technically a prisoner of the Holy Office of
the Inquisition, but has been paroled in the custody of his
friend, Ambassador Niccolini.

FILLIPO
We are happy to have you back, Master Galileo.

GALILEO
(crusty, weary)
Happy or not, I'm back.

FILLIPO
When can you return to Florence?

GALILEO
Who knows?

He holds out the glass for more wine. Allessandro pours, and then kisses the old man's hand.

Galileo starts to drink, and then suddenly he puts the glass down and covers his face with his hands and begins to weep silently. The three stand and watch for a moment and then silently depart. After a moment, he looks up, sees the patio is empty. The telescope stands there pointing at the stars. He gets up and goes to it, pats it.

WALLACE
Galileo?
(Galileo turns into the camera)
What are your plans for the future?

GALILEO
At seventy a man plans from one day to the next.

WALLACE
Is there anything you'd like to say?

Galileo shakes his head, looks up at the sky.

GALILEO
I wonder if the stars heard me today.
(he looks into camera)
Yes, I have plans. My plan is to return to Florence if the Holy Office permits and there complete my works on the new sciences of mechanics.

WALLACE
What do you think the effect of your action today will be?

Galileo points to the telescope and then to the stars.

GALILEO

Both of these remain. Men will look through this and see what is up there.

INT. CBS STUDIOS

CRONKITE

Galileo did retire to his Florentine villa, living in comparative freedom . . . as a matter of fact, completed there his greatest work on the science of mechanics. The controversy in which he was a storm center persisted for years, and it was two centuries before his work and that of Kepler and Copernicus was removed from censorship. Galileo: on the year that *he* died, Isaac Newton was born. The works of Galileo were smuggled out of Italy and, based on the great experiments of this Italian, the Englishman Newton laid the foundations for modern science.

What sort of a day was it? A day like all days, filled with those events that alter and illuminate our time . . . and YOU WERE THERE.

FADE OUT.

THE FATE OF NATHAN HALE

Nathan Hale (b. 6 June 1755, Coventry, Connecticut—d. 22 September 1776, present New York City) was an American Revolutionary officer who, assuming the role of a schoolteacher, attempted to spy on the British and was hanged. A graduate of Yale University (1773), Hale joined a Connecticut regiment after the American Revolution began, served in the siege of Boston, and was commissioned a captain (1776). He went to New York with William Heath's brigade and is said to have participated in the capture of a provision ship from under the guns of a British man-of-war. Hale was captured and hanged by the British after he had almost completed his volunteer mission to enter British lines on Long Island to obtain information.

He is regarded by American Revolutionary tradition as a hero and a martyr and is supposed to have said before his death that his only regret was that he had but one life to lose for his country, a remark similar to one in Joseph Addison's play *Cato* (1713). In Polonsky's teleplay, Hale is shown reading Addison's text, which he describes as "an old favorite" (p. 121). Indeed, most Americans will remember Nathan Hale when they hear Cato saying: "What pity is it / That we can die but once to serve our country!"

❖❖❖

"'The Fate of Nathan Hale' was not simply the story of a young patriot who died for his principles, but of the complex interplay between Hale and his captor, Captain John Montressor. The viewer sees the soul-searching of the two protagonists as they seek to understand each other's views and principles [pp. 114-116, 121-123]. This is accomplished in a crisply written script that avoids the childish and maudlin sentimentality which all too often accompanies interpretations of the Nathan Hale story." (Horowitz, "History Comes to Life," pp. 81-82.)

Note in the teleplay the recurrence of the "informer" or "betrayal" motif (pp. 116-119). This is a continuing thread throughout Polonsky's work: most powerfully in his feature film screenplays of *Body and Soul* and *Force of Evil*; in other episodes of the *You Are There* series, such as "The Tragedy of John Milton," "The Recognition of Michelangelo," and "The Vindication of Savonarola;" and in his novels *The World Above* (Little, Brown and Co., 1951) and *Season of Fear*. It is a thematic element that has been profoundly influenced by the cultural climate of the Cold War and the Blacklist era—and by Polonsky's personal experience. (Polonsky, who appeared before HUAC on 25 April 1951 and refused to affirm or deny Communist party membership, has been informed on by Richard Collins, Sterling Hayden, Meta Reis Rosenberg, Leo Townsend, Charles Daggett, Stanley Roberts, and Leo Townsend—as documented in the *Annual Report of the Committee on Un-American Activities for the Year 1952*.) The dialogue Polonsky provides for Samuel Hale is a subtle adumbration of the dark potentialities in a perhaps unintentional, but nevertheless soul-destroying process of "betrayal."

Nathan Hale was played by Paul Newman. It was his second television appearance; his first was in another celebrated *You Are There* episode, "The Death of Socrates" (air date: 3 May 1953). Charles Russell recalls: "Paul came up to me early in the day while I was standing watching the stagehands setting up the ladder and tying the heavy noose. He stood next to me as we watched the action. I was thinking to myself, how the hell are we going to make this work? Paul asked quietly, 'Charlie, how are you going to do this?' Reassuringly I said, 'Don't worry Paul, it'll look real.'

"Later, in a camera rehearsal for positions in that final scene, Hale is taken to the foot of the ladder braced against the side of the old barn. Above the ladder a hangman's noose is suspended from the crossbeam and as Hale reaches the top of the ladder and stands there, his hands tied behind his back, the noose is adjusted around his neck and secured. On the ground two men seize hold of the ladder ready to pull it away at Provost Marshal Cunningham's order. He asks, 'Is there anything you would say, Nathan Hale, before you fall to your just and dishonorable death as a traitor and a spy against your own king and country?' Hale replies clearly, with defiance, 'I only regret that I have but one life to lose for my country.' There is a flash of triumph on his face before Cunningham bellows, 'Hang him.'

"At that moment, Paul, in his stationary position with his eyes thrown back toward the control room, said, 'Look fellows let's not be too realistic.'" ("In the Worst of Times," pp. 84-85.)

The ending of "The Fate of Nathan Hale" offers a quintessential model of Polonsky's literary vision, which is consistently drawn to conflicts—individuals absorbed in moral and psychological crises—which must be reconciled existentially in terms of personal identity, integrity, and responsibility. The death of an individual—the death of Nathan Hale, "a youth who reached his maturity and death in the same year"—is a crisis of ultimate purity. And, for Polonsky, an existential purity results from the death of a human being "fulfilling the purpose which *in his own mind* was the ideal of his own life, and the nation to come." (See the Introduction, pp. 28-30).

❖❖❖

The Revolutionary War context of the Nathan Hale script will now be used as a springboard to a discussion of "The Crisis at Valley Forge" (air date: 6 December 1953), a teleplay which was also researched and authored by Polonsky. The ambiance of this episode might serve a dual purpose—to underscore the typical thoroughness of the historical research that went into the shows, and to provide a concrete example of the ofttimes bizarre, labyrinthian nature of the fronting process.

Polonsky, in writing the script, selected the date of 28 February 1778 as the focus of the historical crisis of the show's title. Now, in a letter to *The New York Times*, 24 January 1954, viewer Edward Pinkowski criticized this particular narrative for inaccuracy. Confronted by such a rare challenge to the historical validity of the show's dramatizations, the producers felt a response to the charges was imperative. Executive producer William Dozier told line producer Charles Russell to get Jeremy Daniel, as titular author of the episode, to write the response. "Jeremy Daniel" was Polonsky's front for the "Valley Forge" script, so it was, of course, Polonsky who wrote the reply, which was then taken by Russell, who in turn handed it over to Dozier, who sent it to *The New York Times*, which proceeded to print it on 28 February 1954. The following is the rebuttal letter, as written by Polonsky, in which he addressed the critic's specific points:

> Mr. Pinkowski challenges the selection of the date, Feb. 20, 1778, and denies that it was a time of crisis at Valley Forge. Now let's examine Feb. 20: On Feb. 17 the situation at Valley Forge had become so crucial that John Laurens, then a major and highly respected aide, wrote to his father, the then President of the Continental Congress, "Hunger has brought the troops to the verge of mutiny." (*The Army Career of Col. John Laurens*, Bradford Club series.)
>
> On Feb. 16 Washington wrote, "For some days past there has been little less than a famine in camp. A part of the army has been a week without flesh and the rest three to four days." (*Writings of George Washington*, Vol. 2, United States Printing Office, 1933.)
>
> The late Douglas S. Freeman, a recognized authority throughout the world, wrote on Washington (Vol. 4, p. 575), "From Feb. 11 onward Washington, intensively anxious, walked through the camp and heard the ominous chant: 'No pay, no

clothes, no provisions, no rum."' So much for the propriety of Feb. 20 . . . .

Next, Mr. Pinkowski implies that Aaron Burr was no longer a member of Conway's brigade on Feb. 20, and therefore not at Valley Forge. Schachner, in his definitive work on Burr, says it was not before March that Burr's regiment was removed from Conway's brigade and placed on the left wing of Sterling's division.

Next, Mr. Pinkowski denies that Washington ever considered resigning his command to Conway. Conway's treachery is an essential element in this conflict with George Washington, for Conway's cabal was the one important organized conspiracy against the commander of the armies.

Mr. Freeman, in the work already cited, states, "Could the three assumed leaders in the movement (Conway et al) do what Washington's friends feared the trio might . . . put so many obstacles in [Washington's] way . . . that Washington would resign in disgust."

Mr. Pinkowski concluded his criticism, "The entire television program distorted the true story of Valley Forge." The theme of the *You Are There* program is amply justified by the statement of Lyn Montross in his fine work, *Rag, Tag and Bobtail*: "It cannot be said that America had a truly national army until the early spring of 1778." And this was exactly the historical theme of the program.

Thus Polonsky—the historian—disposes of the accusations with specific primary and scholarly sources. But Polonsky—the romantic progressive—adds a note of his emblematic lyricism:

We believe it to be a thrilling conception that men became Americans in this terrible valley of despair, and they were transformed, and lost their colonial identity, and that Virginians, Irish, Levellers, Baptists became a new unity in the world, one with immense duplicating power. [We] feel the scope and beauty and power of their spiritual and moral victory.

Of course, as a blacklisted writer, deep in the labyrinthe, Polonsky's name would not appear on the *Times* letter—and neither, as it turned out, would Jeremy Daniel's. The letter was signed, ironically, by executive producer William Dozier—fronting for a front.

THE FATE OF NATHAN HALE

by Abraham Polonsky

(signed by Jeremy Daniel)

Air Date:

August 30, 1953

YOU ARE THERE

September 22, 1776

FADE IN:

INT. CBS STUDIOS

CRONKITE

Walter Cronkite reporting. The date is September 22, 1776. Last night in New York City a series of great fires broke out in the vicinity of South Street and spread rapidly from the warehouses and shipping there into the heart of the city. More than five hundred houses are destroyed and many more damaged. The fires are not yet under control.

Late last night the headquarters of the British expeditionary force under General Sir William Howe announced that they had definite information that the fires were of incendiary origin caused by colonial rebels. As a result orders were immediately issued to execute by hanging on the spot all rebels caught at the site of the fire.

The majority of the citizens of New York are loyal to the crown and they have organized fire fighting teams to save the rest of the city. The natural resentment of the population is such that here and there suspected rebels have been flung into the flames by the enraged citizens, and mobs are running through the streets searching for those believed to be sympathetic with

(MORE)

CRONKITE (CON'T)
the cause of Mr. George Washington. British troops and a
brigade of Hessian Grenadiers under Colonel Carl Van Doop
are trying to maintain order.

CBS Television has arranged an interview with the rebel
commander, Mr. George Washington, in an effort to discover
whether this scorched earth policy will be followed in every
case where the rebels withdraw after being defeated. All
things are as they were then, except . . . YOU ARE THERE.

INT. WASHINGTON'S HEADQUARTERS

A small group of rather gloomy officers, a few soldiers. An aide is
signing orders.

BURDETT
This is Winston Burdett at Harlem, New York, field
headquarters for the revolutionary army of General
Washington. We've been informed that the General has
prepared a statement in reply to the British charges that rebel
Americans under direct orders from Washington himself set
the disastrous fires in New York City. We expect the General
momentarily. That is Adjutant-General Joseph Reed at the
desk, preparing orders for a prisoner exchange with the
British, scheduled tomorrow. Up here in strongly fortified
Harlem Heights the atmosphere is far from optimistic. The
rebels have suffered a series of shattering defeats, beginning
with the rout in Long Island where Washington himself was
nearly captured. British amphibian landings in Manhattan
have forced a rebel withdrawal to the northern tip of
Manhattan. It is completely doubtful that Washington will be
able to keep a foothold on this island. As you know, the city
itself is in British hands.

A stir and WASHINGTON enters. He is booted and spurred, serious,
and very curt and commanding. An aide proceeds him. Washington is
saluted. The aide hands him a slip of paper.

BURDETT (CON'T)
(very low voiced, quick)
This is General Washington just returned from an inspection of
the lines. He is now ready to read his prepared statement.
General Washington . . .

WASHINGTON
(reading, very dryly)
In view of the baseless accusation made by British invaders of
New York, I wish to state unequivocally that the disastrous
fires in the City of New York were not set by command of the
Continental Army, the State Militia Organizations, or the
Continental Congress. I would like it to be plainly understood
that it was my considered opinion that the city should be razed
and destroyed to prevent its use by the British as winter
headquarters, but the Congress gave orders that the city be
spared, and I obeyed the command. The fires are either of
accidental origin or started by the British themselves in order
to becloud the issues of the war and arouse sentiment against
our fight for freedom.

He lowers the paper, looks around, hands it to his aide and is about to
walk off. BURDETT will ask his questions quickly, on the fly so to speak,
for Washington is eager to be off. If possible, the general will be in
motion with the questioner apparently tagging along.

BURDETT
Thank you, General Washington. You do not, then, intend to
pursue a policy of destroying what you cannot defend?

WASHINGTON
It is the British who do the destroying and we who seek to
preserve our homes, our property and our fortunes.

BURDETT
Can the present conflict be settled by negotiations?

WASHINGTON
We are always ready to negotiate.

BURDETT
I am informed, sir, that when the British Commander, General Howe, approached you earlier with proposals for settling the conflict, you refused to receive his letter.

WASHINGTON
(very stiffly)
It was not addressed to me. It was directed to George Washington, Esquire, a private citizen, and not to George Washington, General of the Continental Army. I consider it my duty to my country and to my position to insist upon a respect which, in other than public view, I would gladly waive. If the British want peace they must recognize our status as a free nation.

BURDETT
Thank you, General Washington.
(but Washington and his aides
are already gone)
We now take you to quarters of the British provost marshal in charge of the execution of those rebels accused of setting the great New York fire. Come in, Edward P. Morgan.

INT. CUNNINGHAM'S QUARTERS

A room in a small farmhouse or greenhouse. A few disreputable loyalist citizens around, a couple of soldiers, and at a table, his feet up on a chair, drinking, is the PROVOST MARSHAL. He is talking to an assistant. This is in background over which Morgan talks.

CUNNINGHAM is historically notorious for his brutality and drunkenness, and he should look the part. He is in that drunken-sober state familiar to all perpetual alcoholics, sometimes belligerent, sometimes curt, sometimes talkative, but he is shrewd and devoted to his side, and not without humor.

CUNNINGHAM
And then find a row of trees because I'll be wanting them to dangle there side by side in the streets to be a lesson for the vicious and bedeviled traitors they are.

AIDE

Yes, Marshal.

CUNNINGHAM

And no man is to be cut down till three days have passed
whether the smell of him gets to Dublin or not.

AIDE

Yes, Marshal.

CUNNINGHAM

And bring me in that young one and have him brought up to
the Dove Artillery Park where my commission says to hang
him at eleven this morning.

AIDE

Yes, Marshal.

He goes out with a few soldiers. While the above conversation is going
on, reporter is over with.

MORGAN

Ed Morgan reporting. We are at the headquarters of William
Cunningham, Provost Marshal to General Howe and
commissioned to execute by hanging all those considered
guilty of setting the great fires. Marshal Cunningham is in
charge of the prison houses. He came to the colonies two years
before the outbreak of the rebellion and was driven out of New
York by the rebels.

Now Cunningham turns to the camera, smiles.

CUNNINGHAM

At your service, sir.

MORGAN

Marshal Cunningham, how many rebels accused of starting
the fires at the lower end of Manhattan have been
apprehended and hung by you?

CUNNINGHAM

I don't rightly know, but I would say more than two, but less
than a dozen.

(MORE)

CUNNINGHAM (CON'T)
(he grins)
I'm not counting those who were found in the vicinity of these
conflagrations and consigned to the flames on the fly so to
speak by the enraged populace of the city.

MORGAN
Were these persons whom you hanged given a trial?

CUNNINGHAM
It wasn't necessary since they were caught in "flagrante
delicto," so to speak.

MORGAN
Some might have been innocent.

CUNNINGHAM
They were all rebels notwithstanding, and the only good rebel
is a dead one as every patriotic Englishman knows.

Behind him, NATHAN HALE, bound, is shoved forward, kicked a few
times, and pushed out of the room.

MORGAN
Is that one of them?

Cunningham takes a nonchalant look around.

CUNNINGHAM
No, that is a more venomous viper in the bosom of our good
King George. He's a rebel spy who undoubtedly was sent in
by that rascal Washington to organize the incendiary action
which has destroyed so much of this fair city. Since the young
villain is an officer in the rebel army, he is being hanged by the
express orders of General Sir William Howe himself.
(he looks through his papers)
Captain Nathan Hale of Knowlton's Rangers.

MORGAN
(sudden interest)
Isn't he a prisoner of war and entitled to the treatment as such?

CUNNINGHAM
He's a confessed spy and entitled to nothing but the rope
which he will receive as per my commission the hour of eleven
in the artillery park near Dove Tavern . . . .

He has been buckling on his sword, and now puts on his hat with a
flourish and leaves.

MORGAN
(excited)
It's difficult to believe that General Howe would order the
execution of a regular officer of the American army since this
might cause retaliation against British prisoners in American
hands. He is at the headquarters of General Howe in the
Beekman Mansion and we will see if we can get a statement
from him . . . . Are you there, Harry Marble?

INT. HOWE'S HEADQUARTERS AT BEEKMAN MANSION

In front of the elegant mantelpiece in the Beekman Mansion. The elegant
and beautifully attired HOWE is in conversation with a Hessian General
and an aide.

MARBLE
(low voiced, respectful, rapid)
This is Harry Marble reporting. We are in the magnificent
mansion of James Beekman, a fugitive rebel. I have submitted
two written questions to General Sir William Howe, and will
question him about Captain Hale if he permits it. General
Howe is talking with General Philip de Heister in command of
the Hessian infantry and Earl Percy commanding the Second
and Sixth Brigades and the Brigade of Guards.

The three men shake hands, and the two leave, as Howe faces the
camera.

MARBLE
(respectfully)
General Howe, will you find it convenient to answer my
proposed questions?

HOWE
They seem innocent enough. You may ask them.

MARBLE

On what basis were the peace negotiations with the colonists
broken off?

HOWE

His Majesty empowered me to settle this matter between the
colonies and the home country by all peaceable means, and I
was prepared to do so. But when the rebel Congress insisted
on His Majesty's government accepting the principles of their
Declaration of Independence as a prerequisite to negotiation,
naturally there was no more to be said.

MARBLE

Will you please explain why not, General Howe?

HOWE

Because a more impudent, false and atrocious proclamation
was never fabricated by the hands of man, and the rebellious
faction has thrown aside all appearance at length and declared
openly for independence and war. I propose to punish them
until they are willing to listen to reason. Your second
question, please?

MARBLE

There have been speeches in Parliament to the effect that you
do not seem to pursue the war with that force and
destructiveness of which your army is capable. For example,
you could have easily crushed Washington after the recent
rout of the rebels at Long Island and yet you did not. Can you
explain your strategy?

HOWE

My strategy is political as well as military. The criticisms you
have heard are the usual fulminations of the Tories whose
stupid obstinacy has driven these loyal colonists into rebellion.
As a Whig, it is my feeling that I can bring the rebels to their
senses without destroying their honor as Englishmen or their
rights as citizens of the empire. Only as a last resort must we
wage total war against our own people. I think that takes care
of your questions. Excuse me.

He turns away.

MARBLE

General Howe?

HOWE

Yes?

MARBLE

I've just learned of an incident that you might clarify if you so
wish. It seems you ordered the execution at eleven this
morning of a young rebel captain.

HOWE
(for the first time, with a certain
anger)

Indeed, I did. He was spying in civilian clothes behind our
lines and apprehended not far from here yesterday night. I
examined him myself. In this very room. He made a full
confession and we found secreted on him plans of our
fortifications and a description of our movements and troop
dispositions. He had no excuse and made none. He claims he
is an officer in the American army, but no true army officer
would violate his code of honor and masquerade in civilian
clothes to spy on enemy forces. There is a certain dignity and
honor in being a soldier. One wins or loses, one lives or dies,
but one does both according to a code of behavior
that no officer and gentleman would violate. This young
schoolmaster. . . what was his name? . . .

MARBLE

Captain Nathan Hale.

HOWE

The schoolmaster, Hale, wore brown civilian clothes and
carried a diploma from Yale college, one of the local
institutions, and passed himself off as a loyal subject of His
Majesty. Amusingly enough, some of his treasonable material
was written in Latin, I presume because he felt that no British
officer would understand that classic tongue. Well, Hale the
spy will find that *"facilis descensus averno,"* which I suggest as
an appropriate inscription on every traitor's grave.

He turns abruptly away.

MARBLE
General Howe's quotation from the Roman poet can be translated as: "Easy is the decent into hell . . . ." Come in, Don Hollenbeck.

EXT. ARTILLERY PARK

An encampment of engineers, part of an old barn with a crossbeam. To one side an officer's tent, etc.

There is considerable activity. A ladder is arranged under the crossbeam, and from it a hangman's rope is being suspended. A few British soldiers are sitting to one side playing cards and drinking rum.

HOLLENBECK
Don Hollenbeck reporting. I'm at the artillery park just north of Howe's headquarters at the Beekman Mansion. We are right in the midst of the reserve Artillery and Engineer Corps, and the tent you see there belongs to one of the officers.

Some of Provost Marshal Cunningham's men are preparing the hangman's rope for the young rebel captain who is at the moment on his way here under guard.

It is a very hot and bright day. There isn't much wind and from the hill just to the west of here, you can see to the south the immense pall of smoke rising from the fires in the lower end of the city. The British soldiers here believe that Captain Hale was sent by General Washington to burn down the city. Facing north from the hill you can see the heights of Harlem, still strongly held by the rebels.
> (a distant roll of cannons)

There is occasional firing and some scouting action but in general things are quiet. In New York City there have been great celebrations to welcome the troops of General Howe . . . . Here they come with Hale now.

Under guard Hale is brought forward to stand in the sun just before the tent. He is dirty, disheveled, and his hands are bound tightly behind him. Cunningham contemplates the scene with a certain professional satisfaction. He turns to Hale, who is breathing a little hard, whether from emotion or being forced on the run, we cannot say.

CUNNINGHAM

Well, my little rebel schoolmarm, you rest comfortable there in the sun while I arrange your farewell party.

The flap to the tent is raised and a British officer steps out. He is a rather handsome and dignified man and carries great authority in his bearing. He is forty years of age, wears a thin fine mustache.

CUNNINGHAM

Sit down and make yourself at home, even though it be for just awhile.

He pushes Hale down roughly. Hale squats there without speaking.

MONTRESSOR

What's this, Marshal, another incendiary?

CUNNINGHAM

Better game, Captain Montressor. This is a rebel spy.

MONTRESSOR
(with a contemptuous look at
the seated Hale)
Then finish the dirty business quickly and make less noise.

He starts to turn back into tent.

CUNNINGHAM

That we shall do. I'll have this Yankee captain up on that beam before you can say George Washington.

MONTRESSOR

What do you mean, "captain"? Is this man an officer in the Continental Army?

HALE

I am Captain Hale of Knowlton's Rangers.

MONTRESSOR looks from Hale to Cunningham. Then he bends down and helps Hale to his feet.

HALE

Thank you, sir.

MONTRESSOR
Captain John Montressor, aide-de-camp to General Howe, at
your service.
(turns to Cunningham)
Under what authority is this man being hanged, Marshal?

CUNNINGHAM
Why cunning little captain was caught last night and brought
before the General himself who personally examined him and
ordered his execution here this morning.

He reaches into his coat and takes out a folded paper which he hands to
Montressor. After reading it, Montressor hands it back. There is a
moment of silence.

MONTRESSOR
(to Cunningham)
How long will it be before you are ready?

CUNNINGHAM
A few brief moments if these fellows will move themselves
along.

MONTRESSOR
(to Hale)
I suggest, Captain, that you come into the tent and rest out of
the sun.
(to Cunningham)
I'll be responsible for the prisoner, Marshal.

He holds aside the flap. Hale looks at the gallows being prepared and
then moves slowly into the tent. Montressor follows. As the flap falls . . .

CUNNINGHAM
(shouting)
Let's move along, my boys, or we'll all be late for our noonday
bite.

INT. TENT

Hale stands in the relative quiet of the tent. There is an improvised desk
with some books on it. Among them Addison's *Cato* and the Bible.
There are writing materials, a bed, etc.

Montressor pushes a chair forward.

>   HALE
>   Thank you, Captain Montressor.

>   MONTRESSOR
>   Why don't you sit down?

Hale does so. They sit in silence for a moment.

>   HALE
>   Might I ask the favor of a drink of water?

>   MONTRESSOR
>   Of course.
>   (he gets a carafe and a wine
>   glass)
>   I have some wine if you would like it.

>   HALE
>   No, thank you.

Montressor holds out the glass to Hale.

>   HALE
>   I'm afraid you will have to hold it for me.

Montressor puts the glass down, takes a bayonet and cuts the rope. Hale
rubs his hands and wrists.

>   IIALE
>   In their eagerness to hang me, I suppose they forgot about
>   food and drink.

He takes up the glass.

>   MONTRESSOR
>   Would you like something to eat?

>   HALE
>   It seems somehow a useless appetite at the moment.

MONTRESSOR
(quite moved)
In my philosophy one should live as one can up to the very
last moment.

HALE
I'm trying to. To your health.

He toasts Montressor and drinks. He drinks with very great pleasure,
slowly. Montressor observes him with great compassion.

MONTRESSOR
You seem very young. How old are you, Captain?

HALE
Twenty-one years.

He sits down again. He rubs his wrists and hands.

MONTRESSOR
Isn't that rather inexperienced for someone to be sent by
Washington behind our lines?

HALE
I volunteered.

MONTRESSOR
They should not have accepted it. A soldier's work is to fight
not to spy.

HALE
Why is it more dishonorable to die by a rope behind the
enemy's lines than by a bullet in front of them, providing I die
for the same cause that I must live for . . . .

MONTRESSOR
(ill at ease, embarrassed)
Is there anything else I can do for you?

HALE
If you please, sir, I asked for the chance to write to my brother
and the commanding officer and Marshal Cunningham
refused me.

Montressor indicates the desk and materials. He hands him the quill and the ink and arranges the desk.

MONTRESSOR

Here you are, Captain Hale. I'll wait outside.

The camera takes him out as Hale turns to his letters, taking up his pen. Montressor stands if front of the closed flap of the tent. Cunningham and his men proceed with their preparations.

HOLLENBECK

Captain Montressor?
                    (Montressor looks into camera)
What is your opinion of this sentence on Captain Nathan Hale?

MONTRESSOR
                    (icily)
I'm an engineer and a human being not a judge and a hangman. I have no opinion.

He turns his back on the camera.

HOLLENBECK

While we are waiting, Harry Marble at the Beekman Mansion, headquarters for General Howe, tells us they have run down a rumor that Captain Hale was betrayed to the British by his own cousin, a man named Samuel Hale, a loyalist and now Deputy Commissary of Prisoners to the British. Come in, Harry Marble.

INT. BEEKMAN MANSION

A man is standing against the mantel. He is thirty years old, in British uniform and quite ill at ease.

MARBLE

This is Harry Marble. We have just been able to find Samuel Hale who is standing here and prepared, he says, to answer any questions we may ask about his cousin, Nathan Hale, the rebel spy. It was Ed Morgan who heard this rumor and traced Samuel Hale to Howe's headquarters here. Ed is here with me. Go ahead, Ed.

Double interview.

MORGAN

You are Samuel Hale, cousin of Captain Nathan Hale?

SAMUEL

I am. My father and his father are brothers.

MORGAN

You're Deputy Commissary of Prisoners for General William
Howe.

SAMUEL

Yes. I was driven out of my home and from my practice as an
attorney because of my loyalty to my king and my country. In
fact I was detained in prison several times in 1775 because of
my principles as a loyal Englishman.

MORGAN

The rumor is, as you must know, that your cousin was in
disguise at a tavern not far from here last night. I believe the
name is the Cedars, and that you were there, recognized him,
slipped out and reported it and thus brought about his
capture.

SAMUEL
(indignantly)
Not one single word of that story is true, not one word of it. I
did not betray my cousin. There is not the least truth in this
infamous accusation. My only crime is my attachment to my
king and my country.

MARBLE
(quickly)
Then can you tell us just how Captain Hale was betrayed and
caught?

SAMUEL

It was both an accident and a result of his own carelessness
and, I might say, inexperience as a spy. Because of the fires in
New York which we believe were set at the instigation of the
rebel Congress despite their denials, everyone was on the
outlook for incendiaries and suspicious characters.

(MORE)

SAMUEL (CON'T)

My cousin tried to pass through the advance pickets, north of here, and go through to his own line. His nervous behavior gave him away.

MORGAN

How did they know he was an American spy?

SAMUEL

By his peculiar actions and the story he gave. He said he was a schoolteacher and produced his Yale diploma.

MARBLE

I still don't see that that would indicate he was a spy. How did they know this?

SAMUEL

He was examined by General Howe himself, and when he was searched they found plans of our fortifications on his person and other incriminating matters. Then he confessed.

MORGAN

I still don't see why a young man of twenty-one found acting suspiciously should be brought before General Howe himself, examined, and searched there. Is that the custom in the British army?

Samuel is quite nervous now.

MARBLE

Can you explain that, sir?

SAMUEL

It was the result of a series of unfortunate circumstances and accidents.

MARBLE

What accidents?

SAMUEL

Naturally I am well known as Deputy Commissary of Prisoners. When my unfortunate cousin was apprehended, he was brought to be booked. One of my assistants noticed that

(MORE)

SAMUEL (CON'T)
the diploma which my cousin used to identify himself and his
disguise as a schoolteacher, bore a name similar to my own.
My assistant made a jest. He asked whether it was a relative,
and when he showed me the diploma, naturally I knew it
referred to my cousin.

MARBLE
You pointed him out?

SAMUEL
(heatedly)
I did not even see him. I have not seen him.

MORGAN
What did you do?

SAMUEL
I simply said . . . that is . . . I remarked . . . that I had a cousin in
the Continental Army whose name was Nathan Hale, and that
he too had gone to Yale.

MORGAN
Did you know your cousin at Yale?

SAMUEL
Of course not. I'm nine years older. I went to Harvard.

MARBLE
To whom did you give this information?

SAMUEL
It came to General Howe's attention, and because of my close
connection with him, my cousin was brought before him.
Nathan made no attempt to conceal his identity. In fact he
proudly stated his name, his rank, and his mission.

MORGAN
So it was your identification of your cousin that exposed him?

SAMUEL
I merely spoke the truth without ever seeing him and without
knowing whether or not some fellow might not have stolen his
diploma.

MARBLE
Any more questions, Ed?

MORGAN
No.

MARBLE
Thank you Deputy Commissary Hale. We return you to Don Hollenbeck.

EXT. ARTILLERY PARK

The arrangements are completed. The gambling soldiers are still playing but ready to stop once the fun begins. Cunningham's assistant is on the ladder testing the rope.

HOLLENBECK
Don Hollenbeck here at the artillery park of the British Army on the outskirts of the Beekman Estate. The arrangements for the hanging of Captain Nathan Hale are completed. Provost Marshal Cunningham is testing the equipment and should very shortly proceed with the execution. Young Captain Hale is at the moment within the tent you see there. We have asked permission to interview Hale but while Marshal Cunningham was agreeable, Captain Montressor, who is standing in front of the tent, refused. He said the last moment in a man's life belonged to himself and his maker and not to the curiosity of posterity.

Cunningham has descended the ladder and approached Montressor. He bows to Montressor with a certain buffoonery.

CUNNINGHAM
Captain Montressor, the equipment for the last journey of the spy is ready, and so are his coachmen. May I have my prisoner?

MONTRESSOR
(with ill-concealed disfavor)
I'll fetch him, Marshal.

He starts into the tent. Cunningham makes a move to follow.

MONTRESSOR
(sharply)
Wait here.

Cunningham resents this but puts on a false smile.

INT. TENT

Montressor enters the tent. Inside Hale is reading a book, Addison's *Cato*. He looks up, rises, smiles a bit wanly.

HALE
With so much time on my hands, Captain, I spent some of it reading.

MONTRESSOR
(Forcing a smile)
Did you know Addison's *Cato* before?

HALE
An old favorite.

He puts the book down regretfully then picks up his letters and starts to seal them with wax.

HALE (CON'T)
I realize however that there is a considerable amount of reading I'll have to forego.

MONTRESSOR
One must be prepared to forego everything in order to enjoy anything.

He watches Hale seal the letters with a certain gloomy admiration.
HALE
I've written to my brother and my commander.
(hands the letters to Montressor)
Will you see that they are delivered, sir?

MONTRESSOR
I will instruct the provost marshal to do so. However, I am going on a flag of truce tomorrow to your lines in order to discuss a prisoner of war exchange. I can deliver an oral message for you.

HALE

Thank you.

MONTRESSOR
(finding it difficult to make this
proposal to a man of honor)
Captain Hale, it may be that it is not too late to rectify this
disagreeable situation. You are, after all, a very young man,
and as such, entitled to make errors that in an older man might
be unforgivable.

He pauses. Hale waits expectantly.

HALE
If you are asking me whether or not I wish to live . . . I do. In
all the deaths that I have seen around me, nothing has become
more precious than my own life.
(with a certain melancholy, his
voice dying away into
memories)
I keep remembering playing football in the Bouery, and once
kicking a ball over the tallest tree . . . or the old house at
Coventry . . . the corn crib in the backyard, and the little pines
my father planted . . . . I keep recalling foolish
things . . . .
(his voice sinks . . . and then in a
fit of anguish)
God knows! I would live . . . and God knows that my life is
gone.

MONTRESSOR
It isn't too late.
(with great vigor and sympathy)
You can abandon your rebellion and join His Majesty's army
as so many of your colonists have done. You can do so, and I
swear to you I will stay this execution and see General Howe
himself and plead your case. I promise you.

HALE
Thank you.

MONTRESSOR
(joyfully)
You accept?

HALE
I refuse, but I thank you for your kindness and concern.

MONTRESSOR
(crying out)
You are too young to die. This isn't patriotism. It's folly.

HALE
(with great simplicity and
sincerity)
Whenever a new country is about to be born someone must
choose to be its patriot. I know I'm quite young. Nevertheless,
I am too old to betray what I believe is just.
(he holds out his hand)
Goodbye, sir.

MONTRESSOR
(taking his hand)
God bless you.
(formally to hide his emotion)
What shall I tell your representatives tomorrow on the flag of
truce?

HALE
(after a moment of thought,
suddenly, quite young and
helpless)
I can think of nothing except goodbye.
(he turns around and clasps his
hands behind him)
You had better tie my hands again since you were not
supposed to free them.

Montressor takes a piece of rope and ties Hale's hands. He picks up the
letters. He turns to Hale, salutes him. Then he goes out, followed by
Hale. Outside Cunningham is waiting.

EXT. ARTILLERY PARK

> CUNNINGHAM
> I hope, my lad, you are as ready as we are.

He takes Hale by the arm, and hurries him along under the gallows. A stir from the crowd . . . not too many present . . . but say a half dozen. . . . at the foot of the ladder Hale stops. Montressor comes up and hands the letters to Cunningham.

> MONTRESSOR
> The prisoner wrote these letters with my permission. See that they are delivered.

He takes the letters and shoves them into his coat. Hale mounts the ladder. The rope is adjusted around his neck. Now he stands there alone.

> CUNNINGHAM
> (he removes an order from his
> coat)
> I will now read the order under whose authority, you, Captain Nathan Hale, are to be hanged by the neck until you are dead.
> (reads)
> Headquarters New York Island, September 22, 1776. Parole: London. Count: Great Britain. A spy of the enemy, one Nathan Hale (by his own confession) apprehended last night is condemned to be executed at eleven o'clock this day in front of the artillery park.
> (he looks up to Hale)
> And as a warning to such others who treasonably would act as spies for the rebels against their own country, you will hang there for three days.

Intercut to Montressor and Hale for emphasis during the reading.

> CUNNINGHAM (CON'T)
> (pause, then)
> Make ready.

> (MORE)

CUNNINGHAM (CON'T)
(two men seize hold of the
ladder to pull it away)
Is there anything you would say, Nathan Hale, before you fall
to your just and dishonorable death as a traitor and a spy
against your own king and country?

Hale looks around. His mouth is dry. His lips trembling. Montressor
looks at him steeling himself against the tragic sense he feels.

HALE

Yes.

CUNNINGHAM

Then speak up and confess your crime and error.

HALE

Yes, I will speak. I know what to say.
(an exchange of looks between
him and Montressor . . . clearly,
with defiance and not regret)
I only regret that I have but one life to lose for my country.

A flash of triumph on his face . . . on Montressor's, a recognition of this.

CUNNINGHAM
(bellowing with fury)

Hang him.

The ladder is drawn away. We see only Montressor's face as he suddenly
turns away but into camera. Pain and anguish . . . . He starts to walk
away . . . . The camera pans with him . . . . He enters his tent . . . . The flap
falls . . . .

CRONKITE
(over this last action)

And so he died, a youth who reached his maturity and death
in the same year. For three days, in the sun, in the dew, in the
rain, his body was dishonored. Provost Marshal Cunningham
destroyed his letters. But the next day Captain Montressor
during the truce told Nathan Hale's story and his last moments
to the Americans, among whom was Alexander Hamilton, and
later to Hale's close friend, Captain, later General William
Hull, and Hale's name became a legend.

INT. CBS STUDIOS

CRONKITE (CON'T)

In a sense Nathan Hale's immediate mission was a failure for the British struck before he was captured and General Washington knew that all of New York would have to be abandoned. But in the sense in which men make their own history, irrespective of immediate events, Hale made his, and made ours. In this profound action we can say that he did not die in vain or too soon, for he died fulfilling the purpose which in his own mind was the ideal of his own life, and the nation to come.

What kind of day was it? A day like all days, filled with those events that alter and illuminate our time . . . and YOU WERE THERE!

FADE OUT.

The Secret of Sigmund Freud

As a physician who specialized in treating the mentally ill, Sigmund Freud (b. 6 May 1856, Freiberg, Moravia, now Pribor, Czechoslovakia—d. 23 September 1939, London) developed a comprehensive theory concerning the psychological structure and functioning of the human mind. He demonstrated that many illnesses with no apparent organic explanation could be treated by psychiatry or psychoanalysis. He identified and explored hidden motivations in the subconscious mind, and he perfected psychoanalytic techniques for analyzing the development and functioning of both normal and abnormal behavior. His original and often controversial ideas have had wide applications—even beyond psychiatry—in understanding processes of artistic creation, education, and political conduct.

In writing what is generally regarded as his major work, *The Interpretation of Dreams* (1899), Freud outlined a main theme: "It seems to me that the theory of wish fulfillment gives us only the psychological solution—not the biological. It seems to me that biologically the dream life proceeds altogether from the relics of the prehistoric period. I surmise the formula: what was seen in that prehistoric period gives rise to dreams: what was heard, to fantasies: what was sexually experienced, to psychoneuroses."

In this work, Freud analyzed the dream mechanisms and discussed the latent content of dreams; he explained the principle of wish fulfillment; he described the Oedipal complex, involving the emotional sexual complications between parents and children; and he showed the overwhelming influence of infantile life in conditioning the human adult.

❖❖❖

Abraham Polonsky was the only logical candidate of Russell's blacklisted trio to write the script on Sigmund Freud, even though when Russell first offered the project, Manoff said, "Give it to Bernstein. He's been in analysis so long he can't think when he's standing up." (Russell, "In the Worst of Times," p. 93.) Indeed, Polonsky had published, two years earlier, an impassioned and brilliantly written novel, *The World Above* (1951), about a psychiatrist's search for a working philosophy that will reconcile his strictly scientific principles with a broadly humanistic faith. In the novel, Polonsky writes: "Superbly Freud had sketched the geography of the human soul so that men could travel through their hearts without fear, but not without danger. For psychic reality was real, unlike storybook ghosts. These spirits of the past were like many an ancient geographer and voyager, while discovering new continents and opening an era, had like them often given these places magical shapes and presences." (Polonsky, *The World Above*, p. 93.)

Freud spent most of his life refining and elaborating the brilliant theories by which he reinterpreted the nature of the human psyche. But the work of Wilhelm Reich, Karen Horney, Erich Fromm, Melanie Klein, and R.D. Laing has revised or further developed his main ideas. Moreover, serious qualifications of the sexual causality of human behavior have been put forward. The power of socio-economic factors in the formation of human personality and the growth of doubt about the exact relation between nature and nurture have blurred theories Freud once thought to be clear and distinct.

Polonsky's teleplay is breathtakingly economical in forging the template for these ramifications. The exchange between Freud (played in the episode by Philip Bourneuf) and Northshield (pp. 148-152) *contrasts* Freud's emphasis on the role that the unconscious mind plays in forcing the repression of natural, "anti-social" instincts *with* an alternative approach which attempts to find explanations in the real objective world that humans exist in. Freud maintains that psychoanalysis "points to the fact that the human mind obeys natural laws as clear and as absolute as the law of gravitation or natural selection." Freud the existentialist teaches "patients, who are badly adjusted to the life in which they find themselves, how to adjust, how to live in the world they exist in."

What is Freud's response when confronted by a world that is not worth adjusting to, when asked (in the teleplay) how to amend a world in which it is unfit to live? Freud: "I'm a psychologist, not a social reformer."

But in *The World Above*, Polonsky's protagonist, Dr. Carl Myers, says: "In every case of mental illness you will find not a single cause, but a whole history of individual defeats that begin in the earliest stages of childhood and continue up to the point of breakdown in the present. Do you think it improper to examine the environment in which this disaster occurs? Whether it is the sexuality of man that takes monstrous shapes, or his dreams, or his acts of social drive within the community, in every case, at every point, the malformations are symptoms, no matter how deeply they exist, even to the earliest days within the parents' house. There is no wickedness in all history that did not come from the social environment, and there is not an act of heroism or goodness that did not issue from the social cause." (Polonsky, *The World Above*, pp. 358-360.)

Polonsky's Freud is a composite of these various currents, who states at the narrative's conclusion: "If men should ever remember Dr. Freud, let them remember that the slogan of my life was: nothing human is alien to me."

❖❖❖

While the episode was in production, Charles Russell received a phone call. "My secretary, Helen, said, 'Dr. Freud is on the line.' I carefully picked up the phone thinking it was some kind of sick joke.

"The voice at the other end identified himself as an analyst and Sigmund Freud's nephew. He continued, 'I would like you to come to my office and we can discuss the content of this script you are doing on your program.' His voice was authoritative and I agreed to meet him.

"'Come in, Mr. Russell. I can see you don't have a copy of the script with you. How unfortunate. Would you be kind enough to tell me what your plans are for this story?' This was the introduction.

"I told him it related to the conflict caused by the publication of Freud's book, *The Interpretation of Dreams*. He then asked, 'What is the implication of the word secret in your title?' (Abe suggested it should be titled 'The Secret of Sigmund Freud.' The series used dramatic nouns in the titles such as, 'The Fate of,' 'The Triumph of,' 'The Death of,' 'The Vindication of,' and so on. I didn't know what the secret was but knew that Abe didn't know either.) I told him, 'There is no implication; it is simply to dramatically emphasize an important person's position in history.'

"He paused, then said, 'When I receive the script and read it I will determine whether I will file suit against your network. Good night.'

"Sigmund Freud's nephew did not consider it necessary to file suit against the network. He actually liked the script and at my invitation came to the studio on Sunday with Ernest Jones, author of *The Life and Works of Sigmund Freud*. They posed together, in one of the sets, with Walter Cronkite looking at a copy of the book he held in his hand. . . and I'm sure Walter was trying to figure out what sort of a day it was. It was like all of our days during that period, filled with dreams and sometimes their fulfillment." (Russell, "In the Worst of Times," pp. 94-95.)

The Secret of Sigmund Freud
by Abraham Polonsky
(signed by Jeremy Daniel)

Air Date:
October 4, 1953

YOU ARE THERE
January 2, 1900

FADE IN:

INT. CBS STUDIOS

CRONKITE
Walter Cronkite reporting. The date is January 2, 1900. All
things are as they were then, except . . . YOU ARE THERE.

INT. WUNDT'S LABORATORY, LEIPZIG

WUNDT has his back to the camera. On the table in foreground are two
cages: one with a rat running in its endless exercise drum, and in the
other a few white rats. When Wundt talks, he stands between cages.

HOLLENBECK
This is Don Hollenbeck reporting from the University
laboratories of Dr. Wundt in Leipzig. Professor Wundt, who is
the leading experimental psychologist of Europe, has kindly
consented to answer a few questions on the significance of the
controversial new book by Sigmund Freud. Professor Wundt?
(Wundt turns into camera)
Have you read Dr. Freud's book, *The Interpretation of Dreams*?

WUNDT
(a deliberate man)
I have read as much of it as I can read.

HOLLENBECK
What do you think of it?

WUNDT
Well, it's an astonishing performance.

HOLLENBECK
In what way, sir?

WUNDT
(severely)
I had been under the impression that Dr. Freud was a modest
scientific observer of nature. It seems, however, that he is
nothing but a medical charlatan.

HOLLENBECK
You mean you don't agree with his theory of the interpretation
of dreams?

WUNDT
His book on dreams is similar to the one my cook keeps in the
kitchen which she consults for her love affairs. You can buy
such articles for a few cents in any cheap bookstore frequented
by shopgirls and servants. We have made scientific
investigations of dreams. Dreams are the insignificant remains
of a previous day's activity plus the accidental stimulation of
temperature, body position and so forth . . . of no significance.

HOLLENBECK
Whereas Freud claims they are of tremendous value in the
interpretation of human behavior in health and disease?

WUNDT
That is his claim.

HOLLENBECK
What do you think of his theory of the unconscious mind?

WUNDT

There can be no unconscious mind. By definition the mental is
the same as the conscious.

HOLLENBECK

But Dr. Freud seems to give case histories and evidence of the
existence of a mental entity which can be called the
unconscious.

WUNDT

Everything depends on method. Whether or not the method is
scientific. No scientific theory can be based on factors which
are not material and quantitative, capable of measurement and
susceptible to mathematical manipulation. Freud's method
seems to consist of endless unmotivated conversations without
logic or any other discipline, moral or scientific.

HOLLENBECK

What do you think of his theory of the role of sexuality in
human behavior?

WUNDT

Being a German and a citizen of Berlin, being so to speak a
civilized European, I can only say that Freud's notions of
sexuality may very well apply to the habits and practices of the
Austrians, especially the Viennese. We are all familiar with the
loose living, the silly customs, the self-indulgence and lack of
seriousness of the Viennese, and Freud's theory is just another
manifestation of the degeneracy of that city. I consider his
work immoral, disgusting and dangerous. Any more
questions?

HOLLENBECK

No, sir. Thank you, Professor Wundt. We now take you to
Vienna . . . and Harry Marble.

INT. GENERAL HOSPITAL AUDITORIUM — VIENNA

FREUD in the center as he faces a wall of empty seats. in front of him on
the closest bench, a woman and a young lieutenant of the Austrian army.
This is his only audience. The lights are out all over except for a few
bulbs that burn above Freud's head. And yet, he seems affable and
undiscouraged.

                              MARBLE
Harry Marble speaking from the auditorium of the psychiatric
clinic, the General Hospital, Vienna. You are listening to Dr.
Sigmund Freud, private docent of the University, delivering
one of his bi-weekly lectures to an audience of two. Here in
these gloomy halls earlier today, Professor Wagner-Jauregg, a
former classmate of Freud and Professor of Psychiatry,
lectured to over four hundred students. Nevertheless, it is
Sigmund Freud who is the center of the present controversy in
psychology. It is rumored that students stay away from his
lectures because they are afraid to incur the enmity of the
doctors and officials who strongly disapprove of Freud's work.

Simultaneously over the quick quiet voice of Marble, Freud lectures. As
Marble finishes, Freud's voice up.

                              FREUD
                      (as marble speaks)
The theories of resistance and repression, of the unconscious,
of the etiologic significance of sexual life and the importance of
infantile experiences—these form the principal constituents of
the theoretical structure of psychoanalysis. We have been
studying and discussing them in turn, and tonight, now that
we have briefly summarized our insights into the mechanism
of repression, we turn to an old topic from a new point of
view . . .

Freud leans affably on the lectern, gazes around at the empty hall, smiles,
and remarks in all mildness . . . .

                         FREUD (CON'T)
I should like to say that this evening we have doubled our
audience, and have twice as many listeners as last time, a gain
of one hundred percent.
                      (the two listeners look around
                      and laugh self-consciously)
I suppose it's because of the main subject of our little talk
tonight. I am going to discuss a very improper subject: the
sexuality of the human being and its relation to health and
disease. Now the deformations and malformations of the
sexual impulse lead to all kinds of peculiar symptoms that
seem to have no connection with sex at all. These symptoms
                                                     (MORE)

FREUD (CON'T)

often mimic other diseases and thus we have hysterical
paralysis of the limbs, loss of appetite, vomiting, nervous
headaches, twitches, loss of memory, and almost any kind of
physical ailment you can imagine, from simulated leprosy to
false pregnancy. Curious, isn't it? The academic psychiatrists,
like those at this very institution, like Professor Wagner-
Jauregg, for example, while learned men and estimable
colleagues of mine, insist on classifying and treating the
symptoms and thus never get at the real causes of the mental
disease. These official doctors remind me of the farmer who
had never seen an electric light. He came up to Vienna, took a
room in a hotel. When the time came to retire, he tried to blow
out the electric light. Naturally he couldn't, although he blew
and blew. He didn't know that in order to turn off the electric
light you had to find the secret switch. Now official doctors
keep blowing at the electric light which is the symptom of the
disease, and never look for the secret switch which is the
strange, the puzzling and wayward sexual nature of man
hidden in the depths of his unconscious.
                    (he chuckles, walks around, is
                    quite informal)
If I say anything you don't understand, stop me. With such an
immense audience, we can afford to be informal.
                    (he looks at his notes . . . drinks
                    some water)
Human sexuality is the second of the unpleasant notions that
psychoanalysis has to deal with. The first unpleasant notion,
as you will recall, is that mental processes are essentially
unconscious. Those ideas which are conscious are
unfortunately merely isolated acts and parts of our whole
psychic nature. To put it another way: psychoanalysis cannot
accept the view that consciousness is the essence of mental life,
and we can accept no modification of this concept. None
whatsoever.
                    (drinks again)
To return now to our investigation of sex. I assert that the
sexual impulses play a tremendous part in the causation of
nervous and mental disorders. What is more, these sexual
impulses have contributed invaluably to the highest cultural,
artistic and social achievements of the human mind.

                                                    (MORE)

FREUD (CON'T)

Therefore, society can think of no more powerful menace to its existence than the liberation of the sexual impulses. It looks upon sex with horror, with loathing, and with concealed passionate interest. As a result, the scientific laws which I have discovered are branded by society as morally reprehensible, aesthetically offensive and politically dangerous. We all know it is a characteristic of human nature to regard anything disagreeable as untrue, anything critical of accepted beliefs as dangerous, and anything that violates the common prejudices as immoral. So be it. We can only follow the truth where it leads us and suffer the consequences thereof.

As Freud continues to speak, Marble will come in. The camera withdraws into the corridor outside while we fade Freud and his next remarks under and then out. What follows is to be used as background to be cut and used as needed.

FREUD (CON'T)

I have already mentioned that my investigation of the precipitating and underlying causes of the neuroses led me more and more frequently to conflicts between the subject's sexual impulses and his resistances to sexuality. In my search for the pathogenic situations in which the repressions of sexuality had set in and in which the symptoms, as substitutes for what was repressed, had had their origin, I was carried further and further back into the patient's life and ended by reaching the first years of his childhood. Since these experiences of childhood were always concerned with sexual excitations and the reaction against them, I found myself faced by the fact of infantile sexuality—once again a novelty and a contradiction of one of the strongest of human prejudices. Childhood was looked upon as "innocent" and free from the lusts of sex, and the fight with the demon of "sensuality" was not thought to exist until the troubled age of puberty. Such occasional sexual activities as it had been impossible to overlook in children were put down as signs of degeneracy and premature depravity or as a curious freak of nature. Few of the findings of psychoanalysis have met with such universal contradiction or have aroused such outbursts of indignation as the assertion that the sexual function starts at the beginning of

(MORE)

FREUD (CON'T)
life and reveals its presence by important signs even in
childhood. And yet no other finding of analysis can be
demonstrated so easily and completely . . . .

MARBLE
We planned to interview Professor Wagner-Jauregg, professor
of psychiatry here, and we are informed that he is now leaving
the hospital and will soon appear in this corridor.

Freud's voice fades, then comes up a little stronger as Marble stops
speaking. We are now in the corridor. In the distance appears
WAGNER-JAUREGG and a couple of younger men. The young men are
laughing as a result of some remark of the professor's.

MARBLE (CON'T)
The older man is Dr. Julius Wagner-Jauregg, professor of
psychiatry and discoverer of the fever therapy treatment of
paresis. He was associated with Freud in certain experimental
work in neuropathology.

Wagner and the young doctors stop at the open door and listen to Freud
whose voice sounds indistinctly off.

STUDENT DOCTOR
He's got a full house tonight.

WAGNER
(with cynical amusement)
He'll soon discover that the sexual is less sensational than he
imagines.

MARBLE
Professor?
(Wagner into camera, the other
two student doctors forming a
background)
Have you read Dr. Freud's new book on the interpretation of
dreams?

WAGNER
Indeed I have.

MARBLE
Would you like to make a comment?

WAGNER
It seems to be rather autobiographical.

MARBLE
I mean as to its scientific value.

WAGNER
I didn't think it was meant to be a contribution to science.
(the students laugh)
I was sorry to see that he was willing to confess in public his
obsession with sex.

MARBLE
You find the book valueless?

WAGNER
Au contraire. I find it intensely interesting, for in it I see the
story of a man whose sober work in science brought him no
satisfaction and insufficient fame, with the result that he
plunged into these strange aberrations.

MARBLE
You ascribe his present work to his ambitions to be famous?

WAGNER
We are all weak in that direction. I think mainly his new work
stems from his work with Charcot and Bernheim. The French
are naturally prone to an overestimate of the role of sex in
human life . . . no doubt from personal experience.

The students laugh.

MARBLE
You knew Freud as a student?

WAGNER
Indeed and as a neurologist, too. He was always a hard and
devoted worker but he had a fatal tendency to go overboard
and ride some fact or theory until it broke down. He had, so to
(MORE)

WAGNER (CON'T)

speak, a medieval tendency to find a single all comprehensive
answer to some complex affair. I remember how he lost his
head over cocaine.

The students are interested.

STUDENT DOCTOR

Didn't Dr. Freud write the first paper on its uses?

WAGNER

The story is more interesting than that. When the cola leaf was
brought to Freud's attention he initiated a series of tests on
himself and his friends, in searching for a drug that would be
useful in the treatment of neurasthenia. He dispensed it so
liberally that he never noticed its tendency to become habit
forming. He tried cocaine for everything. Strangely enough in
the two most important uses of the drug, surgery of the eye,
and nerve blocking, it was not Freud but Carl Koller and a Dr.
Halstead of the United States who made the final discoveries.
Freud was a monomaniac on cocaine and yet not thorough
enough. An interesting irony. He spread the bad effects not
the good. I often wonder if he is not doing the same with his
theory of psychoanalysis.

As he says these words, Freud appears followed by his two listeners and
overhears the final remarks. He frowns.

FREUD

Good evening, Professor.

WAGNER
(a little upset)
Good evening, Dr. Freud.

FREUD
(ironically)
You were reminiscing?

WAGNER

I'm getting old.

FREUD

And to be old is to be forgetful as well we know . . . although it is possible to be young and forget what we find disagreeable to remember. It was my paper and my verbal suggestions to Koller that cocaine could be used in the treatment of diseases of the eye . . . that put him on the path. In his first paper he mentioned my name. In his later papers he forgot to. Such slips of memory we find quite interesting in analysis. And perhaps you might recall, Professor, that I made the first attempt to use cocaine to relieve trigeminal neuralgia by injections into the nerves.

WAGNER
(stiffly)
I believe, sir, that was what I said.

FREUD

We don't always hear what we say or say what we think we are saying. Goodnight, sir.

Freud stalks off followed by the woman. The lieutenant remains behind, curious.

MARBLE

Professor, do you believe that Dr. Freud has made any real contribution to the treatment of the mentally ill?

WAGNER

He has certainly listed a great many interesting new mental peculiarities. He claims that he has discovered them by the use of psychoanalysis.

MARBLE

Doesn't Freud in effect claim to have discovered the mechanism of all mental illness?

WAGNER

We other psychiatrists feel that his claims are a little far reaching. As I said before, in his passionate devotion to his work he has a tendency to find what he is looking for. We all know, those of us who are familiar with the mentally ill, that
(MORE)

WAGNER (CON'T)
such patients are hypersensitive in one direction . . . they are
very suggestible. They are like blotting paper and soak up the
suggestion of the physician without even knowing it.

STUDENT DOCTOR
As in hypnosis?

WAGNER
Precisely. Under hypnotism the patient can be made to have
all kinds of symptoms. I believe under analysis by the process
of transference and dependence on the physician the patient
learns to find those symptoms and connections that he feels
the doctor would like him to have. The whole thing is quite
subjective and until objective verifiable criteria are established,
reputable psychiatrists will simply have to suspend judgment.

He nods to his students who join him as he leaves.

MARBLE
Thank you, Professor Wagner-Jauregg.

Only the lieutenant is left. He stands watching Wagner leave and then
turns to the camera.

LIEUTENANT
Sir?

MARBLE
Yes.
(recognizing him)
Weren't you one of the two people listening to Dr. Freud's
lecture?

LIEUTENANT
I was. I'm a former patient of Dr. Freud's. I think you might
interview some of his patients as well as the doctors.

MARBLE
Dr. Freud helped you?

LIEUTENANT
He gave me back my life.

(MORE)

LIEUTENANT (CON'T)
(pause)
I had been to these other respectable doctors. They all
diagnosed my case and then folded their hands. They were
glad to give my illness a name and consign me to those refuse
cans of our society . . . the mental hospitals. They know what
my sickness was. I fitted into their formula. But they
abandoned *me* . . . . Dr. Freud didn't see me as an example of a
disease. He saw me as an individual . . . human. . . suffering. . .
worthy of his time . . . worthy of being saved for life. He saved
me.

MARBLE
By the use of psychoanalysis?

LIEUTENANT
Yes, sir. By his patience, his kindness, his understanding, he
freed me from those obsessive ideas that were slowly
destroying my health, my honor, my mind, my career, my
family. He knew, as every suffering neurotic knows, that
mental pain is real pain and not malingering . . . that psychic
reality, as he says it, is as real as material reality . . . and I say
God bless him and save him from these old fashioned and
blind men who cannot see that a miracle is happening under
their very noses.

MARBLE
What is your name, sir?

LIEUTENANT
What's the difference? I'm anyone who has found himself
suddenly unable to deal with life and but for the helping hand
of a Dr. Freud would be dead, either actually, or in one of
those institutions which are living graves.

He turns away and marches off erect and militarily.

MARBLE
We are a little late now . . . and must omit our scheduled
interview with Dr. Breur, Freud's first collaborator and co-
discoverer of the cathartic treatment of neurosis. We take you
to Dr. Freud's home . . . and Robert Northshield.

INT. FREUD'S HOME AND OFFICE — VIENNA

The reporter and camera are in the study/library. Just behind, the examination room. The door to the examination room is open.

> NORTHSHIELD
> (almost in a whisper, very close
> to microphone)
> This is Robert Northshield in the study of Dr. Sigmund Freud's office. The open door just ahead leads to his examination room. In a few moments we shall go inside, and, by arrangement with Dr. Freud and with the consent of the patient, be able to see briefly something of the course of a psychoanalytic treatment. Naturally this violates the intimacy of such therapy, but we believe that even a rough approximation will be of public interest. We will not show the patient's face to preserve her privacy. Miss X is, according to Dr. Freud, suffering from a case of hysteria. Freud's home and office are located at 19 Bergasse between Vienna's historic junkmarket and the modern cathedral, a position which Dr. Freud has said, is most appropriate for his profession . . . symbolically, that is. I believe it's now time to go into the examination room.

The camera starts to move slowly. We see into the room. Freud smoking a cigar. A couch on which GIRL is resting. We cannot see her face. This should all be revealed slowly, as if unveiled. The girl is talking as we come in.

> GIRL
> . . . and I was very angry. Quite. I don't know why. I couldn't stand the sight of him anymore. Why should I? I'm free to do anything I please. I'm free to get up and walk out of here. You can't make me stay here.

> FREUD
> (calmly . . . blowing out smoke)
> I'd be the last to try.

Now there is silence as if the girl was quite aware that the camera had come into the room.

GIRL

I don't want to talk about that anymore.

FREUD

Some other time then.

GIRL

Would you like to hear a dream I had?

FREUD

When did you have it?

GIRL

Last night. I've had this dream before. Always the same one
more or less . . . .
              (a slight pause . . . a
              remembering voice)
A house was on fire. My father was standing beside my bed
and woke me up. I dressed myself quickly. Mother wanted to
stop and save her jewel case; but father said: "I refuse to let
myself and my two children be burnt for the sake of your
jewelcase." We hurried downstairs, and as soon as I was
outside, I woke up.
              (pause)
I dreamt this dream three nights in a row just after my father's
friend kissed me.

FREUD

How long did you stay up in the country after that scene?

GIRL

Four days more. On the fifth I went away with father.

FREUD

Did you ever have this dream before your father's friend tried
to kiss you?

GIRL

I don't remember.

FREUD

I'm certain you never did. You're just trying to wipe out the
connection in your mind by pretending it might be related to

(MORE)

FREUD (CON'T)

something else. But the days don't fit in yet. If you stayed in the country four more days why didn't you dream the dream four times? Perhaps you did?

GIRL

In the afternoon after that scene, I had gone to lie down as usual on the sofa in the bedroom to have a short nap. I suddenly awoke and saw my father's friend standing beside me.

FREUD

In fact, just as you saw your father standing beside your bed in the dream?

GIRL

Yes. I asked him sharply what he wanted there. He said he was not going to be prevented from coming into his own bedroom when he wanted to. Besides, there was something he wanted to get. This episode put me on my guard. The next morning I locked myself in when I was dressing. In the afternoon when I wanted to lie down on the sofa and lock the door, the key was gone. I made up my mind not to stay there without father. I was always afraid that my father's friend would come in while I was dressing . . . so I always dressed myself very quickly.

FREUD

As in your dream . . . . On the afternoon of your second day you resolved to escape from the persecution of your father's friend . . . and during the second, third, and fourth nights you repeated that resolution in your sleep. Your dream corresponded to a resolution and a resolution remains in effect until it is carried out or otherwise discharged. You said to yourself as it were, I shall have no rest and I can get no quiet sleep until I am out of this house. In your account of the dream you turned it the other way and said: as soon as I was outside I woke up. Now we know why you dreamed it, but let's proceed to find out what it really means and what it is hiding. What is this about the jewel case your mother wanted to save?

He motions with his hand for the camera to withdraw.

                    GIRL
Mother is very fond of jewelry and has had a lot of it given her
by father.

The camera is withdrawing.

                    FREUD
    And you?

                    GIRL
I used to be fond of jewelry once but I haven't worn any since
my illness.

Just as the camera leaves the room, the girl should turn and we get a look
at her tragic suffering face.

                    NORTHSHIELD
You have just witnessed a brief portion of an analysis. The
young woman is suffering from definite physical symptoms. . .
an apparent lameness in one foot. . . a difficulty in breathing. . .
and other symptoms which have no organic cause. By this
process of analysis Dr. Freud is trying to find the psychological
reason for these symptoms and thus eliminate them. We will
return later to interview Dr. Freud, but first we take you to
Berlin where we hope to throw some light on the origins of Dr.
Freud's book on dreams. Come in, Edward P. Morgan.

INT. FLIESS' OFFICE — BERLIN

FLIESS is waiting to be interviewed. He seems ill at ease, a man with a
very intense personality about the same age as Freud, but quite good-
looking and dashing.

                    MORGAN
This is Edward Morgan in Berlin. We're in the office of Dr.
Wilhelm Fliess, a nose and throat specialist. Dr. Fliess has
been Sigmund Freud's intimate friend and confidante during
the past five or six years. They met in Vienna thirteen years
ago. Dr. Fliess?

FLIESS
(with an embarrassed but
charming smile)
Ask away.

MORGAN
As you know we would like for historical purposes to find out
just what it was that led Dr. Freud to pay attention to dreams?

FLIESS
The fact that his patients mentioned them all the time.

MORGAN
I know, sir, but all mental patients mention them and it was
only Freud who started to study these dreams in a way that
might illuminate their significance.

FLIESS
That might have been due to my friendship with him.
Indirectly, so to speak. Because of my interest in the sexual
factors in disease we began to write to each other and later
used to meet quite frequently so that we could discuss our
common scientific interests. Our interests soon led to a more
intimate friendship. From time to time we would both steal
away from our respective homes and meet for a few days in
another city . . . to have the privacy and so on to continue our
discussions. Freud as you know was at that time interested in
seeing if there was a biological and even mathematical basis to
his theories.

MORGAN
Are you a mathematician?

FLIESS
I have originated a numerical theory based on the numbers
twenty-three . . . the male principle . . . and number twenty-
eight . . . the female principle. By combining these in various
ways you get a system of periodicity which explains the
frequency and occurrence of all kinds of diseases.

MORGAN
(a little embarrassed)
I see . . . and was Freud a believer in this system?

FLIESS

He was enthusiastic . . . for some time . . . and then also I
introduced him to the notion of bisexuality as a main factor in
human life and disease. In addition to this, he and I
experimented together with cocaine.

MORGAN

But how did all this influence his interest in dreams?

FLIESS

It was all too human rather than scientific. I began to resent
his influence on me as he no doubt resented mine on his. It
was a challenge to my independence of mind. We began to
disagree more frequently, and then it was . . . a year or so ago
. . . that Freud in an effort to break off his relations with me
entered upon self-analysis . . . the first in human history. It
was his way of freeing himself from me . . . he told me of it.
Naturally the material available for self-analysis is mainly
one's own dreams . . . and his theory of dream interpretation is
based on his own psychic life.

MORGAN

You mean that Dr. Freud felt he was also suffering from some
form of neurosis?

FLIESS
(grimly smiling)

Who doesn't? The brilliance of his work, his immense genius
lies in his profound insight, that between the neurotic and the
normal, between the sick and the well, is not a chasm . . . not
an absolute break, but complete continuity . . . and in this way
he points to beginnings of a real science of psychology.

MORGAN

Are you and Dr. Freud no longer friends?

FLIESS

Let's say, we are no longer intimate friends. He has a way of
making enemies of his old friends when he no longer needs
them. I suppose there is some profound need in him to do so
. . . to free himself . . . to go forward intellectually and

(MORE)

FLIESS (CON'T)
emotionally. As for myself, all I can say is . . . it was an honor
to have known so closely a man whose genius will some day
transform the world.

Very moved as he turns away.

MORGAN
Thank you, Dr. Fliess. We return you to 19 Bergasse in Vienna.

INT. FREUD'S OFFICE — VIENNA

We are in the study, surrounded by the books and the objects of Freud's
collection. Freud has changed to a smoking jacket, and has a fresh cigar.
His wife brings in coffee in a silver service. Freud talks quietly with her,
pouring himself coffee. On the desk are playing cards, cigars, cigarettes,
etc.

NORTHSHIELD
This is Robert Northshield again in the study of Dr. Freud at 19
Bergasse. The lady with whom Freud is talking is his wife. Dr.
Freud has consented to answer any questions we wish to ask
concerning his theories and work . . . "within the limits of
medical propriety," he added. The objects d'art you see
around us have been personally collected by Freud and
represent his interest in the symbolic past of the human mind
which he believes exists on as the archaic in our own.

Coffee in hand, cigar, Freud turns to camera as his wife leaves. As she
goes she looks back curiously.

FREUD
We have a few minutes before my guests arrive.
                    (he indicates the cards and
                    table)
This is my weekly evening for playing cards with a few
friends. I never break the custom if I can help it. It takes one's
mind off the burdens of daily life and is not without its
contribution to psychology.

NORTHSHIELD

I should like, if I may, Dr. Freud, to press a little harder with some of the questions. I'm afraid we don't see eye to eye on everything.

FREUD

By now I'm familiar with the resistance that most people have to my theories.

He drinks and he smokes. From time to time he can move around.

NORTHSHIELD

What scientific proof have you found for the existence of an unconscious mind?

FREUD

The same kind of scientific proof that we have of the existence of atoms . . . or to use a medical analogy . . . the same kind of proof that we have that there is a virus that causes the common cold. With one exception, I know more about man's unconscious mind than man knows about the common cold.

NORTHSHIELD

There is no objective proof of such an entity as the unconscious . . . isn't that correct?

FREUD

Naturally. Our unconscious is hidden from us. It manifests itself in actions of one kind or another . . . and from my experience of hundreds of cases I've been able to demonstrate its nature and the laws under which it operates. Tell me, why do you resist the idea that people have unconscious minds whose role in human life is of central importance?

NORTHSHIELD

Isn't it unscientific to ascribe to the unknown explanations which can be found in the real objective world around us?

FREUD

People always say that in order not to consider the subject. You don't really object to my theory of the unconscious mind, but my description of its role in human life. It's in the

(MORE)

FREUD (CON'T)

unconscious mind that the sexual instincts strive with each
other, struggling to break into the world and its objects; and it
is into the unconscious that the world forces man to repress
these powerful instincts with the resultant diseases of
sublimations. This is what you object to . . . not the idea of the
unconscious.

NORTHSHIELD

In other words, whoever disagrees with you is afraid to
recognize the truth and whoever agrees is a liberated intellect?

FREUD

Precisely.

NORTHSHIELD

Aren't you being a little one-sided in your characterization of
human nature? Human beings have other interests beside
sexual ones.

FREUD

Their other interests exist, but most of them are the result of
the repression of the sexual instincts. And what is repressed
one way must come out another. Let me sum up for you.
Psychoanalytic investigation demonstrates that the essence of
human nature consists of elemental instincts which are
common to all men and aim at the satisfaction of certain primal
needs. These instincts have no morality and no conscience and
to satisfy themselves would refrain from nothing, including
murder . . . as when we wish someone we love to die because
they frustrate some profound impulse of ours.

NORTHSHIELD

You mean man's natural instincts are anti-social?

FREUD

They seem so.

NORTHSHIELD

And yet man never has existed apart from society.

FREUD

Well, I know I can't convince you by logic when your feelings
are aroused. You can find reasons enough to back up your
feelings, for reasons, as Falstaff said, are as common as
blackberries.

The door opens and in comes DR. KONIGSTEIN, about six years older
than Freud.

FREUD

Excuse me. This is Dr. Konigstein, one of my card partners.

Konigstein bows toward camera and goes to table. In background he
lights cigar, pours himself coffee, riffles cards as Freud speaks.

FREUD (CON'T)

Dr. Konigstein was the first to use cocaine in the treatment of
eye diseases when I indicated the possibility.

NORTHSHIELD

Dr. Freud, do you deny that man can perfect himself?

FREUD

I would say you can never eradicate his basic instincts,
although you can modify them drastically . . . remembering
always that too severe a repression leads to mental disease, the
main characteristic of our times.

The door opens and two men enter.

FREUD (CON'T)

Excuse me.
                    (to camera)
Dr. Rie and Dr. Rosenstein.

The men bow, go to the table and take their places. They too light cigars
and take coffee.

FREUD (CON'T)

I'm afraid you'll have to excuse me. Now is my time to forget
the world and its illnesses.

NORTHSHIELD

Dr. Freud, just exactly how do you help your patients?

FREUD

Well, in general my patients are badly adjusted to the life in which they find themselves, so I teach them how to adjust, how to live in the world they exist in.

NORTHSHIELD

Suppose the world around them isn't worth adjusting to? Suppose it's unfit to live in as in so many of the cases which you have described?

FREUD

I'm a psychologist, not a social reformer.

NORTHSHIELD

Dr. Freud, what do you think is your main contribution to science?

FREUD

(he thinks for a moment)

Science is based on the liberation of man from his historical illusions. In the eighteenth century, as a result of the work of Newton, man learned that his planet as well as the most distant stars obeyed the same inalterable laws. In the nineteenth century because of Darwin, man learned that he belonged to the order of organic life and obeyed the same laws as the mouse or the rose, the cabbage or the mosquito, that his flesh was of their flesh and therefore his destiny was a natural one. Today we stand on the brink of the twentieth century, and I hope on the verge of new discoveries and our liberation from a final illusion. Psychoanalysis points to the fact that the human mind obeys natural laws as clear and as absolute as the law of gravitation or natural selection. I think it is quite interesting that it was through the study of the sick, the ill, the despised, the condemned, through the study of what people refuse to admit existed, through what people avoided, that we found a clue to the secrets of the human mind in general. And if men should remember Dr. Freud let them remember that the slogan of my life was: nothing human is alien to me. Goodnight.

NORTHSHIELD

Goodnight and thank you, Dr. Freud.

Freud is closing the doors.

INT. CBS STUDIOS

CRONKITE

Thirty-eight years later, two years before he died, Sigmund
Freud's books were burned by the German and Austrian Nazis
but by that time psychoanalysis had penetrated the intellectual
life of western civilization. Its words and ideas had become a
commonplace in education, literature, law and medicine, and
everybody was psychoanalyzing everybody else. Today
mental illness is increasing in our own country, and the truth
or falsity of psychoanalysis is more important than ever.

What sort of a day was it? A day like all days, filled with those events
that alter and illuminate our time . . . and YOU WERE THERE.

FADE OUT.

THE RECOGNITION OF MICHELANGELO

One of the major sculptors of all time, Michelangelo, full name Michelangelo di Lodovico Buonarroti Simoni (b. 6 March 1475, Caprese, Italy—d. 18 February 1564, Rome), won incomparable recognition during the Renaissance for his paintings, architecture, and drawings. After the tardy appearance of his poetry in 1623, he slowly emerged as one of the most significant and personal poets of his age, his sonnets and madrigals appearing in almost all recent anthologies of Italian literature. So extraordinary was his influence on the history of art that the word Renaissance (Italian *rinascita*, "rebirth") was coined to characterize the leap or saltation of the fine arts under Michelangelo and Raphael. According to the historian Giovanni Papini, the Reformation, as well, owes its very existence to Michelangelo. Papini reasons that Pope Julius II so increased the sale of indulgences to ensure the magnificence of his tomb, which Michelangelo was to execute, that Luther and others rebelled and split the Church in two. Still a third definable age is occasionally credited to Michelangelo, who is often hailed as father of the Baroque for such tortuous and tense figures as the Haman of the Sistine ceiling. It is an overwhelming honor—if a debatable one—to be credited with the existence of the Renaissance, the Reformation, and the Baroque age, yet these claims at least suggest the influential role that Michelangelo played in the history of the fine arts.

The worlds of fine art and politics commingle, as they do in most of his writings, in Polonsky's "The Recognition of Michelangelo." In 1501, Michelangelo signed a contract for the marble "David," which, upon completion in 1504, was hailed by Florentines as "the Giant." It was viewed by the democratic Commune as an allegory on the moral strength of Florence. In the teleplay the statue is used to symbolize the triumph of the Florentine republic over the banished Medici. In so doing, Polonsky allows the "betrayal" theme to emerge: this time Michelangelo himself, in the view of Cardinal Giovanni de Medici, expediently and opportunistically violated past loyalties and affiliations.

Giovanni remembers Michelangelo as a friend of his youth, one who was embraced by his own family, who received the sponsorship of Giovanni's father. But now Michelangelo has completed a giant statue "which represents the shaming of Giovanni's family," the Medici, which political currents have now discredited.

COMMENTATOR

The statue we are informed was directly commissioned by the republic. Do you expect artists in Florence to refuse such commissions?

GIOVANNI

I expect men to live and die by their ideals, but artists, I suppose, are less than men and work for whomsoever pays them and for whatever cause! (p. 162)

The rendering of a statue—Michelangelo's sublime act of creation—is played by Polonsky for maximum ambiguity. Giovanni views the work of art as a personal betrayal of his family, and indicts an artist's willingness to sell out his art for a price (see Introduction, pp. 21-22). The 1950s/1990s parallels remain constant.

On a lighter note, Polonsky depicts Pier Soderini, the chief magistrate of Florence who gave Michelangelo the commission for the statue, as a prototype of a modern-day film producer, or as a variation of those non-creative "executive" types who feel they must justify their participation in a project by imposing changes on their hireling's work. [Peter Shaffer's Emperor Joseph II, in Amadeus, is such a character. The scene (Act One, Scene 8) in which Joseph tells Mozart that his "The Abduction from the Seraglio" has "too many notes" is an example of this sort of artistic meddling.] Here, Soderini says to the master Michelangelo: "I feel . . . that the nose seems a trifle long and takes away from the full dignity of the work."

Michelangelo performs a mock alteration of his masterpiece, and Soderini leaves happily content that his suggestion had been accepted. The experience leads Michelangelo into some observations on the nature of "art criticism": "The eyes of even the untrained can see beauty when it masters them, and I for one prefer the praise of those who pass in the street to those who sit in the palaces. In the palace, art is a form of pleasure. But the ordinary man when he loves a worthy work, a painting by Botticelli, a Madonna, a Christ, then his life is altered thereby and the high design of the artist is made flesh" (p. 178).

Polonsky has his Michelangelo state: "it seems to me that I can discover but one art or science, which is design, and that all the works of the human brain and hand are either design itself or some branch of that art" (p. 178). Indeed, it was Michelangelo's unifying embrace of

Humanism, its unitarian drive, that led him to adopt as his personal emblem three circles interwoven, as he explained, to show the interdependence of each on the other two. Many of his comments shattered the rigid distinctions among the parallel arts. He knew that, "philosophically speaking," the underlying unity of art was to be found in design (in Renaissance Italian the "fine" arts were then called the "arts of design"), and his insistence on the oneness of the arts issued from this knowledge. Design, draftsmanship, drawing—this was the basic talent he demanded of his colleagues and assistants.

Thus, this unitarian tendency as a Renaissance thinker led the artist, so ungregarious and unaccommodating as an individual (Raphael called him "the hangman") to become conciliatory in the areas of aesthetics and philosophy, uniting artistic theory and practice, Christianity and paganism, and the three arts of design. Michelangelo's slogan, in Polonsky's vision, thus becomes the same as Sigmund Freud's: "Nothing human is alien to me."

❖❖❖

Producer Charles Russell: "I called Bob Markell and casually told him we would need the statue of David for the Michelangelo show. Bob, the stoic set designer who was accustomed to these crazy and impossible requests on our small budget, dropped the phone. I could hear it hit the floor then thud against his desk. After a moment I could hear his voice, very calm and controlled, 'Charlie, you know how much I enjoy working with you on this series, the scripts are great and I get tremendous satisfaction out of doing the show . . . you mean you really need the statue of David?'

"Abe had already told me it would be impossible to do the show without the statue. He was above such practical matters. Bob and I finally figured out a way to do it. He knew of a museum in Boston that had a four foot replica of David that we could buy. Bob then had a miniature set built, to scale and detail, of Michelangelo's studio, and the replica worked in that set. Then he was able to get a life size plaster cast made of the head of David which was used in the actual set. From the head down what was supposed to be the rest of the sculpture was covered by burlap and we could see the actor dealing with the final touches on the head.

"When the burlap is pulled off we see the committee's reaction. Then we cut to the replica as the camera moves and pans exploring the statue in detail, giving it a kind of living motion with Michelangelo's voice over the movement: 'David is a young giant, but so are men young giants seeking with courage and nobility to find their way among the torments of the earth and the vices of cowards.'

"After dress rehearsal Bill Dozier came up to me and said, 'You have to put a fig leaf on that statue.' I said, 'If you insist, Bill, but every knowledgeable person in the art world will crucify you if you do.' I suggested a little pencil shading in the genital area and he agreed.

"I talked to Markell into letting me have the replica of David and after the erasures were made it was given to Abe and [his wife] Sylvia for their 81st Street apartment." (Russell, "In the Worst of Times," pp. 101-103.)

✛✛✛

You Are There, Charles Russell, Sidney Lumet, and the clandestine writers' unit were nearing the completion of almost a year of celebrated collaboration. Here is a halftime report, so to speak, from Walter Bernstein:

Schools across the country asked for copies of the shows for their history classes. We found ourselves with a hit on our hands.

The position was curious. We could get no credit for the success and could not build on it, since that would give the fronts too much exposure. It meant nothing to our own careers because we had no careers. When the show began winning prizes and receiving awards, we could not appear to claim them. Russell could, but he was usually shunted aside by Dozier, who saw no reason why he shouldn't take the credit. None of this mattered. We were having too good a time. We were choosing subjects of controversy and importance: Galileo, Savonarola, John Milton, Cortez, Joan of Arc, Dreyfus, Benedict Arnold, Susan B. Anthony, Freud, Tom Paine, Socrates, Beethoven. We did the Scopes trial and the fall of Troy, the death of Cleopatra and the impeachment of Andrew Johnson. We roamed fall and wide. . . .

CBS let us [do the show], which caused some perplexity among its employees. . . . No one knew how [we got away with it.] . . . Most likely because the show was successful or perhaps someone high up in CBS thought this was something worthwhile. . . . [But] the success of the show also had ancillary benefits. We were able to give work to other blacklisted writers. While the three of us wrote almost all the shows, there were some we didn't have time for. Russell gave a few of these to unblacklisted writers, but kept a few for some blacklisted ones we suggested. . . . If the other blacklisted writers had no fronts, we lent them ours. This arrangement worked because we could guarantee the scripts. In the rare event a script was not adequate, we rewrote it. The other writer still got the script fee.

Our little group became the axis of my life. I saw my two children on weekends and I had other friends, but the group was both work and play, an oasis in a desert of discouragement and fear. We were making enough money now to pay our expenses; we believed in what we were doing, believed it was of value, enjoyed one another's company. We criticized one another with ruthless abandon and accepted it as love. We felt ourselves lucky. (*Inside Out*, pp. 221-223.)

THE RECOGNITION OF MICHELANGELO

by Abraham Polonsky

(signed by Jeremy Daniel)

Air Date:
November 15, 1953

YOU ARE THERE

January 25, 1504

FADE IN:

INT. CBS STUDIOS

> CRONKITE
>
> Walter Cronkite reporting. The date is January 25, 1504. All things are as they were then, except . . . YOU ARE THERE.

INT. VATICAN CORRIDOR

> LESEUER
>
> This is Larry LeSeuer. We are in the corridor that leads to the reception room of His Holiness, Pope Julius II. A new spirit is present in the Vatican now that Cesare Borgia is a prisoner in Spain and the years of poisonings, assassination, terror and immorality have come to an abrupt end. There is a sense of hopefulness, of change, and in line with this new atmosphere, an audience has been granted to Cardinal Giovanni de Medici.

A figure passes from camera right and starts down the corridor. It is the cardinal in full state robes.

                                   LESEUER
The subject of the audience is Florence, City of Flowers and the
former center of the financial power of the Medici. That is
Cardinal Giovanni de Medici. Your Eminence . . .

The cardinal pauses, turns back to camera, inclines his head slightly.

                              LESEUER (CON'T)
If you have a moment.

Cardinal takes a few steps toward camera which moves in on him.
GIOVANNI is a man of twenty-nine, of a rather scholarly and sweet
disposition.

                                   LESEUER
Has His Holiness indicated whether or not he intends to
intervene on behalf of your family with the Florentine
republic?

                                   GIOVANNI
We have spoken of the affair, but there is no question of
intervention.

                                   LESEUER
Of negotiation with the republic?

                                   GIOVANNI
There is no republic of Florence. Turmoil, terror and death are
the citizens who elect the officials. The Bargallo resounds with
the screams of honest men, and the Arno receives the bodies of
the innocent who are daily murdered there. When His
Holiness and I have mentioned Florence, we spoke not of
interfering but of saving her, of restoring to her the peace and
glory which was her fortune under the Medici.

                                   LESEUER
It's reported that the city is preparing to celebrate the
expulsion and outlawing of your family by erecting a
monument.

                                   GIOVANNI
I have heard the same.

LESEUER

The monument is supposed to represent the triumph of
republican freedom over Medician tyranny.

GIOVANNI
(coldly)

Monuments can not only be erected. They can be torn down.

LESEUER

Have you any immediate plans?

GIOVANNI
(cryptically)

Since the death of my brother, Piero, I am unfortunately the
material as well as the spiritual head of my family.

LESEUER

Would you then contemplate military action?

GIOVANNI

I cannot say.

LESEUER

Is there any further statement you would like to make, Your
Eminence?

GIOVANNI

Nothing.

He turns to go.

LESEUER

Thank you.

GIOVANNI
(stopping, turning back)

A small matter, but symbolic I think of the ingratitude of a city
whose glory has so long been associated with the fame and
fortune of my family. When I was a young man there was
another my own age, who lived in my father's palace with my
father's sons like one of them. He studied with us under the
great humanist Poliziano, and ate with the artists and scholars
and poets at my father's table, sitting closer to him than we,

(MORE)

GIOVANNI (CON'T)
his own sons. In the square of St. Liberata between the
baptistery and the Duomo, there were steps of white marble
and there we stretched on summer nights and improvised
songs and he was one of us.
(bitterly)
It was the time of our youth and we were friends, and Florence
was the chief state of the civilized world under the guidance of
my father, Lorenzo the magnificent. This young man was
supported by my father and his father received public offices...
from us.

LESEUER
You mean Michelangelo Buonarroti?

GIOVANNI
(passionately)
I mean he who has now it is rumored, completed the giant
statue which represents the shaming of my family.

LESEUER
The statue we are informed was directly commissioned by the
republic. Do you expect artists in Florence to refuse such
commissions?

GIOVANNI
I expect men to live and die by their ideals, but artists, I
suppose . . .
(with savage sarcasm)
. . . are less than men and work for whomsoever pays them
and for whatever cause.

He turns away and he walks away from camera.

LESEUER
We have just interviewed the Cardinal Giovanni de Medici, an
exile from Florence. We now take you to the City of Flowers
on the Arno. Come in, Edward P. Morgan.

INT. SHED OF MICHELANGELO

Studio in deep background. MICHELANGELO washing his arms and hands in a wooden tub. In the foreground a young apprentice is sweeping up.

> MORGAN
> This is Edward P. Morgan in Florence. We are in the
> workshed of Michelangelo Buonarroti within the precincts of
> the Opera Del Duoma, headquarters for the guilds that do
> repairs and decorations on the great cathedral. The young
> sculptor, who is washing up there in the rear in preparation for
> a visit from the art committee, has agreed to answer a few
> questions providing there is no discussion of politics.

As Morgan talks Michelangelo comes forward, drying himself vigorously. He has a rough, careless and rather surly air. He indicates to the apprentice to sweep elsewhere.

> MICHELANGELO
> Now, what is it that you would like to know?

> MORGAN
> Messer Buonarroti, when will the statue by unveiled?

> MICHELANGELO
> I don't know.

> MORGAN
> Can it be seen now?

> MICHELANGELO
> No.

> MORGAN
> Can you tell us what the subject of the statue is, what it
> represents?

> MICHELANGELO
> It is a statue of David who slew Goliath.

> MORGAN
> Who selected the subject?

MICHELANGELO
(hesitates)
I did . . . and so did Pier Soderini who gave the commission.

MORGAN
(a low explanatory voice)
Pier Soderini is the chief magistrate and Gonfaloniere of the
republic.
(then in question again)
Did he have any particular reason for suggesting the subject of
David?

MICHELANGELO
(irritably)
How should I know the inner mind of Soderini any more than
you or he can know mine!

He turns to his table loaded down with the tools of his craft. A small half
worked block of marble lies there. He stands and runs his hand over it,
feeling it as if truth were in the marble and not in the conversation.

MORGAN
(more persistent)
Well, what was in your mind? Did you have any particular
reason for selecting the theme of young David?

MICHELANGELO
(suspiciously)
What do you mean?

MORGAN
Well, why for instance, didn't you decide to do a Ganymede,
or some other theme from antique Rome and Greece?

MICHELANGELO
The great Donatello did a David and so did Verrochio. I, being
Michelangelo Buonarroti, decided to do one also.

MORGAN
No other reason?
(Michelangelo shrugs his
shoulders)
We hear that attempts have been made to injure the statue.
(MORE)

MORGAN (CON'T)
(persuasively as Michelangelo
shrugs again)
I don't wish to engage you in any discussion of Florentine
politics, but you know that the Cardinal Giovanni de Medici
has objected to your making this statue.

Michelangelo shrugs. He takes up a chisel and taps on the marble.

MORGAN (CON'T)
When the commission to make a statue was first discussed two
years ago, both Leonardo da Vinci and Andrea Contucci
requested the work. Why did you take it? Did you have any
particular reason?

MICHELANGELO
(breaking out angrily)
I had two reasons, one to live, because sculptors, like
Cardinals, must live. And the second was because the
commission was a challenge. It was said that nothing could be
done with this piece of marble. It was spoiled, very long and
narrow like a column and it had lain rotting and dead here in
the Opera for one hundred years. Agostini di Guccio had
slaughtered it, hacking it about the base, and cutting too
deeply. Both Leonardo and Andrea wanted to add pieces of
stone to it, but I believe I could make something of it as it was,
keeping its full height.

MORGAN
May we see it now?

MICHELANGELO
No.

MORGAN
Has any pressure been brought on you not to complete this
statue?

MICHELANGELO
(furiously)
A statue is a statue. I tried to breathe life back into the dead
marble and rescue it from its grave, but now I wish to God I
never had seen it, heard of it, or returned to Florence.

As he breaks out, a file of men starts to enter from behind the camera.

MICHELANGELO
(roughly to Morgan)

Go now. The committee is here.

As the camera starts to back away, as the men come in, Morgan low voiced and hurriedly begins to identify them.

MORGAN
(as Botticelli comes by, old and
weary, leaning on two canes)

That is Sandro Botticelli, perhaps the supreme lyrical painter of the time. He became a follower of Savonarola and very devout.

(now Leonardo—handsome,
richly dressed, elegant—
followed by a servant
companion)

Leonardo da Vinci, the mysterious man of the age, inventor of a new method of painting, scientist, man of the world.

(now an old gay blade, Piero di
Cosimo)

Piero di Cosimo, one of the favorites of Lorenzo de Medici, inventor of festivals, carnivals, circuses, and an extraordinary painter.

(now another)

Messer Francesco Filarete, chief herald of the ruling council.

There are others but Michelangelo has been walking toward the camera, pushing it out so to speak, and now we pass through the door which is closed into the camera.

MORGAN (CON'T)

This committee will judge whether the statue is worthy of being seen and then decide where it is to be placed. We will try to get a view of the statue later, but meanwhile we have arranged an interview with Pier Soderini, the head of the Florentine republic. Come in, Harry Marble.

INT. OPERA DEL DUOMO

A soldierly man, straight, simple, with an air of complete candor, sits on the edge of the table and faces into the camera.

> MARBLE
>
> Harry Marble here in the council room of the Opera Del Duomo. You are looking at Pier Soderini, Gonfaloniere of the republic, elected for life, and the supreme head of Florence. He rules with the assistance and help of a council and is sworn never to permit the return of the outlawed Medici. The Gonfaloniere has kindly consented to answer any questions we may put. Your Excellency, what would be your position if the new pope, Julius II, should support the attempt of the Medici to return?

> SODERINI
>
> The same answer we made to the last pope . . . war.

> MARBLE
>
> We understand that there are important sections of the population who would welcome the return of the Medici to Florence.

> SODERINI
>
> Without doubt there are those who have not yet learned to love and live with the republic.

> MARBLE
>
> The people you refer to say that there is more crime, lawlessness, corruption and anarchy in the city than in the days of the Medici.

SODERINI gets up. He grows sterner.

> SODERINI
>
> The lawlessness is the illegal action of factions, of the Palleschi as these followers of the Medici call themselves. They make riots and secret plots. They bribe officials. They spread rumors. They have even thrown stones into the workshop of Michelangelo and tried to break the statue he is making for the republic.

MARBLE

Then the statue of David is supposed to represent the triumph
of the republic over the outlawed and banished Medici.

SODERINI
(with great pleasure)

Indeed, that is my hope. Since this is a republic, the artists will
judge the work and the artists will select the site upon which it
will stand as an example to the citizens and to confound our
enemies.

MARBLE

Do you have any particular site in mind if the statue is
worthy?

SODERINI

For my part, as a simple soldier, I would select the place
directly in front of the entrance to the Signory. There
dominating the great square sacred in Florentine history, it
would replace the statue by Donatello which only is a
reminder of the rule of Medici.

MARBLE

Was the rule of the Medici unqualifiedly bad? Didn't they
raise Florence from a simple Italian town to a great city and
make it the center of the revival of classical learning and the
new Tuscan art?

SODERINI

How often I hear that argument . . . and yet did the Medici
make me a great soldier or did I the soldier make the Medici
great? Were the superb talents of the Florentine people, the
talents of the Medici . . . or did our scholars, our poets, our
artists in developing this renaissance of human life and human
worth carry along with them the pampered Medician rulers.
And today, when the Medici are gone, the most marvelous
artists of the world work here: Botticelli, Andrea Del Sarto,
Leonardo da Vinci, Fra Bartolomeo, Perugino . . . and two of
great promise, Michelangelo Buonarroti and young Raphael.
It is a sorry thing to hear intelligent men transfer to the Medici
the talents, the skills, the work of the Florentine citizens.
People love symbols.

MARBLE
And is that why you wish to have a symbol of the republic
erected in the square?

SODERINI
Precisely, but my symbol will be a work of art, not a tyranny of
men.

MARBLE
Thank you, Messer Pier Soderini. We now take you back to
the workshop of Michelangelo and Edward P. Morgan.

EXT. MICHELANGELO'S SHED

The closed door and part of the wall.

MORGAN
We are outside the workshop of Michelangelo Buonarroti. Just
a few minutes ago the committee of artists left after viewing
the statue. We tried to talk to some of them, but none would
make any comment . . . and no one is permitted to enter the
workshop until the decision is announced. The members of
the committee . . .

The doors open and the apprentice comes out. We see Michelangelo bolt
the door closed behind him.

MORGAN (CON'T)
. . . seemed to be in a state of high excitement and there was a
great deal of argument going on. The young man who just left
the workshop is the apprentice of the sculptor. From his bottle
and basket we gather he's going to market.

As he speaks, two bully boys with swords and capes come up. One
carries a jar and a brush. They knock on the door and it opens. We can
see Michelangelo shaking his head.

MORGAN (CON'T)
(as the action goes on)
I suppose those men are trying to get in also, but they're
having the same luck as we did a moment before.

Michelangelo slams the door in their faces. One of the men kicks the door. The other dips the brush in the jar and crudely paints on the door the coat of arms of the Medici.

> MORGAN (CON'T)
> That's odd . . . .
>> (as the man starts painting)
> Those two are evidently members of the Palleshi, the faction that supports the Medici, for that is the Medician coat of arms they have just painted on the door. It's a warning to the sculptor not to show his statue. There have been any number of stabbings over this in the past months.

One of the men kicks at the door and the other flings the jar and the brush over the paling. The men run off. But nothing happens. The door remains locked.

> MORGAN (CON'T)
> Michelangelo is not the kind of a man to come out and carry on a streetfight about things like this. In fact, his reputation is one of timidity.
>> (the door remains closed)
> I suppose the door will remain closed. So back to the council chamber and Harry Marble.

INT. COUNCIL ROOM OPERA DEL DUOMO

The committee of artists is in session, some gathered around the table, some standing. As Marble talks, the CHIEF HERALD should arise and take his position as the chairman.

> MARBLE
> We are back in the council chamber of the Opera Del Duomo where the committee of artists has just returned from a viewing of the statue of David by Michelangelo. That is Messer Francesco Filarete, chief herald of the Signory, who is rising to address the meeting.

> FILARETE
> Citizens, the young David, called the Giant, whom we have just seen certainly bears the palm among all modern and ancient works and on this we all agree. The statues of the past,
>> (MORE)

FILARETE (CON'T)

Greek or Roman, the Marfario of Rome, the Tiber and Nile of
the Belvedere, and the colossal statues of Montecavallo do not
compare with the David of Michelangelo in beauty or
proportion. The legs are finely turned, the slender flanks
divine, and the graceful pose unequaled, while such feet and
head and hands have never been excelled. After seeing this no
one need wish to look at any other sculpture or the work of
any other artist. The next question before us, is the placing
thereof. I have turned over in my mind those suggestions
which my judgment could afford me. You have one place
where the statue may be set up to honor our city and proclaim
the defeat of the Medician tyranny and the triumph of our
republic. That place is where the Judith stands, for she is a
symbol of the Medici and an omen of evil, and no fit object to
stand there in front of the Signory where all the world may
see. So I counsel you to remove the Judith and place there the
Giant, David.

Pan shot on the artists as they listen to this. They are obviously
disturbed by this suggestion.

FILARETE (CON'T)

Who is it that would like now to speak?

A certain hesitancy, into which in quick low tones . . .

MARBLE

It's quite obvious that the officials of the Republic want the
statue placed where it will most offend the Medici and their
followers . . . and it is equally obvious that the artists here have
had pressure put on them from all sides . . . .
   (Botticelli is rising)
That is Sandro Botticelli about to speak.

BOTTICELLI

It is my view, considering the beauty and divine religious
nature of the statue that it be placed in front of Duomo where
the worshippers going to and fro from their religious
devotions can take strength from the Giant.

As Botticelli sits down, SAN GALLO rises.

MARBLE
(rapidly)

Giuliano San Gallo, a great architect, is about to speak.

SAN GALLO

I agree as to the immense perfection of the statue, and will say
that nowhere in our time or even in the past has such art and
ingenuity come to so great a triumph. But the marble of the
statue has been exposed to rain and wind and storm for a
hundred years and it is of a soft and bad quality. If the David
should stand out in the elements time will destroy
it . . . and with it the art of the divine Michelangelo Buonarroti.
I suggest therefore that it be placed in the middle of the Logia
dei Lanza where the Giant will be under cover.

FILARETE
(angrily)

And out of sight.

As San Gallo sits down, Leonardo rises.

MARBLE
(in a quick undertone)

Leonardo da Vinci.

LEONARDO

I agree with Giuliano San Gallo.

FILARETE

I don't agree. There the statue will not be seen and it will risk
injury from scoundrels who have come to believe they can
destroy the republic by destroying the statue which stands for
our triumph.

LEONARDO

It is not a matter of the use to which the David shall be put
either by us or the enemies of our state. It is a question of the
marble itself and our desire to preserve for eternity what so
impresses our sense. Can the herald deny the stone is of a soft
and inferior quality.

FILARETE
(strong and sarcastic)
I'm afraid there are soft hearts here who have listened too
much to the threats of idlers and the grumbling of factions.

There are protests from the artists and further uneasiness.

MARBLE
(quickly)
No doubt the artists are reluctant to go on record here, for the
results of this meeting will be known immediately in the city,
and almost all of these men have worked for the Medici and
hope, if the times should change, to work for the Medici again.
The herald naturally represents the republic and his position is
clear.
(a man rises among the buzz of
confusion)
Peiro di Cosimo, the painter and close associate in former
times of the Medici family.

PEIRO
I have listened to the arguments and they are all sound.
Certainly the greatest place of honor would be to stand in the
entrance to the Signory, and *likewise* before the Duomo. In
truth, those of us who love art would like to preserve the
statue for all time and prefer to see it in a sheltered place. But
since we all admit that this work is of such a divine merit, we
should say further that the sculptor has by this work leapt at
one bound into the realms of the immortals and stands with
Phidias and the great sculptors of antique Greece. Let us,
therefore, do him the honor which he has won by his hand.
Let us come to the following decision: in recognition of the
supreme genius of Michelangelo Buonarroti, he himself shall
decide where his statue shall stand.

An uproar. The artists clap, cheer . . . this is solution.

MARBLE
(in the hubbub, dryly)
Of course, this will take all the artists out of trouble and put
the whole responsibility on Michelangelo.

FILARETE
I am opposed to that. The responsibility was given to this committee by Pier Soderini . . . .

A group forms around him arguing.

MARBLE
As the council thrashes out this decision, we take you back to the workshop of Michelangelo to see if we can view the statue which has received such unanimous praise, and yet, by its great beauty, precipitated this crisis among the factions of the city. Come in, Edward P. Morgan.

INT. WORKSHOP OF MICHELANGELO

Close shot on Soderini. He is looking up at the statue.

MORGAN
With the arrival of Pier Soderini, Gonfaloniere of the Republic, we were able to gain admittance to the workshop. In a sense, the statue has become public property now that the artists have decided that the David is worthy of being shown.

Cut to shot of Michelangelo on catwalk near the head of the statue. The statue is draped except for the head and shoulders and the artist is about to cover it completely.

MORGAN (CON'T)
That's Michelangelo up on the little catwalk built around the roof of the shed. We get a real sense of its enormous size from down here.

Michelangelo starts to put the drape on. Cut to Soderini.

SODERINI
One moment. I wish to observe the head once again.

Cut to Michelangelo waiting, looking down. Cut to Soderini.

SODERINI
Like the others I have been overwhelmed by the beauty of your work, and yet . . .

(MORE)

SODERINI (CON'T)
(he holds up a hand making a
kind of telescope with his
fingers)
... I feel ... if I may say so ... that the nose seems a trifle long
and takes away from the full dignity of the work.

Cut to close shot of Michelangelo. A wrathful look clouds his face. He
stares at the head which dwarfs his own. A slow arc to bring out the
superlative proportions of the head.

MICHELANGELO
(he roars it out)
Giulio!

Shop where the apprentice is busy scrubbing the Medici arms off the
door which is opened inward.

GIULIO
(jumping up)
Master.

Cut to Michelangelo.

MICHELANGELO
The Gonfaloniere of the republic considers the nose of the
Giant to be too long. Bring me some tools.

Cut to Soderini.

SODERINI
A trifle ... at the most a trifle ... and you need make no
changes ... but it seems to me that you miss perfection by a
trifle ... a hair.

The boy comes running by and goes up the ladder and disappears out of
the frame as Soderini looks up and talks. Cut to Michelangelo.

MICHELANGELO
I have labored all my life for perfection and why should I now
pause ... for a hair?

He turns to the boy who come to him. As the boy hands him the chisel
and hammer, Michelangelo whispers.

MICHELANGELO (CON'T)
Give me a pinch of marble dust . . . .

Michelangelo turns to the statue.

MICHELANGELO (CON'T)
Is it at the very end, Your Excellency?

Cut to Soderini using his hand as a telescope again.

SODERINI
To the left a little . . . a protuberance . . .

Cut to Michelangelo, indicating a position on the nose.

MICHELANGELO
Here?

The boy comes up and surreptitiously he puts a handful of marble dust
in Michelangelo's hand.

GIULIO
(whispering)
It is perfect, master.

MICHELANGELO
(whispering)
But men are not.

Close shot as he transfers dust to hand holding the chisel. He holds the
chisel with its blade covered from Soderini's view by his palm and takes
a position at the nose.

MICHELANGELO
Here?

SODERINI
There . . . but carefully . . . strike softly . . . .

MICHELANGELO
I was fed by the wife of a stonemason and grew up with the
stone cutters on the hills of Fiesole. I strike as they do, like
thunder.

He hits hard, the chisel rings, and the marble dust falls from his palm. The boy turns his face to the wall, laughing.

> MICHELANGELO (CON'T)
> Well, Your Excellency?

Cut to Soderini, a little dust falling in front of him as he surveys the statue.

> SODERINI
> Well struck . . . . Perfection . . . . It will be a great honor to us
> to have it stand to the right of the entrance to the Signory, and
> when the counselors come and go they will always be
> reminded of the indomitable spirit of this city which rises to
> conquer its enemies. I will post guards outside the shed and
> we will see to it that no harm comes from those devils of the
> Palleschi.
> > (he turns to go)
> Farewell.

Cut to Michelangelo and boy.

> MICHELANGELO
> Farewell.
> > (he watches and grins
> > sarcastically, then softly)
> Farewell.

He opens his hands and drops the rest of the dust down. He takes a polishing tool from his pocket and works at the neck while the boy sits down on the catwalk and watches.

> MICHELANGELO (CON'T)
> When you work in a Duchy, then the Duke is the art critic, and
> when you work for a king, then the king is, and if you work for
> a pope, then the pope . . . but, when you work in a republic,
> every fool is an art critic.

> GIULIO
> Do you think he could see whether the statue is great or not?

> MICHELANGELO
> I believe so. Pier Soderini is an honest man, but like all people
> he must speak when it's better to hold his tongue.

GIULIO

Does he love the design?

MICHELANGELO

I believe so. Two years ago when we began, I made him a line drawing of this David and he saw at once its secret and its strength . . . for the eyes of even the untrained can see beauty when it masters them, and I for one prefer the praise of those who pass in the street to those who sit in the palaces. In the palace, art is a form of pleasure. But the ordinary man when he loves a worthy work, a painting by Botticelli, a Madonna, a Christ, then his life is altered thereby and the high design of the artist is made flesh. Sometimes when I meditate on these topics, it seems to me that I can discover but one art or science, which is design, and that all the works of the human brain and hand are either design itself or some branch of that art.

He is showing in this the other side of his character, when suddenly he sees something below.

Voices off camera.

LEONARDO

Michelangelo.

MICHELANGELO

The politicians have arrived. Undrape the statue.

He starts to climb down. Cut to Leonardo, Botticelli and Piero di Cosimo entering. They approach the base of the draped statue as Michelangelo comes down the ladder.

MICHELANGELO (CON'T)

Is there some little detail of the David that you would see again?

LEONARDO

We come to praise you, Michelangelo. The committee has decided to let you choose where the statue shall stand.

MICHELANGELO
(understanding the trick, angrily)
So much honor will make me lose my head if the Medici return.

BOTTICELLI

The Gonfaloniere is determined that it shall stand in the one
and only place of supreme honor in the city, before the
Signory.

PEIRO

But it need not, for we all know that the stone is soft and the
statue should be protected.

Giulio joins them now.

PIERO

Look at it.

Cut to the statue in full. The camera slowly moves in upon it as Piero
speaks.

PIERO

It is a marvel, how out of that thin elongated column of spoiled
marble you could put together a statue that seems to spring
into action while it stands at rest . . . .

Cut to group. Michelangelo stands and glowers.

MICHELANGELO

I want no choice of where the statue should stand, and beside
Piero, men put together festivals and carnivals, but my David
lay hidden in that block of marble and I, like a discoverer,
found him there in his prison of stone crying to be set free. I
do not make him. I uncover him chip by chip, working around
him to loosen those members that protrude furthest from the
trunk. He comes to life as I release him from his marble bonds
. . . and now that he is free, let the republic choose where he
shall stand, for I am through with him.

Cut to group.

BOTTICELLI

He deserves the place before the Signory, for your David is
beyond question of supreme nobility and will be an inspiration
to our youth and a reminder to our old men when they forget
that we do not live on earth for our ease but for our journey to
God.

LEONARDO
(judiciously)
I admire the work, but I think that it has certain limitations.
Observe for a moment the statue . . . .

Cut back to full shot, then moving in closer to the statue.

LEONARDO (CON'T)
In the first place, as we view it, it can be seen that the hands,
the head and the legs are out of proportion to the trunk which
is too narrow. If the statue is placed under cover the shadows
will hide these deficiencies whereas broad daylight will expose
them. In the second place, we all admit the stone is soft and
should be protected. But in the third place, there is another
reason for the statue of David to be placed in some less
prominent place. The work upon it is excellent, but the idea
fails. The story of David tells us that a slim youth of delicate
strength overcame a giant Philistine, and overcame him only
because God himself came to the aid of the boy. But this
David is a giant himself. What help does he need from God?

MICHELANGELO
(passionate and furious)
God is in all of us and in David, too. And God was in me
when I loosed him from his marble grave. And you,
Leonardo, who have begun so many things and finished so
few, do not know the spirit that leads a man to actions that
complete the nature which lies hidden in things and men.
(he turns to the statue)
Behold my David.

Cut to full shot. Now the camera suiting its motions to Michelangelo's
words should explore the statue in detail, giving it a kind of living
motion.

MICHELANGELO (CON'T)
The block of marble was so thin I could not give to David the
beginning of the action itself, so I gave to him that profound
moment of will when he arrived at the decision to move
forward, to unleash the strap and let the stone fly, and yet,
nevertheless, he is at rest and at ease for the action is still
potential. So the action of the statue is of the mind, and you,
(MORE)

MICHELANGELO (CON'T)
Leonardo, who paint the smiles of women, know the difficulty
of executing in material objects the divine motions of the
human mind.

Be on the face at this moment which is heroic and divine indeed.

MICHELANGELO (CON'T)
As for the hands . . .

Go to the hands.

MICHELANGELO (CON'T)
. . . they are like mine . . . .

Cut to close shot of Michelangelo holding his hands up for Leonardo to
see. Cut back to the statue.

MICHELANGELO (CON'T)
You cannot break out of the stone the innumerable forms that
are hidden there with the luxurious hands of a lover of sensual
pleasure. My hands, like his, are those of a stone mason or a
warrior in whom the spirit of the just God is moving. God
gives us courage but we are his instruments and the
instrument must have the strength and force. And as for the
soft stone . . . I do not give my life to my art to make a
monument for my eternal fame. The stone will outlast us and I
live for my work in my time. Let God grant that the men of
the future find merit in my labors, but I, and only I can labor
for the elevation of the men of my own time. David is a young
giant, but so are men young giants seeking with courage and
nobility to find their way among the torments of the earth and
the vices of cowards.

Cut to Michelangelo. He is uplifted on his own words.

MICHELANGELO (CON'T)
Let David stand before the Signory and sound the trumpet of
his spirit to awaken us here in Florence. I care not for this
republic or the Medici, but only for the spirit of man, and he
who serves that spirit serves God. Let David stand there.

There is a grave silence.

PIERO
(softly)
And if the Medici return?

MICHELANGELO
They will meet my Giant in the Piazza della Signoria, and
I . . .
(he pauses)
. . . and I will run away to Rome.

BOTTICELLI
Michelangelo.

He embraces him as the other two stare. the boy smiles . . . and turns to
look at the statue. Final shot on the statue.

INT. CBS STUDIOS

CRONKITE
And there the statue stood for more than three hundred years,
exposed to rain and wind and storms and the violence of the
revolutions and wars until we in our time moved it for
safekeeping to a museum. The Medici returned and the
Cardinal Giovanni became pope, known as Leo X.
Michelangelo left Florence and went to Rome.

In Rome, Michelangelo dominated the world of art both as a
sculptor and painter, creating on the ceiling of the Sistine
Chapel the works that have been the marvel of the ages. And
in the end, honored, an old man, he was called upon to build
the immense dome of St. Peter's by the very Cardinal Giovanni
who had become pope. In that David which we have seen was
first manifest what the Italians call *terrabilita*, the awe-inspiring
energy and force, austere and overwhelming, which is the sign
of great art, great men and great actions.

What kind of a day was it? A day like all days, filled with
those events that alter and illuminate our time . . . and YOU
WERE THERE!

FADE OUT.

THE VINDICATION OF SAVONAROLA

The famous 15th century Italian preacher, reformer, and martyr Girolamo Savonarola (b. 21 September 1452, Ferrara, Italy—d. 23 May 1498, Florence) was educated by his paternal grandfather, Michele, a celebrated doctor and a man of rigid moral and religious principles. From this elderly scholar, whose own education was of the 14th century, Savonarola may have received certain medieval influences. In his early poetry and other adolescent writings the main characteristics of the future reformer are seen. Even at that early date, as he wrote in a letter to his father, he could not suffer "the blind wickedness of the peoples of Italy." He found unbearable the humanistic paganism that corrupted manners, art, poetry, and religion itself. He saw as the cause of this spreading corruption a clergy vicious even in the highest levels of the Church hierarchy.

The ambiguities of the historical context, along with their contemporary implications, of "The Vindication of Savonarola" are discussed in the "Introduction" (pp. 23-25). But this text is also an appropriate framework for a discussion of Polonsky's emblematically piquant and lyrical writing style, his proclivity for flamboyant, provocative, bravura characters who are shocking, darkly humorous, perversely ironic. In "Savonarola," Cesare Borgia (played in the episode by David J. Stewart) defines this role: "He is beautifully dressed in a hunting costume. He carries a little whip with which he sometimes strikes his hand or boot to make a point. He is very young, very handsome, and very sure of himself." He is asked to comment on the Florentine situation, and, in the process, he discourses on the adroit manipulation of political power. This is a scene, quintessentially Polonsky, of high literary style, sardonic wit, and an all-too-realistic existential cynicism:

BORGIA
There are three methods of bringing an end to the disunity
within a city or state. Firstly, by murdering the party leaders.

COMMENTATOR
Did you say murdering the party leaders?

I did. Secondly, by removing them from power. Thirdly, by winning them to peace through compromise and agreement. The last is most dangerous. The first is most secure. Force, courage, violence are the weapons by which quiet is imposed on states. They do not always suffice, for we cannot kill everyone. Therefore, fraud and stratagem are necessary. If the citizens are used to the words of liberty, then we embrace the word; if they despise war, we oppose war; if they like ease and contentment we promise them both; if they cherish independence we extol it. By such means we gain power and, although they will have lost liberty, be at war, have neither ease nor contentment, and be slaves, the citizens will think they have all. For human nature is unchangeable. It is foolish, and only good rulers can like good shepherds protect the flock while gathering the wool and eating the fattest lambs.
(p. 195)

Does this have a ring of political modernity? Is this the application of irony to historical necessity?

"Cesare Borgia is expressing from the most practical point of view the attitude of a true politician and how you achieve and hold power. And at the same time the way I express it makes the audience listening to it realize that I don't approve of such things. Nevertheless, many things happen in history you don't approve of. Huey Long [flamboyant and demagogic governor of Louisiana whose social reforms and radical welfare proposals got mired in the unprecedented executive dictatorship that he perpetrated to ensure control of his home state] said fascism will come to America and call itself democracy. He knew that. Savonarola knew that. And every politician knows that. And so, in my summarizing it this way, I make it obviously a wrong set of attitudes, where if you stretch it out and you play around with the idea, it begins to have some sense and you take away the bite and savageness of it. That is what you might call the blackest of black humor—and quite appropriate to a residential existentialism."

(Abraham Polonsky, Interview with Editor, 15 July 1989)

❖❖❖

"Abe still thought he was in Hollywood working with a feature film budget," writes producer Charles Russell: 'The gaggle of narrow streets were filled by milling throngs of carnival-costumed celebrating people. High above the city Savonarola exhorted the people below in the square to burn the vanities. The people did and we see the precious objects burning before our eyes in a variety of angles.' This was a beautifully described cinematic sequence . . . but there was a slight problem. It was live TV in a small studio on a program with a smaller budget.

"After reading the script and a short discussion, set designer Bob Markell managed to construct a couple of L-shaped alleys with ceiling pieces, and the square became the barren space where the alleys ended. The few extras we could afford would run down one alley and around the end of the flat, change their masks or hats and come running out again in the other direction.

"For the shot of Savonarola high above the city addressing the crowd below in the square, we had the front of a small balcony along with two pilasters, black velour, and a flaming torch. The shot was done using a guillotine, a two mirror arrangement where the camera image of one mirror is reflected in the other, creating a sense of height. It wasn't high above the city but at least it was an effect.

"The studio was above Grand Central Station, and on air day I learned that fires were not allowed in the studio. An off-duty fireman was recruited and paid to squirt the feeble flames with his extinguisher when they were off camera. During rehearsal, Savonarola, played by Joseph Wiseman, is preaching from the balcony. An organ note sounds, as the sentences roll like doom from his mouth: 'Behold the flames for they are like the flames of hell. Think deeply, for in these flames you will burn if you do not mend your ways. Remember, those of you who speak against the liberty of people, that God intends man to be free. Pray, those of you who seek deliverance from the corruption of Italy.' [p. 205]

"This speech went on for three pages. During a pause an extra in the front row, off camera, muttered something derogatory about Joe's acting style. I think the word 'ham' was used. Joe had been having trouble with this speech all day. He lost concentration and overheard the remark. That did it. He stepped off the platform, brushed past that extra and walked out of the studio.

"Sidney [Lumet] called a five-minute break and we went out to the hall where Joe was furiously pacing up and down. I left Sidney to appeal to Joe while I went back to the studio and rearranged the extras. The offender was placed in the rear row behind a tall burly man and told to pray on his knees. Savonarola wanted death and salvation: I settled for the latter.

"This was my Renaissance period." (Russell, "In the Worst of Times," pp. 103-105.)

THE VINDICATION OF SAVONAROLA
by Abraham Polonsky
(signed by Jeremy Daniel)

Air Date:
December 13, 1953

YOU ARE THERE
February 7, 1497

FADE IN:

INT. CBS STUDIOS

CRONKITE
February 7, 1497, Walter Cronkite reporting.

Within the hour a great bonfire will blaze out in the heart of
Italy, and in the flames an era will expire. In the city of
Florence there were strange processions today. Groups of
children clad in white, bearing olive branches and singing
hymns, went from door to door collecting works of art,
dresses, wigs, articles of pleasure and joy, and these are to be
burnt in the great square along with the books and
manuscripts which are considered "vanities." Florence, which
symbolized the beginning of a new age of learning, art and
splendid life, is now ruled by a Dominican monk named
Girolamo Savonarola. His strange and magnetic personality
seems to have hypnotized the city and transformed it, pointing
to a change in the religious and political life of Europe.

Today is the last day of the Season of Carnivals in Florence,
(MORE)

CRONKITE (CON'T)
Italy. Where once the cavaliers rode forth in gay carnival
costumes and the greatest poets made songs and created
processions and floats, spectacles of fireworks and dancing . . .
where once the torches flamed all night as men, women and
children celebrated with a kind of wild forgetfulness . . . now
all is strange, almost still, hushed. The city broods, and
powerful factions move uneasily in the streets. The burning of
the vanities is scheduled at nightfall and with it threats of civil
war against the influence of a new prophet of piety, patriotism,
doom and destruction, the monk . . . Savonarola. We take you
to Florence. All things are as they were then, except . . . YOU
ARE THERE.

EXT. A STREET IN FLORENCE

MARBLE
This is Harry Marble in Florence. We are in one of the dark
twisting streets off the great Piazza della Signoria where the
burning is scheduled.

Three children in white come running by.

MARBLE (CON'T)
There go some of the children who all day long have been
collecting the statues, paintings, books, masks, wigs, mirrors
. . . all things which Savonarola, prior of San Marco, calls
vanities. These have been piled in the square.

A hooded monk and two citizens in plain clothes hurry by carrying
objects.

MARBLE (CON'T)
The monk and those two you see are followers of Savonarola
whom their enemies call the Piagnoni, the wailers, the
mourners.

From a sidestreet, some hoots and refuse thrown at the three who ignore
everything. A quick pan to reveal DOFFO SPINI and a couple of gaily
clad bravos.

MARBLE (CON'T)
The mixture of devotion and resentment is intense and boils over into little riots and quarrels all through the city.

Spini is nailing up a piece of paper on post or door.

MARBLE (CON'T))
The young man with the sword is Rudolfo Spini, leader of the bad companions, or the Compagnacci as they are called here, a dissolute crowd who wish to revive the old carnival spirit and thrust the monk from power.

Move in on Spini who tuns from his paper nailing to face into camera.

MARBLE
You're Rudolfo Spini, aren't you?

SPINI
Doffo Spini.

MARBLE
The leader of the Compagnacci?

SPINI
I have a few friends and we sometimes meet, and meeting sometimes we talk, and talking sometimes we find that we all detest this ruin of Florence which that fanatical monk has brought down on us.

MARBLE
What's that you nailed up there?

SPINI
A poem.

MARBLE
Against Savonarola?

SPINI
It is not for him.

MARBLE
Aren't you afraid of the officials of the republic who support the friar and his policies.

SPINI
(proudly)
We are the republic and not those apothecaries, monks, and
children, weavers and porters. I come from one of the noble
families whom the Medici plundered and exiled. Now we are
back and we do not plan to see our republic fall from the
hands of the Medici tyrants into the arms of the monk and the
mob.

MARBLE
Why do you oppose Savonarola?

SPINI
Because while he speaks against tyranny he wishes to play the
tyrant. He is blinded and inflamed by vice, dominated by
pride. He falsely asserts to have discoursed with Almighty
God himself. He believes that he is to give order and laws to
Florence and through Florence to the world as if he were
Moses himself.

MARBLE
Didn't Savonarola save the city when the Medici wanted to
give it up to the French?

SPINI
The Medici wanted to save the city, but for themselves.
Likewise, the fanatical monk. But Florence belongs to its great
families and its followers. The monk is mad.

Some children come by with vanities.

SPINI (CON'T)
He has piped a tune and misled the children. He burns the
glories of our city. He destroys our carnival time. But I tell
you when night comes not only will the fire burn but those
wailers will mourn for many other things besides.

He runs down the street with his friends as the camera moves in on the
poem.

MARBLE
The habit of putting up rhymes and jokes as part of an attack on a man or a party is common here.
>   (reading poem)
> *O popolo ingrato,*
> *Tu ne vai preso alle grida,*
> *E drieto a una guida*
> *Piena d'ipocrisia.*

This one reads something like this:
> *O ungrateful people,*
> *You are caught up by a cry*
> *and follow a guide*
> *All full of hypocrisy . . . .*

Things will be livelier down here at nightfall. Meanwhile we will take you to the convent of San Marco which is under the rule of Savonarola.

EXT. CONVENT OF SAN MARCO — A LOGGIA AND GARDENS

HOLLENBECK
This is Don Hollenbeck in the convent of San Marco, home of the Dominican order of friars of which Savonarola is prior. The church and cloisters here are among the most beautiful in the world, and from this place of rest and retreat the prior meditates the sermons which he has delivered with such overwhelming and extraordinary results to the city. That is Fra Girolamo Savonarola himself who is pacing beneath the arches, and here is Fra Domenico de Pescia, one of Savonarola's most faithful and devoted followers.

DOMENICO waits with simple humility to be interviewed. From time to time he will turn a glance of great devotion upon Savonarola as he passes behind in his slow and steady pacing and deep introspection.

HOLLENBECK (CON'T)
Fra Domenico, may we interview the prior?

DOMENICO

We may not interrupt him now as he communes with his
spirit. He is going to preach tonight from the Signory when
the vanities are burned.

[HOLLENBECK

On what grounds did Savonarola order the burning of these so
called vanities?

DOMENICO

He did not order them burned. He merely suggested that it
would be more fit to end the carnival with the destruction of
life's vanities than with its celebration.

HOLLENBECK

Aren't you then calling for the destruction of valuable
property?

DOMENICO
(smiling)
Indeed, valuable. A great Florentine merchant offered twenty
thousand crowns for the lot. Our answer will be to burn his
portrait along with the other vanities that mislead men.

HOLLENBECK

Do you think it's wise to use children to collect these objects
and involve them in these struggles? After all, you know
many are opposed to the burning.

DOMENICO

The uncorrupted innocents used to beg the street during
carnival time. No one objected. Now that they ask money for
the poor and collect obscene and disgraceful objects for the
bonfire, it is said that we misuse them. I taught them. I
instructed them. They will lead us to virtue and grace this way
and grow up to be lovers of republican liberty instead of
libertines.]

HOLLENBECK

Would you call the atmosphere in the city a healthy one?

DOMENICO
(surprised)
What do you mean?

HOLLENBECK

It seems to border on hysteria. [Crowds of children stopping grownups, unbraiding them for their sins. Children accusing householders. Children carrying works of art to bonfires. Orators suddenly appearing in the streets proclaiming, as does Savonarola, doom and destruction, attacking the good name and reputation of citizens. Brawls . . . street fights . . . the word traitor on everyone's mouth. And tonight this fire, and the mounting tension and emotional violence.] Can a city live this way and carry on its normal life?

DOMENICO

This is a time of change. The fat easy days are now through and the citizens who lived luxuriously under the tyranny of the Medici must now pay for their indifference to liberty. Liberty returns and it comes with God's word, and it comes with repentance and suffering. But if we are righteous then these times will pass.

HOLLENBECK

Thank you, Fra Domenico. May we speak to the prior?

Savonarola is still pacing and Domenico shakes his head.

DOMENICO

Not now. Later perhaps.

HOLLENBECK

Thank you.

DOMENICO
(making sign of the cross)

God be with you.

HOLLENBECK

We take you to the city of Rome now and another point of view on the situation of Florence.

INT. THE BORGIA PALACE — ROME

BURDETT

This is Winston Burdett in the palace of the Cardinal of
Valencia, Cesare Borgia.

A huntsman with a falcon on his wrist stands in the background as
BORGIA walks into the shot. He is beautifully dressed in a hunting
costume. He carries a little whip with which he sometimes strikes his
hand or boot to make a point. He is very young, very handsome, and
very sure of himself.

BURDETT (CON'T)

Because of his connections with the Holy See and the armies of
the papacy, Cesare Borgia along with his brother will play a
crucial role in the present struggles in Italy. We have asked
him to make some comments on the Florentine situation and
His Eminence has agreed. [Your Eminence, do you believe
that the situation in Italy would be more stable if the Medici
were still in power in Florence?

BORGIA

Were they not in power when Italy began to collapse into ruin
and war?

BURDETT

But they offered a rallying point for the center of the peninsula.
They made a stable center for political power where there is
now a vacuum.

BORGIA

True enough. But the son of Lorenzo was and is a weakling,
and the family no longer holds out any hope of strength and
energy.]

BURDETT

What do you think of the present government of Florence?

BORGIA

Savonarola is a fanatic and a fool and he has given power to
the lowest elements in the city.

BURDETT

Do you think he will be able to establish a stable republican government?

BORGIA

A republic is the worst form of government. By making all equal, it reduces all to nothing. What the citizens share in common is not power but servitude and weakness.

BURDETT

It was these very people who saved their city from the French when the Medici deserted them.

BORGIA

History contains many axioms and principles, one of which asserts that what war unites, peace separates. Moreover, the Florentines are like wild, ferocious animals always fed behind bars. Such a people can only with great difficulty be trained to live in true freedom.

BURDETT

Is there no solution to the problem?

BORGIA

The times will work out their own solutions.

BURDETT

And what of the men of these times?

BORGIA

Men? Let us say *a* man. It must be clearly seen that in Italy, by reason of her corruption, there is little or nothing to hope, save by the daring and violence of some great man, who may be willing and able to strive for her improvement.

BURDETT
(after a pause)
Is there such a man?

BORGIA

Perhaps.

BURDETT

How would he, for example, solve the situation in Florence?

BORGIA
(softly)
I have given it some thought. There are three methods of
bringing an end to the disunity within a city or state. Firstly,
by murdering the party leaders.

BURDETT
Did you say murdering the party leaders?

BORGIA
I did. Secondly, by removing them from power. Thirdly, by
winning them to peace through compromise and agreement.
The last is most dangerous. The first most secure. Force,
courage, violence are the weapons by which quiet is imposed
on states. They do not always suffice, for we cannot kill
everyone. Therefore, fraud and stratagem are necessary. If the
citizens are used to the words of liberty, then we embrace the
word; if they despise war, we oppose war; if they like ease and
contentment, we promise them both; if they cherish
independence, we extol it. By such means we gain power, and
although they will have lost liberty, be at war, have neither
ease nor contentment, and be slaves, the citizens will think
they have all. For human nature is unchangeable. It is foolish,
and only good rulers can, like good shepherds, protect the
flock while gathering the wool and eating the fattest lambs.
(pause)
Have you any further questions?

BURDETT
No, Your Eminence.
(Borgia turns to his falcon)
We return you to Florence and Don Hollenbeck.

INT. CONVENT OF SAN MARCO — DUSK

HOLLENBECK
This is Don Hollenbeck and we are back again at the convent
of San Marco. Savonarola is preparing to go into the heart of
the city as the time for burning the vanities approaches.
However, we have been promised a short interview.

First one monk and then another passes. Then Domenico.

[HOLLENBECK (CON'T)
In Rome we interviewed Cesare Borgia, considered by many as
perhaps the supreme representative of one of the most evil
families in Italy. Savonarola is considered, on the other hand,
to be a man of utter selflessness and piety, a holy man.]

He appears, coming to camera, where he pauses.

HOLLENBECK (CON'T)
(quickly)
Here he comes now. Fra Girolamo, a number of accusations
have been made against you. Would you care to answer them?

SAVONAROLA
My life answers them.

HOLLENBECK
Some very honest men question your right to burn works of
art, for example, that you just happen not to like. These men
say that you are hostile to learning, to art, and would reduce
all men to simple obedient creatures.

SAVONAROLA
[(with a sweet smile)
I would raise men to simple faith. I would make them
obedient to God. I would return them to freedom.]
(quietly, factually)
I am not hostile to art. When the great library of codices and
miniatures, the books and manuscripts collected by the Medici
were offered up for sale to be dispersed through the world, we
monks at San Marco sold our lands, we beggared ourselves
and paid the money. We brought the library here, and here in
all Italy is the one place where anyone can come and read and
study without bending a knee to a prince or merchant or
priest. Is this to be hostile to art?

HOLLENBECK
Well, no, Father, but these books are books of the past, and it is
the artists of the present you condemn.

SAVONAROLA
(more sharply)
I do not condemn artists but only those knaves who prostitute
their art and skill. All the world knows that the most eminent
artists and poets of our city are my friends, and, in the sense
that I follow God, my followers. Does not Fra Bartolomeo love
me as I love his paintings? And della Robbia, whose
sculptures the world acclaims, acclaim my teachings? I have
led the two of them into the monastic order. And Lorenzo Di
Credi, Cronaca, Botticelli. And even the young Michelangelo
Buonarotti came from the Medici palace to hear my sermons
when I unbraided his master.

HOLLENBECK
Yes, I know, Father, but those great artists are your *followers*.
What of the others who are not?

SAVONAROLA
I know whom you mean, those men who are bought and sold
in the market place like sheep and goats. They work for
wicked princes whose courts and palaces are the refuge of all
the beasts and monsters of the earth. These wretches flock to
their halls because it is there that they find ways and means to
satisfy their evil passions and lusts. These are the false
councilors who continuously devise new taxes and burdens to
drain the blood of the people. These are the flattering
philosophers and poets who by force of a thousand lies praise
the destroyers and with a million arguments justify, gild, and
make palatable the evil that is corrupting the citizens. Such
artists, I must condemn.

HOLLENBECK
There are citizens who say that you meddle in the affairs of the
state.

SAVONAROLA
(passionately)
Because I have suggested good laws for the well being of the
people and its liberty? All *that* has been to the glory of God . . .
and those men would stone me for my good work! They go
about crying: the Friar would have money, the Friar would
play the tyrant, the Friar would have a cardinal's hat.
(MORE)

SAVONAROLA (CON'T)
And I tell you that had I desired such things, I should not be
wearing a tattered robe at this hour.

He points to his robe which is worn and drab and torn in one place,
frayed. And then with another gesture to the wall where a crucified
Jesus hangs in its niche. The cry of prophecy leaps in his voice.

SAVONAROLA (CON'T)
I would be glorified only in Thee, my God! Neither mitres nor
cardinals' hats would I have, but only the gift that thou has
conferred on thy saints—death! A crimson hat, a hat reddened
with blood such as the martyr's wear . . . that is my desire.

He crosses himself as the other monks join him and all leave.

HOLLENBECK
Night is here. As Savonarola leaves for the great bonfire of the
vanities, we will go down into the streets and try to bring you
the feeling of the moment, the strange atmosphere of this city.
Come in, Harry Marble.

EXT. THE STREET

Night has fallen. Blazes of light from a window on high, or a door.
Perhaps a torch in the wall. Some men and women in masks and
costumes run through the streets. Far off the gigantic murmur of the
crowd, music off, etc. A sense of a great square nearby where people are
moving through the streets. The first effect on the cut as the reporter's
voice comes in should be a woman flinging a shower of confetti.

MARBLE
Harry Marble here. The last night of the carnival, and the
strangest in all Florentine history. Those in the costumes and
masks you can be sure oppose Savonarola, but to what faction
they belong is hard to tell.

Two children in white bearing vanities pass.

MARBLE (CON'T)
There go two children who have been collecting the vanities,
begging from door to door for objects which the Piagnoni say
represent the evil of life . . . in this case a gilded looking glass, a
statue of cupid. In their enthusiasm some people are burning
what should be preserved, it seems. What's going on in your
bailiwick, Ned Calmer?

EXT. ANOTHER PART OF THE STREET

CALMER
This is Ned Calmer. We're having a little fracas, it seems. A
couple of celebrants have cornered one of the followers of
Savonarola . . . .

We see a man, dressed in plain and sober clothes, pinned in a cranny of
the street. In front of him some masked men and women are laughing.
When he tries to break out, they push him back. They pull off his hat.
They throw confetti in his face. They offer him a drink.

CALMER (CON'T)
The feeling is very intense, explosive, I'd say . . . and even the
goodnatured fooling suddenly gets mean.

Comes closer with camera. Suddenly the man darts through his
tormentors and away. They throw confetti at him.

CALMER (CON'T)
(to masked man)
Messer . . . aren't you going to celebrate the burning of the
vanities?

MAN
I am . . . for I am Vanity and I celebrate myself.

He laughs as do his companions. A woman kisses him, raising her mask
to do so. The man's voice is very cultivated.

CALMER
I suppose then you aren't a follower of Savonarola?

MAN

I, a groaner, a wailer, a howler, one of the Piagnoni. No, I'm a
laugher, a dancer . . .

(he kicks up his heels)

. . . and I celebrate the last night of the carnival in memory of
the days when on these nights all was laughter and gaiety in
the streets . . . and even the old were young, and every girl was
love and every boy a cupid.

CALMER

To what faction do you belong?

MAN

I belong to life. Death and the fanatical monk are the factions.

The woman takes his arm, and they start to run down the street. Man
turns and shouts back as he disappears.

MAN (CON'T)

Life and the Medici will return.

CALMER

He is one of the Bigi, as they call them in Florence, those who
wish to restore the Medici to power. These people are hated
even more intensely than Savonarola by followers of Doffo
Spini.

Some children in white come in bearing their offerings. A woman
accompanies them. She is simply dressed, handsome, grave.

CALMER (CON'T)

More gifts for the fire. There are three main factions: the party
of the Medici, the nobles who hate the Medici who exiled
them, and the followers of the monk. Signora . . .

(he stops the woman)

I presume you are one of the Piagnoni?

WOMAN

(smiling)

So they call us . . . but it seems we sing more often than we
groan; only to sinners the song to God seems like a groan.

CALMER

May I ask your name?

WOMAN

I am of the family of the Strozzi.

CALMER

(a little surprised and
impressed)

Then yours is a noble family . . . . But other people of your
wealth and position are determined enemies of the monk . . .

WOMAN

Because they fear God and liberty. I am proud to be a Strozzi,
but prouder to have sold my jewels and devoted myself to the
poor and the sick and the needy, for I would live free on earth
and in eternal grace in paradise. God praise and keep Fra
Girolamo.

CALMER

Thank you, Signora.

The woman goes off. Some revelers appear.

CALMER (CON'T)

Anything special going on near the big square? Are you there,
Harry Marble?

EXT. ANOTHER PART OF THE STREET

Quite dark, grotesque shadows here. Some men rush by in costumes. A
woman laughs out from the dark.

MARBLE

This is Harry Marble. I've just come down from the tower of
the Signory, one of the highest points in the city next to the
Duomo itself. The immense square below was filled with a
pyramid of vanities, some sixty feet high and about two
hundred and forty feet in circumference. It seems as if the
entire city was looted of every portable object from statues and
paintings to fancy books, pornography, wigs, dresses. Each
person seems to have chosen one single object that would
represent his vanity in life and given it to the fire. When the
signal is given, the fire will be lighted by four guardians . . . the
bells will toll . . . .

As he rapidly speaks a file of children come round the bend, each bearing an object. Some are carrying masks to be burnt, one a painting of a nude, some gambling toys, etc. They approach all alone through the dark street.

> MARBLE (CON'T)
> And here are more offerings to the fire that is supposed to cleanse Florence of its sins.

Suddenly from the dark doorways some men in costumes and masks spring out. One is dressed like death and carries a sword in his hand. He shouts. The children huddle together. The men seize the objects from them and the children flee screaming.

> MARBLE (CON'T)
> This is the first violence I've seen directed at children.

The man dressed as death takes off his mask. It is Doffo Spini. The others are laughing.

> MARBLE (CON'T)
> Of course, Spini, leader of the wild Compagnacci . . . .

Now followed by the children a few citizens run in. They shout and make for the maskers. They brawl in the darkness. Suddenly a scream. The maskers flee and a citizen lies on the ground. Someone kneels over him. The children are huddled against the black wall like white moths.

> MAN
> Call the guard. This man is dead.

The survivors run off calling. The camera moves in on the dead man.

> MARBLE
> There have been stabbings, beatings, brawls everywhere tonight, rising in violence as night came on. Yet, nevertheless, the never-ending stream of people moves to the square, and soon Savonarola will preach. Is there any sign of him yet, Ned Calmer?

EXT. THE FIRST STREET

It is littered with confetti and maskers in motion. Far off a *Te Deum* can be heard, and still further the murmur of the crowd like the sea.

CALMER
(excited)
I can begin to hear the chanting now. I can hear the voices.
Savonarola will soon be here.

A bunch of maskers come running toward camera and out. Suddenly
the street is empty. The singing grows nearer. The roar of the crowd
mounts. A file of children . . . then a monk.

CALMER (CON'T)
Here he comes!

Proceeded by monks, etc., Savonarola. The procession heads for the
camera. Great individual faces . . . ecstatic, marvelous, exalted. They
pass one after the other, the emotion made physical by the great swelling
of the voices singing. As the last one passes . . . .

CALMER (CON'T)
He's just passed here. Come in, Harry Marble.

EXT. THE OTHER SECTION OF THE STREET

The man is propped against the wall. A soldier and a citizen stand with
him. The voices and singing around the bend.

MARBLE
The man was mortally wounded, but he is still alive.

The two with him hear the procession nearby. They run to the corner
and look. Their backs are to us. The camera moves in.

MARBLE (CON'T)
Fra Girolamo Savonarola is passing down the next street,
beyond the bend.

A great roar of sound goes up, drowns out everything. it should roar on
as high as possible from now on, without halt . . . except to take a short
interview.

MAN
(in pain)
Where is he?

MARBLE

They are going by in the next street.

MAN

Fra Girolamo . . . .
(in a whisper)
O God, I am dying . . . .

MARBLE

Who are you?

MAN

A weaver and a dyer . . . a man . . . a man dying.

The singing off, the voices crying out, the roar like the sea. The man raises himself and with a last energy, he makes the sign of a cross in the air. He cries out.

MAN (CON'T)

Comes Christ the Tiger!

As the roar goes on, deafening now, the camera moves in on the man's face.

MARBLE

We'll wait here until the guard returns. You better come in, Ned Calmer.

EXT. THE FIRST STREET

People pressed into the bend as if looking on the square.

CALMER
(as a thunderous roar,
contiguous now, endless,
deafening sounds)
Savonarola has appeared before the crowd . . . . The monk who has by the magic of his oratory, the fervor of his faith, his passion and power, transformed the greatest city of Italy, is about to speak.

THE WINDOW

In the window, Savonarola holds out his hands, and the crowd noise
ceases . . . utter silence.

> SAVONAROLA
> (with great solemn power)
> Let the guardians light the fire.

The great bell of the signory starts to toll. It should toll very slowly.

THE STREET

The fire is lighted. The flames rise. The roar of the crowd sounding
again. The singing. The tolling of the bell. Close-ups on faces as the fire
springs alive on each. Λ rhythm. The last one: Spini, as he removes his
mask. Close-up on Savonarola as the fire flames in his eyes. it burns
brighter and brighter and then the camera pulls back as he slowly raises
his arms. Voices down. We hear the flames . . . the crackle. The bell tolls
very slowly.

> SAVONAROLA
> *Ecce ego adducam aquas super terram!*

Low rumble of noise from the crowd. The people fall to their knees by
the light of the flame.

THE WINDOW

Savonarola preaches. He is not a shouter, a screamer. The sentences roll
like doom from his mouth . . . an organ note.

> SAVONAROLA
> Behold the flames for they are like the flames of hell. Think
> deeply, for in these flames you will burn if you do not mend
> your ways. Remember, those of you who speak against the
> liberty of the people, that God intends man to be free. Pray,
> those of you who seek deliverance from the corruption of Italy.
> (pause)
> What do the corrupt most fear? I recall when this fair city of
> Florence was ruled by Lorenzo the Magnificent, and the hour
> came when he heard death hovering above his head.
> (MORE)

He called his priests; but, although they confessed him in the
end, he wished to see me. I was the enemy of his rule and yet
he wished to see me. So I came there, and pale and shaken, he
lay at death's door, and there was no peace in him for his
crimes burnt before his eyes as these flames shriek before ours.
He wished to be absolved from his sins. Then I said to him,
three things are needed.

> (extending his right hand and
> holding one finger out)

Firstly, a great and living faith in God's mercy. He replied, I
have the fullest faith in it. It was easy to say. Secondly, I said,
you must restore all the wealth you have robbed from the
people of Florence.

> (pause)

At this, the Magnificent was struck with surprise and grief, but
when I remained unbending, he nodded his head. He cowered
in his bed with fear, and in the room the wings of the angel of
death obscured the sun. Lastly, I said, you must restore liberty
to the people of Florence. And what did he do, my children?
A cold look came upon his face and he turned to the wall and
died miserably like a dog before he could restore liberty to us
. . . for the greatest wealth of the powerful is not gold but the
slavery of the people of Florence.

> (pause)

So we seized our liberty, but we will not keep it if we yield to
the corruption of the times. Italy, mend your ways or a
scourge is at hand. I announce to you, Italy and Rome, that the
Lord will come forth out of His place. I tell you, God will
draw forth the sword from the sheath. He will send the
foreign nations and such bloodshed shall there be, so many
deaths, such cruelty, that you shalt say: Yea, the Lord is come.
I prophesy that He will come down and tread upon the high
places of the earth. I say to you, Italy and Rome, that God will
tread upon you. His feet shall be the horses, the armies of
foreign nations, and all the great men who corrupt and
mislead shall be trampled down. I warn you. God will not
suffer the iniquities of our people. The blood cries up to Christ
to come and chastise all of you.

Intercut the above, etc. Bring up bell and the crowd noise at end.

INT. CBS STUDIOS

CRONKITE

And as Savonarola prophesied, so it happened. Italian freedom perished in tyranny, in flames, in blood, as the monk himself did a few years later, burning in that very square where the vanities were consumed. The powerful nobles, having seized the republic, destroyed Savonarola and vindicated his life with martyrdom. But the image of the passionate friar remained alive in the minds of the great artists and the ordinary man who amidst plenty and the soft luxury of decay recalled the hard days when life was dangerous but every man was free.

The figure of Savonarola has been a puzzling one for historians. Did he look backward toward the intense spirituality of the medieval era, or did he look forward to the age of reform, an age which unloosed personal freedom and political democracy in Europe and thus changed the face of the entire world?

What kind of a day was it? A day like all days, filled with those events that alter and illuminate our time . . . and YOU WERE THERE.

FADE OUT.

MALLORY'S TRAGEDY ON MT. EVEREST

Mount Everest, a peak on the crest of the Himalayan range in Asia, is the highest mountain on earth (29,028 feet; 8,848 metres). Because of its commanding size and height, Everest was known in the Tibetan language as Chomolungma, "Goddess Mother of the World." Its identity as the highest point on the earth's surface was not recognized, however, until 1852 when the governmental Survey of India established that fact. In 1865 the mountain—previously referred to as Peak XV—was renamed for a British official, Sir George Everest, who was surveyor general of India from 1823 to 1843.

Attempts to climb Everest began with the opening of the Tibetan route in 1920. Seven successive attempts on the Northeast Ridge (1921-1938), including the Mallory expedition (1924), as well as three missions up the Southeast Ridge (1951-1952), failed because of the combined difficulties caused by cold arid air, high winds, difficult terrain, and high altitude.

Everest was finally surmounted in 1953, as the result of efforts by an expedition sponsored by the Royal Geographical Society and the Joint Himalayan Committee of the Alpine Club. Open- and closed-circuit oxygen systems, especially insulated boots and clothing, and portable radio equipment were used by the climbers. On 29 May 1953 Edmund Hillary, a beekeeper from New Zealand, and Tenzing Norgay of Nepal ascended the Southeast Ridge, past South Peak, to the summit. Since then, four expeditions sponsored by different nations—Swiss (1956), American (1963), Indian (1965), and Japanese (1970)—have scaled the peak. The Japanese party was the first to include a woman.

It has been suggested that the theme of existential struggle is a coherent thread linking all of Polonsky's major works ("Introduction, pp. 28-30). *A Season of Fear*, his novel of rich autobiographical undertones, asserts that an exile must "passionately struggle to return home, to overturn the government which has banished him or pursued him—a man must love his native land and refuse to give it up." Even losing fights must be fought. "Somebody has to be in the losing fight or else nothing would ever happen." (Polonsky, *A Season of Fear*, pp. 52, 158.)

This volume presents poetic and passionate examples ("The Fate of Nathan Hale," "The Torment of Beethoven," "The Tragedy of John

Milton") of human beings attempting to achieve some sort of "separate peace" or accommodation with their private or public crises—attempts to impose a meaningful order on a chaotic environment through their art, physical endurance, or an integrity of the spirit. The doomed Mallory expedition offers Polonsky one more historical opportunity to engage the notion of the nobility of struggle.

Mallory, who will perish in the pursuit of his goal, says: "Whatever the past announces as the limit of human ability, effort, power, and growth, is wrong. That is the one absolute and universal rule: the possibilities of the human are infinite." (p. 223) "There is for every man his own Everest which he must surmount, for if he does not, if he turns back, then he has lost the reason for life. Neither pain nor death nor the moment of victory is decisive. It is the act of attempt, the assault on the unknown, and every man or woman who has struggled or perished for an ideal knows this." (p. 225) More than physical endurance is necessary. Polonsky calls this "an affair of the heart, the will, the soul—an experiment in life—a proof of man's unconquerable will, the lesson that we have learned from the moment that we, like this very mountain, rose from the primeval sea." (p. 233)

❖❖❖

"Abe suggested that a show should be done on Mallory, the English mountain climber and his effort on that final day of the expedition to reach the summit of Mt. Everest," writes producer Charles Russell. "His suggestion was greeted with some derisive comments by his friends around the table, but as usual Abe was able to rise above them. Any negative response to any of his ideas was simply a springboard for his invention. He launched into a very articulate story presentation outlining the theme of the show. There was a boldness to the idea that was appealing and exciting as well as demanding.

"In Bill Dozier's office the next day I outlined the idea for a show on Mallory, but Bill was not familiar with Mallory and less familiar with the unconquered summit of Everest. He said, 'It sounds pretty dull, let's forget it.'

"Some time after this, my secretary handed me a copy of *The New York Times*. The front page was made up of photographs and columns describing that moment of triumph as Hillary and Tenzing reached the summit of Mt. Everest. I couldn't resist and I tore off the front page, enclosed it in an inter-office envelope addressed to Bill Dozier with a note, 'Dear Bill, this is Mt. Everest.'

"The next day Dozier called and 'suggested' that I accompany him to lunch with the advertising agency executives representing the sponsors of *You Are There*. After the usual greetings, trivia, and martinis, we sat down to lunch. The executive at the head of the table enthusiastically said, 'Why don't we do a show about the climbing of Mt. Everest. It's topical.'

"I looked at Dozier without any reaction. I was waiting for him and he was waiting for me. Finally he said, 'Strangely enough, Charles and I were discussing a story along those lines. It's about an English mountain climber named Mallory and his attempt to climb Mt. Everest. What year was that again, Charles?' I told them it was 1924 and filled in some of the details. They thought it was a tremendous idea and approved it immediately.

"The problem now was how to do it on live TV.

"I was able to get a nine foot piece of film made by the British expedition of Mallory and Irvine climbing a steep glacier. The film was rocked and rolled in the lab in order to stretch the moment; dupes were made of the print so the shot could be used several times. There was some expedition footage of the guides with the supplies approaching Camp 3 on the Rongbuk Glacier. This was to be used for a short cut to establish the terrain. Some footage was located of long pans up and down the snowy, windswept icy glaciers: to be used as transitional devices to move from camp to camp and to dramatically emphasize how unclimbable the mountain is. Then I managed to get two frames of film from different elevations and angles of the mountain. Blow-ups and transfers were made for stereopticon slides that were used for backgrounds in two interview scenes.

"For these interview scenes, set designer Bob Markell had some two and four foot platforms arranged to mask the bottom of the screen, and that's what they looked like—instead of slopes of snow and ice with irregular form. I suggested that to break up the sharp lines and give them some definition, we wad up some wet balls of newspaper and throw them at the platform.

"Bob said, 'I've got a great idea. I'll go up on the grid and throw them down so they'll splatter and look irregular.' He did and I discovered later he was afraid of heights. (For this personal conquest of Everest he won the Emmy award for set design.)

"These platforms—as well as the green linoleum studio floors— were painted white. If we are on Mt. Everest, we should have an icy glare not a green glow. The word 'glare' brought a strong reaction from the video man and the lighting director. In the early 1950s on live TV, white was a difficult color to control in picture quality. The main source of lighting in live TV in those days was provided by scoops and pans of six fluorescent tubes rigged high and tilted down into the set. We had the pans moved back and lowered and killed a few tubes in each.

During the interview scenes, the lights were seen reflected in the dark goggles of the climbers when facing the camera. I had some black tape put over each lens, leaving a tiny slit in the middle so the actor could read the teleprompter during the interview. Depending on the eyesight of the actors, while trying to locate the teleprompter, they appeared to be looking around the mountain for any sight of Mallory.

"In the scene between Mallory [played in this episode by Leslie Nielsen] and Irvine [played by Francis Bethencourt] in their tent before the assault on the summit, we could use only one small 'noiseless' fan for the sense of wind and two stagehands outside tugging at the tent to try to get some feeling of the weather outside. And for the last two minutes, over the film of Mallory and Irvine climbing, intercut with the long pans of the icy glacier and the plumes of snow from the peak, we used every effects record available of screaming, howling winds at a high level." (Russell, "In the Worst of Times," pp. 107-112.)

MALLORY'S TRAGEDY ON MT. EVEREST
by Abraham Polonsky
(signed by Jeremy Daniel)

Air Date:
January 3, 1954

YOU ARE THERE
June 8, 1924

FADE IN:

INT. CBS STUDIOS

                    CRONKITE
June 8, 1924, Walter Cronkite reporting. At this moment an
assault team of two climbers stands ready to attempt to scale
the top of Mount Everest, the tallest mountain in the world. It
is five and one half miles high and is known to geographers as
the third pole of the Earth. Whether human beings can
actively survive at that elevation is questionable. Many have
already died in the attempt. Ice, snow, wind are the enemies
which defend the white fortress against adventurers. It is the
very top of our world and the question has been raised, what
use is there in reaching it? We shall take you to the high
Himalayas to find the answer.

On March 25th, the British Everest Expedition left Darjeeling
in India and plunged into the mystery of Tibet. A month and
nine days later a base camp was established near the Rongbuk
monastery. Two thousand miles of mountains here form the
backbone of the earth. It is here in Asia that the human race
originated, and here that civilization began,

                                              (MORE)

CRONKITE (CON'T)
and here finally that men will try to conquer an extravagant
dream: to set foot on the highest place on earth. A chain of six
camps have been placed after painful and heroic effort along
the great Rongbuk glacier and the northern ridge of the
mountain. We take you to Camp 3 on the Rongbuk Glacier in
Tibet, Asia. All things are as they were then except . . . YOU
ARE THERE.

EXT. CAMP 3

MARBLE
This is Harry Marble.
    (a long shot of Everest)
You are looking up at Mount Everest from Camp 3 of the
British Everest Expedition on the Rongbuk glacier. The tallest
mountain in North America is Mount McKinley. Everest is
nearly two miles higher. The tallest mountain in Europe is
Mount Blanc. Everest is nearly three miles higher. Here in the
Himalayas we now stand twenty-one thousand feet above sea
level, higher than McKinley, higher than Mount Blanc, and the
snowy summit you see before you is still eight thousand feet
above us, defended by walls of ice, slopes of snow, abysses of
space, storm and wind.

Into live shot of Camp 3 exterior. A few sherpas looking up. NOEL
peering up through binoculars, before Norton's tent. HINGSTON stands
looking up also.

MARBLE (CON'T)
Since dawn all eyes have been pointed up to the tiny tent just
under the northeast shoulder of Everest. This tent is placed at
26,800 feet, and in it are two men, George Mallory and Andrew
Irvine. It is their job to reach the summit. We are going to ask
Captain John Noel, the expedition photographer, to sketch out
the plan of assault for us. Captain Noel is one of the chief
organizers of this expedition and himself explored Tibet in
1913, disguised as a native. Captain Noel . . .
    (the man with the binoculars
    turns into the camera)
Just how will this particular attempt to climb Everest be made?

NOEL

Under perfect conditions, the plan is like the others, except that
we all now know this is our last chance before the mountain
becomes unclimbable. We are in Camp 3 of the ladder of
camps up the side of Everest. Above us on the ice cliff is Camp
4. Then Camp 5 on the North Ridge at 25,200 feet. Above that
Camp 6 from which Mallory and Irvine must have already
begun their dash to the top.

(he smiles a little)

By dash, of course, I mean a slow and painful step by step
progression across steep and icy rocks and snow, hanging
above disaster while your heart labors like mad and your
breath chokes you and your legs and hands are like lead, and
nothing keeps you going but the dream of taking Everest by
storm.

(he looks about)

Naturally the camps above us are more primitive than this one
. . . if you wish to call this luxury.

He looks up again.

MARBLE

What will the other parties on the mountain do?

[NOEL

They must support the final climbers closely and be ready to
go to their aid at once, if they are late or missing. So long as a
single man, native or European, is alive on that mountain, we
must be ready to rescue them no matter what the danger.
Specifically, Odell who is at Camp 5 will descend this evening
and leave the tents vacant for Mallory and Irvine, but he will
not go down until the last moment in case we receive any
distress signal from the final climbers. You see, no one should
spend more time than absolutely essential in Camp 6.

MARBLE

Because of the altitude?

NOEL

That and the temperature which hardly ever goes above zero
and most often is below. What's worse, the small tent of

(MORE)

NOEL (CON'T)
Camp 6 is perched over a precipice, exposed to wind and storm. There is no spot on the whole mountain level enough to place a sleeping bag at full length in any direction.]

MARBLE
Will Mallory and Irvine use oxygen equipment?

NOEL
Yes. The experience of Norton and Sommerval shows that men lose strength so quickly at that altitude as to make an attempt on the summit without oxygen utterly precarious.

Hingston has just helped NORTON whose eyes are bandaged to sit down on supply case in front of one of the tents. Noel and the camera look at him.

NOEL (CON'T)
There is Captain Norton now.

Noel points his glasses at the mountain again.

MARBLE
Captain Noel, why do you think Everest is worth climbing?

NOEL
The people of India call the Himalayas the roof of the world. Well, the world is my home and I'm curious to know what's in the attic.

He looks up again.

MARBLE
Thank you, Captain Noel.

As Noel turns again to search the mountains with his glasses. Long shot: a party in single file making its way up the glacier.

MARBLE (CON'T)
We are going to take you to Camp 5. You see before you a relief party heading up the glacier for the ice cliff. They are bringing further supplies of food and oxygen in case they are needed.

Pan shot going up mountainside.

MARBLE
Are you ready, Ed Morgan? Ed Morgan . . . at Camp 5?

EXT. CAMP 5

Two tents in waste of snow and mountain. Film: a downward pan across mountains to tent.

MORGAN
This is Edward P. Morgan at Camp 5 of the Everest expedition.
We are over 25,000 feet above sea level and you can feel it in
each breath you take.
                    (a distant moan of the wind
                    which sighs in and out from
                    time to time)
That whine you hear is the wind higher up among the icy cliffs
and cornices.
                    (a distant rumble)
And that is an avalanche falling. Somewhere always an
avalanche is falling, peeling off from these precipices and
plunging ten thousand feet to the glacier on the north or
fourteen thousand feet to the glacier on the south. The land
mass of this massif of mountain giants is so immense that
water is affected by it, drawn by the very gravitation of the
mountain. The mountain makes its own weather. No bird
flies here. Nothing. A waste of snow hanging over the land of
men so far below.

On move, cut to: Live. The two tents. A man is sticking his head out.

MORGAN (CON'T)
That is N. E. Odell who was called back from Persia to take
part in the expedition as a scientist. He is an explorer and a
geologist.

As camera moves in, ODELL is getting out of his tent. He is adjusting
his gear and making a load for himself which he will carry above. But
first he rakes the hills with binoculars.

MORGAN (CON'T)
Any sign of Mallory and Irvine, Mr. Odell?

                    ODELL
Nothing.
                (turns to camera)
But we are pretty effectively blocked off from seeing them
from here. We're too high up. The crags are in our way.

He bends down and straps up his load.

                    MORGAN
It looks like a pretty clear and calm day.

                    ODELL
Clear, calm . . . and ominous. The mountain is always
dangerous and can kick up a gale and blizzard in ten minutes.
                (the wind sighing off)
There was snow yesterday.

                    MORGAN
It doesn't seem to have been very heavy.

                    ODELL
The sun evaporates it.

                    MORGAN
Are you alone here?

                    ODELL
Yes.

                    MORGAN
I thought all parties were to consist of at least two men?

                    ODELL
Well, the mountain has been pretty savage with us, and we
don't have enough climbers who are fit. I had to send my
sherpa down because he was mountain sick.
                (he looks up to the heights)
There may be sun above the clouds.

                    MORGAN
You think Mallory and Irvine are on their way up?

ODELL

Oh, yes You see, they must get up to the top before late afternoon or else they'll never get down before nightfall. By the way, Mallory sent a note down last night with his porters.

He finds it.

MORGAN

Would you read it, please?

ODELL

Certainly.
            (reading)
Dear Odell,—We're awfully sorry to have left things in such a mess-our Unna cooker rolled down the slope at the last moment—
            (looks up)
That's quite a roll from there . . . .
            (reading again)
Be sure of getting back to 4 tomorrow . . .
            (looking up)
That's today, of course . . . .
            (reading)
. . . in time to evacuate before dark, as I hope to.
            (explaining)
They intend to reach the top today and then come down and sleep here or even below if there's time enough.
            (reading)
In the tent I must have left a compass—for the Lord's sake, rescue it since we are without. To here on ninety atmospheres. . .
            (looking up)
That refers to the amount of oxygen they have left . . .
            (reading)
. . . for the two days . . . so we'll probably go on two cylinders, but it's a load for climbing. Perfect weather for the job. Yours ever, Mallory.
            (looking up)
I don't think much of oxygen myself.
            (produces compass)
And here's his compass.

MORGAN

What are your plans, sir?

ODELL

I propose to scramble about a bit and do a little geologizing on my way up to Camp 6. There I'll leave the compass and some extra food in case they do have to stay there overnight. Then I'll toddle down, pass this perch by and go down to 4 on the North Col.

MORGAN

Have you made any interesting scientific discoveries so far?

ODELL

Hardly. Most of the time we spend trying to keep warm. But I've knocked out a few fossils up here.
(he waves his hand)
So you see these mountain giants were once the bottom of a primeval sea before the tormented earth pushed them up so high.
(looking around)
Incredible, isn't it?

MORGAN

It is. And is that why you were eager to climb Everest?

ODELL

Heavens, no. No scientist in his right mind would bother. In fact, I'd rather hoped to get a chance at the summit myself, but Mallory picked Irvine as his partner.

MORGAN

Is Irvine a very experienced climber?

ODELL

Not in these regions. But I was with him last year on a sledging expedition to Spitzenberg. He is very good, handy with the oxygen apparatus. Very strong. Very young. Only twenty two and I know desperately anxious to reach the top.

MORGAN

And Mallory?

ODELL

I suppose you could say he has a genius for it as other men
have for poetry or science. He's the very best. And he knows
as we all do that this is the last chance, the very last this year to
attempt the summit pyramid. Bad weather will break at any
moment and only the Grand Lama of Tibet himself knows
when foreigners will get another chance to come back to
Everest.

Odell is loaded up and ready to leave.

MORGAN

How long will it take you to reach Camp 6?

ODELL

Three or four hours. Distance here is not feet but time.

MORGAN

Sir, can you tell us why you want to climb Mount Everest?

ODELL

If you can't feel the magic of these mountains, explanation is
useless.
                    (pause as the wind whines in
                    and goes)
Let us say that Everest is the last great undiscovered adventure
in the exploration of the earth.
                    (he points aloft)
Let us say, for example, that nature lies crouching with her last
secret in that citadel above us, and we cannot rest at ease until
we have breached the ultimate mystery.
                    (he starts)
Or just say I like climbing mountains.

As he starts off into the waste, cut to: Film.

MORGAN

Fifteen hundred feet above us is Camp 6, as high as we can go.
The ridge mounts rapidly here until it meets the great
northeast shoulder. The air is still clear, the wind moderate,
                                                    (MORE)

but freshening. The snow is dry and unconsolidated and here
and there plumes up into space. There is no doubt that
conditions are excellent for success. We take you to
Camp 6.

CAMP 6

Cut to: Film.

CALMER
This is Ned Calmer up at Camp 6.

Film: a downward pan to the camp. Live: the tent. Mallory stands in
front, looking up at the mountain. Around him is scattered extra oxygen
apparatus, etc., dismantled . . . and the two rucksacks to be carried. The
ice axes are plunged into the snow.

CALMER (CON'T)
We've got bad news here. The assault party which should
have left long ago has been unable to start yet. They are
having trouble with the oxygen apparatus. That is Mallory
you see there. Irvine is in the tent working the valves which
have become loosened. It is so cold outside that the parts of
the apparatus to be repaired have to be heated over a candle to
make them touchable by the bare fingers.

The camera is moving in on Mallory . . . into a big head close-up of him,
the handsome intense face, the eyes narrowed against the summit and
the goal.

We can hear the wind. Infrequent flakes of snow fall. The wind
suddenly sounds up, then dies down again, as Mallory turns slowly
looking up into the sky. His face darkens as a patch of cloud covers the
sun, then sunlight again and the snow stops. The wind catches at his
hair. Another angle: as he bends down and crawls into the tent.

Inside the two leveled floor, IRVINE is busy on the apparatus. He heats
a coil over a candle and then works on it and the pressure dials.

MALLORY
(as he crawls in)
Any success?

IRVINE
I'll know shortly. What's it like outside?

MALLORY
Good enough. A bit of wind, a snow flurry dancing over the
slabs, but the summit is still there.

IRVINE
I think the oxygen will work . . . but we're wasting time.

Mallory makes himself comfortable above as Irvine works below.
Mallory nibbles on a biscuit.

MALLORY
Take your time. We'll gain the hour back if the oxygen works.

IRVINE
And if it doesn't?

MALLORY
We'll make it in any event. I've determined to do it.

Suddenly a gust takes hold of the tent and shakes it as a terrier does a rat.
Both men look up suddenly. The wind dies down again. It is still except
for the distant sighing like someone in tears or pain.

IRVINE
Breezy.

MALLORY
Oh, we haven't yet seen the end of the tricks Everest will play
to keep us from the top. We must expect no mercy from
Everest . . . .
            (he laughs)
I remember in twenty two when Bruce was turned back at
twenty seven thousand two hundred, he said . . . just you wait,
old thing, we will get you yet . . . . And we shall today.

He opens a thermos flask.

MALLORY (CON'T)
Some tea?

IRVINE
Please.

Mallory pours some. Irvine sips and goes back to work.

> MALLORY
> The moment you've done, we're off. Everything's ready.
> (pause as he sips)
> The way I see it, Sandy, there's just one really bad place where we will have to exert ourselves . . . and the oxygen will help us save time there.
> (he watches Irvine)
> This is quite different from the Alps, isn't it?

> IRVINE
> Much.

> MALLORY
> The Alps have become a technical problem in the main . . . but here we begin to touch the limits. The very limits.
> (he smiles)
> I recall when they said no man could move about above twenty four thousand foot. Norton went over twenty eight. We're working and sleeping over twenty six.
> (sips)
> You know, Sandy, that is the one absolute truth about the human universe . . . whatever the past announces as the limit of human ability, effort, power, and growth, is wrong. That is the one absolute and universal rule: the possibilities of the human are infinite. Are you convinced we shall make the summit today?

> IRVINE
> Absolutely.

> MALLORY
> (almost to himself)
> I can't see myself coming down defeated.

In the constricted place, with Irvine faced sideways to camera and Mallory lying there, above, they are in a close two shot. Mallory broods, Irvine is intent on his work. A gust of wind, not as strong as the first one, billows the canvas, and as it does, so Irvine looks up as if to the sky, listening. The wind cries again and grows still. The canvas flaps. Mallory broods.

MALLORY (CON'T)

I remember when on the very first expedition here we reached the Rongbuk Valley. The Tibetans had told us about the Sacred Monastery, the valley of the hermits and the Lama who they say is a living reincarnation of a god who dwells in the snows of the mountain. Pilgrims come here to worship him. And we too were pilgrims, pilgrims of adventure come to wrestle with the mountain and not to pray to it. Have you ever read the historic document that first let us into Tibet?

IRVINE

No.

MALLORY

It speaks of this land as I see it. It began something like this: to the West of the Five Treasuries of Great Snow (within the jurisdiction of White Glass Fort, near Rocky Valley Inner Monastery) is the Bird Country of the South . . . . Strange, isn't it? And so we came here. We had mounted a thousand feet when we stopped to wait for what we had come to see. As the clouds rolled asunder before the heights, gradually, very gradually, we saw the great mountain sides and glaciers and ridges, now one fragment, now another, through the floating rifts, until, far higher in the sky than the imagination dared to suggest, a prodigious white fang—an excretion from the jaw of the world—the summit of Everest, appeared.

(Irvine has stopped his work
and looked up at him)

It became at that moment a symbol for all my life.

(he looks at Irvine, who hastily
turns back to his work)

Those who don't climb mountains wonder why we do . . . but we wonder ourselves. What is it for you, Sandy, simply an adventure?

IRVINE

Not Everest. This mountain is too big. It is too big to be simply an adventure.

MALLORY

It asks too much of each man who steps upon it to be merely an adventure . . . and yet it is most supremely that. Has anyone ever asked you what good it is to climb?

IRVINE

They have . . . but I've never bothered to answer.

MALLORY

Why not?

IRVINE

I don't know how.

MALLORY

There is fame, of course, and men understand fame since they want it so badly. And there is triumph and men understand that since so few ever triumph . . . the sense of victory. And there is knowledge in a geographical sense which people pretend to understand although they never explore their own backyards. And, if a pot of gold were on top of Everest, the mountainside would be strewn with corpses all year round because people who are prepared to kill for money will die for it also. But really none of these things are actually here on Everest.

IRVINE

I see the mountain . . . and I would like to be among the first to stand on the summit.

MALLORY

There is for every man his own Everest which he must surmount, for if he does not, if he turns back, then he has lost the reason for life. Neither pain nor death nor the moment of victory is decisive. It is the act of attempt, the assault on the unknown, and every man or woman who has struggled or perished for an ideal knows this.

A moment of silence.

IRVINE

We're ready.

The wind jumps at the tent like a mad thing and shakes it violently.

> MALLORY

Then let's go.

They start to crawl out of the tent. Snow and wind, not overwhelmingly but hard enough, force their way in.

> MALLORY
> (shouting)

It's just a flurry.

The tent is rattling. Empty now, It beats in the wind. We can hear the wind wailing outside. The bottom flap of the tent jerks up and a few objects roll.

Cut to: Film. A pan down the mountain showing height to two men beginning to walk into the waste and wilderness.

> CALMER

The assault on the summit has just begun. We take you back to Camp 3.

EXT. CAMP 3

Film: pan down to glacier. Some sherpas coming toward the camera, etc.

> MARBLE

This is Harry Marble in Camp 3. Everyone knows the last chance to capture the peak of Everest is now being taken, and all the months of preparation, the grueling struggle to establish these camps is being tested somewhere above us over five miles high, somewhere in the region of twenty eight thousand feet.

To: Live. We can see Noel, Hingston and Norton. We move past a couple of sherpas talking and looking up.

> MARBLE (CON'T)

These Tibetan hillmen whose incredible endurance and devotion to the job makes Himalayan climbing possible, have their own opinions of what Everest means. They call it Chomolungma, the Goddess Mother of the World. The one on the left is Lakpa who reached twenty seven thousand feet

> (MORE)

                    MARBLE (CON'T)
carrying supplies, and the other is Dorje Passan.
                    (Noel comes by)
Captain Noel, will you help, please? I'd like to ask these
Sherpas a few questions.

                    NOEL
I'll do my best.

                    MARBLE
Could you find out why these men who have lived here all
their lives have never tried to climb Everest, although by
nature, custom and training they are most fitted for it?

                    NOEL
Very well.

He moves to the sherpas, his back to the camera. The sherpas talk
together. Finally Noel turns to the camera.

                    NOEL (CON'T)
Their answer is, briefly, they never thought of it. The
mountain is the residence of the gods. And now . . .
                    (the sherpas chatter, smiling)
. . . now this is their job and they are doing it.

                    MARBLE
Thank you. Is our view still blocked by clouds?

                    NOEL
                    (looking up)
Yes, but we did catch glimpses of Odell moving along toward
the shoulder.

We pass on to Hingston and Norton. Hingston is adjusting the
bandages.

                    MARBLE
That is Major Hingston, medical officer, and Colonel Norton,
leader of the expedition. Norton made the first attempt to
reach the summit on June fourth. With him was Theodore
Somervell, a physician and missionary who is now in the
                                                (MORE)

MARBLE (CON'T)
lower base camp, ill with a pulmonary infection from frost bite
of the throat. Norton himself was snowblinded. Colonel
Norton, Major Hingston.

Both men turn briefly toward camera. Then Hingston goes on with his
work while Norton keeps his head vaguely in the proper direction.

MARBLE
How are you this morning, Colonel Norton?

NORTON
I'm beginning to see a little again.

HINGSTON
You'll be perfectly all right if you do as you're told.

NORTON
No sign of them?

HINGSTON
There's a smear of cloud in the way.

NORTON
It feels like a good day for it.

HINGSTON
If the monsoon holds off.

MARBLE
Precisely how does the monsoon affect climbing on Everest?

NORTON
Tell him, Hingston. You pretend to be a scientist.

HINGSTON
Yes, I keep up the pretense that this expedition has some
scientific value. Actually, we are here to climb the mountain.
The rest is flim-flam.

NORTON
(grinning)
The monsoon.

HINGSTON

As you know, that is a soft southwest wind which advances up
the Bay of Bengal bringing rain where it is warm and snow
where it is cold. The monsoon usually arrives at this time and
large wet flakes begin to fall, and, very soon, howling
blizzards and wild gales make Everest a soft white cemetery of
avalanches.

NORTON

There is a preliminary monsoon current which I believe we
have passed through. Then there is a brief lull of fine weather
and then the monsoon proper.

MARBLE

And you believe we are in the lull?

NORTON

I hope we are. I've tried to have telegrams sent from Ceylon
and the Malabar coast where the weather breaks about three
weeks earlier than here at Northern India. But no telegrams
have arrived.

MARBLE

To what do you attribute, Colonel Norton, your own inability
to reach the summit?

NORTON

Human weakness.

HINGSTON

Men deteriorate very quickly at such altitudes. They forget
how to eat. They can't sleep. And all the while their bodies
are being starved for oxygen.

MARBLE

How high did you reach?

NORTON

By theodolite we estimate it was 28,126.

MARBLE

No human being has ever climbed higher.

NORTON

I hope Mallory and Irvine have.

Noel strolls into shot.

HINGSTON

Anything?

NOEL

Nothing. Bit of wind is kicking up there. Some snow.

MARBLE

Is Mallory going to use the same route you did, Colonel?

NORTON

No. We had a mountaineer's disagreement on that. I
preferred the yellow band, below the crest, in order to avoid
those two steps of stone there which look anywhere from sixty
to a hundred feet high and quite steep and smooth. I realize
that the slabs are dangerous, since they slope so steeply down,
almost like roof tiles. I mean, of course, dangerous when there
is snow on them. And then, of course, there is the couloir to
cross with its rather powdery snow. In fact, I rather lost my
nerve going by it and was glad to turn back.

NOEL

The fact is, by the time Norton reached there, Somervell had
stopped, unable to go on. Norton was alone, and besides, it
was so late that even had he reached the top he would've been
unable to return by nightfall . . . and on Everest that means
certain death. It was wise to turn back. This is
mountaineering, not suicide.

NORTON

We'll leave climbing by night on Everest to braver men.

MARBLE

Does the summit look difficult?

NORTON

Not particularly. Of course, it's not quite like a stroll along
Piccadilly Circus, but all the tricky part is before it, although I
can't say just what it is on the route that Mallory is taking.

MARBLE

By the way, if you were snowblinded, Colonel Norton, how did you get down?

NORTON

It didn't hit me until I was in Camp 4 on top of the ice cliff, and Hingston and the sherpas got me down. They placed my feet and hands and I did the moving until we got down on the glacier here where I was carried to camp. By the way, Hingston, that was the first you ever climbed, wasn't it?

HINGSTON

The next man will have to come down himself.

NORTON

Nothing, Noel?

NOEL

Nothing.

NORTON

They must be well on their way by now and perhaps with oxygen they'll make it. Without oxygen you slowly get the feeling that it isn't worth the effort. It would be such a relief to stop, to lie down, to put an end to the struggle . . . and that is fatal to the will . . . .

HINGSTON

Into the tent with you.

NORTON

No sign?

HINGSTON

We'll let you know.

Noel and Hingston help Norton into tent.

MARBLE

We are going to take you back to the highest camp . . .
on 6 . . . . There seems to be something of a wind blowing up there now.

Cut to: Film. First shot of the snow blowing off the ridge . . . but far shot.

MARBLE (CON'T)

Whether this is the monsoon beginning or just a local Everest storm is important. If it is the monsoon, there is danger to all men on the mountain. If the storm is local, only to Mallory and Irvine.

EXT. CAMP 6

Film: the snow blowing off the crestline. Sound: the wind off, but beginning to scream. Rumbles of snow slides.

CALMER
(loudly)

The wind is beginning to kick up here at Camp 6. But the main force is still above, higher than the climbers have gone. You can see Mallory and Irvine there . . . .

Film: the climbers in the chimney.

CALMER (CON'T)

They are still protected by the rock and snow parapet from the force of the wind which is above. It is difficult to tell whether this is a local storm or not. If it is the monsoon then every effort should be made to retreat from the mountain at once. But Mallory and Irvine are moving ahead now, quite rapidly for this altitude, in an effort to make up for lost time. They must reach the summit before late afternoon, if they can reach it at all.

(to the storm on the mountain)

As the wind increases it gathers its forces like an army with snow banners.

(the great fans in the downward
pan)

The velocity of the gale easily rises to one hundred and sixty miles an hour, pouring tons of snow, rocks, ice before it, sweeping in vast waterfalls of debris down the immense and almost perpendicular slope of this giant mountain. On top of Everest itself the great plume of windborn ice is tattered and

(MORE)

CALMER (CON'T)

torn. Air currents plunge into the depths and the temperature
drops rapidly until it is beyond all human endurance.

(cut to men)

Yet Mallory and Irvine are still climbing. They will soon reach
into the open. We are here at the top of our world and it
resists us. When Mallory was asked, a year ago in New York,
why men climbed mountains, skirting death and destruction,
he replied that men climb mountains because they are there.
Whatever exists is a challenge of man's role on earth, a
necessity of his life, a condition of his survival.

(pause)

It is strange, it is odd, and yet it is somehow most eloquently
human that at this moment two men, roped together in
comradeship and hope, are climbing into the roof of the world.
More than physical endurance is necessary. This is an affair of
the heart, the will, the soul. It is not something that all men do
or can do. It is not something that all men will want to do, or
should do. But those men who find here in the savagery of
this mountain, in the wilderness here of rock and snow and
wind and storm, an experiment in life, a proof of man's
unconquerable will, read us the lesson that we have learned
from the moment that we, like this very mountain, rose from
the primeval sea.

(the mist is drifting over them)

We will soon lose sight of Mallory and Irvine. They are
moving into the unknown to make it known, into the
unendurable to make it endurable, into the future to make it
present.

Pause. A wild blast of wind. Mallory and Irvine disappear. Sound
effects now. Storm on mountain as long as we can with the whole
orchestra of sound effects. Then to Live: the interior of the empty tent.
Blow the tent up. Blow snow in it. Let the snow gather and rage within
the tent which, empty, is the symbol of the climb and finally of the death
of Mallory and Irvine. Now, keeping picture of the agony of the empty
tent, sound effects out and Cronkite's voice in.

                    CRONKITE

Mallory and Irvine went into the mystery of the summit of
Mount Everest and never returned. For one whole day Odell
searched for them at the utmost peril and found nothing . . .
and then finally the signal of death was given to the party
below and Norton ordered the men off the mountain. The
summit of Everest was still supreme and unconquered.

In 1933 another British Everest expedition attempted to
conquer the mountain. They failed, but high up on the slabs
they found Mallory's ice axe. There were seven expeditions in
all, all failures, and then last year another British expedition
sent two men to the summit, but from the Nepal side of
Everest. The men were a Tibetan Sherpa and a New
Zealander. They found no signs of Mallory or Irvine on the
summit but they knew that it was Mallory and Irvine and all
the others, named and unnamed, European and Asian, who
had made the moment of triumph not only possible but
inevitable.

What sort of a day was it? A day like all days, filled with those
events that alter and illuminate our time . . . and YOU WERE
THERE.

                                        FADE OUT.

THE EMERGENCE OF JAZZ

Although nobody has ever satisfactorily defined it in technical terms, jazz diverges widely, even violently, from all previous canons of musical composition and performance and is immediately distinguishable. What can be said with confidence is that, whereas in more conventional musical areas the artist is fundamentally an executant expressing the findings of the creative mind of the composer, in jazz the performer is usually his or her own composer. The customer unable to acquire the recording of Brahms's *Fourth Symphony* conducted by Herbert von Karajan would probably settle for someone else's recording of that work, but the buyer thwarted in the attempt to buy the jazz musician Duke Ellington's version of "Caravan" might well accept as a substitute anything else played by Ellington. That is why, in jazz, there is at least one truism that has always applied: the performer playing a theme always tries to make it sound not like itself but like himself or herself.

In the social life of the Black American, in Louisiana in the early years of the 20th century, community music played a more prominent part than perhaps can be easily comprehended. There was almost no social activity in New Orleans then that did not imply a musical corollary. There was live music for births, weddings, christenings, funerals, picnics, parades, marches, and all kinds of celebrations.

Although the myth-making process has drawn a picture of jazz limited strictly to the brothels and sporting houses of Storyville, the town's bordello district, there were, of course, many instances of the music splashing over into the life of the city at large. Nonetheless, jazz, linked to the Black performer and the social events of Black life in the city, retained a connotation of sin and dissipation for many years after the New Orleans pioneers were forgotten. The saxophonist Sidney Bechet, one of the most gifted of all the New Orleans musicians, insisted in his autobiography that the word jazz in its original form of *jass* was local slang for sexual intercourse, and the evidence in favor of Bechet's assertion seems overwhelming.

These brothels were thus a link in the jazz musician's economic chain, for many employed bands or, at the very least, a house pianist whose job was to thump out ragtime rhythms against a background of red plush and gilt. The collapse of the Storyville economy was naturally disastrous for the working musician. In 1917 the United States Secretary of the Navy decreed that, in view of the repeated fighting and violence involving seamen on leave in the city, the New Orleans red-light district must be closed down.

The closing of Storyville did not stop jazz in New Orleans, nor was jazz unknown in the North. As early as 1917, the year of the Storyville edict, the Original Dixieland Jass Band, a group of white Southerners with a comically inflated sense of their own importance as musical innovators, had introduced jazz to the patrons of Reisenweber's restaurant in New York and recorded two compositions.

The main force pushing the New Orleans musician north was his need to find employment, and perhaps the most significant sequence of events after the closing of Storyville was that involving Joe "King" Oliver. Early in 1918 Oliver, acknowledged trumpet champion of New Orleans, migrated north to Chicago. By 1920 he had become a popular bandleader there, and two years later, wanting to increase the size of his band, he sent to New Orleans for a star disciple, one of the most brilliant of the jazz musicians who came out of the city, Louis Daniel Armstrong. From this point on, jazz evolved from a local musical dialect into an international language, proliferating in geographical range and in stylistic variation to a degree that astonished those of the New Orleans founding fathers who lived long enough to watch the process for themselves.

❖❖❖

"For 'The Emergence of Jazz,'" writes Charles Russell, "I became an entrepreneur—the last of the big spenders.

"I booked Louis Armstrong to play that legendary cornet player King Oliver, along with Louis' backup group which included Trummie Young on trombone, Barney Bigard on clarinet, and Billy Kyle on piano. I booked Zutty Singleton to play Louis Mitchell, a Black drummer from New Orleans who had brought jazz to Paris before the first American troops had arrived, who referred to himself during the Paris interview as 'just a trap drummer.'

"I continued my binge and booked Bobby Hackett, a great trumpet player, to be Nick La Rocca the cornet player in the Original Dixieland Jazz Band that included Larry Shields on clarinet, Daddy Edwards on trombone, Henry Ragas on piano, and Tony Sbarro on drums.

"I was on a roll and had booked Billy Taylor, a marvelous piano player, to be and play 'Jelly Roll' Morton. He plays throughout the interview, never stopping even when he speaks, the harmonies and rhythms of his blues improvisations underlying his explanations of how this new music came about.

"Sidney Lumet had returned from his vacation and we were in rehearsal—I seemed to have spent more time at the rehearsals on this show than usual. Louis would be walking up and down the corridor outside the rehearsal hall, trumpet in hand warming up his 'chops.' He told me, 'I go home at night and my wife hides my mouthpiece because I like to sit and listen to records and play the music with just my mouthpiece. She doesn't know I've got another one hidden from her.' In the morning his wife would pierce the blisters on his lips with a needle and then apply some homemade ointment. He carried a jar of this stuff with him at all times.

"If I had sense enough to sell tickets to the CBS personnel who 'just happened to be in the vicinity,' to peer in and listen during the week's rehearsal, I would have been able to retire. My secretary, Helen, got through the onlookers and told me, 'Mr. Dozier called. He wants to see you in his office as soon as possible.'

"Bill Dozier's desk was always immaculate, the desk pens at the proper angle, the blotter exactly in the center of the desk, and the phones artfully placed near his elbow. He was behind the desk when I came in and talking to Albert Taylor, head of Business Affairs.

"'Charles,' Bill said, 'Albert tells me you have been spending money on the Jazz show in a very cavalier way.' He looked at Albert who said, 'Yes, Charles, you have presented us with a *fait accompli*.' I said, 'Look, the overage will made up on the next show, which is not heavy in cast or physical production requirements. Trust me.' As Albert was leaving he said, 'I never trust a man who says trust me. I'll keep an eye on that show.'

"As I started to leave Bill said, 'Charles.' I turned and watched him pull out a copy of the Jazz script from a drawer in his desk and place it on the blotter on top of his desk. He looked at me and said, 'Tell Abe I think it's a good script.'

"There was only one Abe writing for the series and that was Polonsky. So I called him. Abe's reply was, 'Did he say that? Oh God, we're in real trouble now. The man has no taste.'"
(Russell, "In the Worst of Times," pp. 126-130.)

THE EMERGENCE OF JAZZ
by Abraham Polonsky
(signed by Jeremy Daniel)

Air Date:
September 5, 1954

YOU ARE THERE
November 12, 1917

FADE IN:

INT. CBS STUDIOS

                    CRONKITE
Walter Cronkite reporting, November 12, 1917.

Our featured story today will be a new fad that's making
wartime New York sound like a French battlefield. But first a
roundup of the important headlines of the month. The big
news is still Russia, and today Premier Kerensky announced
the near collapse of the Bolshevik Revolution. In Petrograd,
Leo Trotsky was greeted with taunts and laughter when he
came to take over for the Reds.

On the battlefront, the Germans have again defeated the
Italians, but generally the picture is brighter and General
Pershing announces that supplies from America are arriving in
volume. In Washington, President Wilson is still being
besieged by the suffragettes, some of whom have been arrested
for picketing the White House to enforce their demands for
votes for women. As if to forget their troubles, New Yorkers
are going crazy over the music called jazz. War years always
                                                        (MORE)

CRONKITE (CON'T)
bring on new fads and tastes and the strangest taste around is the excitement generated by the musical noise called jazz. This strange music has been accused of everything, including: the present decay in morality, the bad weather, and the desire of the women for the vote. We take you now to a musical recording studio in New York where some of this wild music is being recorded for posterity. All things are as they were then except . . . YOU ARE THERE.

INT. VICTOR RECORDING STUDIO

REPORTER 1
Here we are in the Victor Recording Studio in New York City. The wild racket coming from behind those closed doors is what they call jazz, and is being made by the Original Dixieland Jazz Band. The little orchestra is cutting a record of one of its famous numbers called the "Dixieland Jass One Step," popularly known as "Mutt and Jeff."

We are in a corridor facing a closed door which mutes without sweetening the music. A porter sweeps the floor aimlessly because he is listening with a smile. Half-facing into camera is MAX HART, the agent. The porter is black; the agent is white.

REPORTER 1 (CON'T)
This five piece dance band from New Orleans has caused a sensation at Reisenweber's Cafe, just off Columbus Circle. The thing called jazz has hit New York like a new intoxicant.

The music ends and Max turns full into camera. He is grinning.

MAX
Sensational, isn't it?

REPORTER 1
That's the most moderate thing you can say about it. The gentleman with the cigar is Max Hart, a booking agent. It was he who discovered the band and brought it to New York where it has electrified the town and achieved notoriety plus the condemnation of some of our leading citizens.

MAX

Now wait a minute. Fame, yes. Blame, no. A few blue faces,
that's all.

REPORTER 1
(dryly)

Let me quote: "Jazz is dirty music, mongrel music." And a
leading minister has said, quotes open: When America regains
its soul, jazz will go, not before. That is to say, it will be
relegated to the dark and scarlet haunts whence it came and
whither unwept it will return after America's soul is reborn.
Quotes closed.

MAX

Spare me. There's always someone to say that what they never
heard before is bad. They said Beethoven was bad. What's
wrong with Jass? People like it. They jump, they jiggle, they
dance. They forget their troubles. It fits in with the modern
spirit of devil-may-care. So what of it if a minister says it's the
music of the devil? With a big war on, people want to know
the devil a little better.
(he laughs)
Don't quote me. You want to meet the boys?

REPORTER 1

Surely.

Max opens the door which emits smoke and a few tootles and chords.

MAX

Do me one favor, keep an open mind.

He goes in. As the camera follows, it passes the porter who smiles.

PORTER

If you like this, mister, you should hear it when it's real.

REPORTER 1

What do you mean real?

PORTER

Like they play it in New Orleans, at Pete Lala's where it's
music.

REPORTER 1

Are you from New Orleans?

PORTER

No, sir. Mobile. But I've been to New Orleans. I've heard.
Yes, sir, I sure heard it.

REPORTER 1

Do you like this music?

PORTER

Well, this music here is different. I mean, it's not exactly how
they play it there. It's more nervous, you see, not so easy.

REPORTER 1

Well, how do you like it?

PORTER

It's music . . . .

He goes off whistling and sweeping, and the camera enters the room.
The five musicians are taking their break, smoking. The engineer and his
assistants are fiddling with the acoustical equipment. RAGAS and
SHIELDS are at the piano with Max.

MAX
(with a sweeping gesture)
I want you to meet the boys: Nick La Rocca, cornet; Larry
Shields, clarinet; Daddy Edwards, trombone; Henry Ragas,
piano; Tony Sbarro, drums. All New Orleans boys.

All nod except Ragas.

RAGAS

Come to hear the noise?

REPORTER 1

Come to find out what makes it so noisy.

RAGAS

Just a little bit of hopped-up ragtime like it's been played for
years.

HART

But not in New York. These boys have something altogether new. It's different. I heard them in Schiller's Cafe in Chicago and I said, New York must hear this. This is for the big town. So I brought them. Nothing. Then one day, fame. And the next day, respectability. They play a concert with the great Caruso. That's show business.

REPORTER 1

Why do people like it? I mean why do they either hate it or love it? Do you know?

RAGAS

Well, I guess people are looking for a little excitement with no killing in it, so they come and listen and dance and forget their troubles. Do you like it?

REPORTER 1

I never heard anything like it before, and I've been to many dances.

RAGAS

It doesn't come from a respectable dance hall. It comes from a honky-tonk, long after midnight when all the nice people have quit counting their money and gone to bed.

SHIELDS

Yes, sir, man. That's the way we heard it in the town we was born in, in uptown New Orleans, on Magazine, and Third and Fourth Street, or downtown of Louis Street. Yes, sir. This is the way we heard it when we were kids and hung around Storyville. People there have heard this music.

He blows a run on his clarinet.

ENGINEER

We can try the fast one now.

REPORTER 1

Who invented this kind of music? Where did it start?

RAGAS

Mister, this is the way the colored play it. That's where we learned it, from them, down in Storyville.

"Tiger Rag," is that it?

EDWARDS
That's it. All right, boys. Let us see if we got the strength to
hold that tiger.

He raises his trombone. He beats the time. The band jumps in, and the
infernal din rises. Play off on the recording devices of the day as the
music proceeds.

REPORTER 1
We are going to take you to New Orleans to get the story on
this fad which is sweeping New York and Chicago. Come in,
Harry Marble.

INT. MAYOR'S OFFICE NEW ORLEANS

In the mayor's office, the MAYOR and two women. Far off, the music of
"Did you Ramble."

MARBLE
This is Harry Marble and we are in the office of his honor,
Mayor Martin Behrman, of the city of New Orleans. We had
come down here to find out what jazz was, but it seems we are
going to witness the end of this fad before it even comes alive,
for the mayor is closing Storyville, the home of vice and jazz,
tonight. It is, as he says, the end of an era. Mayor Behrman.

BEHRMAN
Personally, you understand, sir, I am opposed to the
elimination of Storyville from our city. It is my opinion, sir,
that by enclosing and supervising those vicious elements
which pander to the baser appetites of man, we are better able
to control them. This was why in 1897, Assemblyman Story
introduced an ordinance to confine the vices to a specific
section of the city, which unfortunately became known as
Storyville.

MARBLE
Then why is Storyville being closed down?

BEHRMAN

The war, sir, has brought a great number of soldiers and sailors into New Orleans and the federal government feels it can best protect the morals of these young men by closing down Storyville. We have no choice. Tonight at midnight, it exists no more.

WOMAN

As a representative of the Louisiana Federation of Women's Clubs I can only applaud a government wise enough to remove this blight on New Orleans. Storyville has been for years a center of gambling, drinking, a home for thieves and murderers and worse.

MARBLE

We heard it was the home of jazz.

BEHRMAN
(as music fades in from the
streets)
There goes a street band returning form a funeral. That's a kind of jazz, too. Always had it in New Orleans.

WOMAN

Jazz, sir, is a direct cause of the degradation of the mind and morals which feeds on vice. I should like, sir, if I may, to read a part of an editorial written in one of our leading papers, the *Times-Picayune*.

She fishes around in her bag for it, and the other woman, GERTRUDE DIX, smiles ironically. Gertrude is as beautiful as the other woman is nondescript.

MARBLE
(to Gertrude)
Is that your opinion, mam?

WOMAN

Her opinion!

GERTRUDE

I'm one of those who has tried through the courts to prevent the closing of Storyville, but I've failed.

WOMAN
(waving the editorial)
As vice will always fail before virtue, and evil fall before good,
and the devil before the Almighty.
(she reads)
What is jazz music and the jazz band? It is a manifestation of a
low streak in man's tastes that has not yet come out in
civilization's wash. Indeed we might go further and say that
jazz music is the indecent story syncopated and
counterpointed. Like the improper anecdote, also, in its youth,
it is listened to blushingly behind closed doors and drawn
curtains, but like vice, it grows bolder until it dares decent
surroundings. On certain natures, loud and meaningless
sound has an exciting, almost intoxicating effect, like crude
colors and strong perfumes, like the sight of flesh or the
pleasure of blood. It is a point of civic honor to repress it.

MARBLE
What do you think of jazz, Miss Dix?

GERTRUDE
The customers in my cafe like it. I always give them what they
like.

MARBLE
Do you think the closing of Storyville will put an end to this
music?

GERTRUDE
You can't pass a law against what people really want.

MARBLE
(to mayor)
Mayor Behrman, do you think jazz music leads to vice?

MAYOR
How should I know, sir?

MARBLE
From your observation of Storyville?

MAYOR

Good people looking for vice lead to vice, sir, but the
government and these fair ladies, at least one of them,
disagree, so tonight Storyville ends.

WOMAN

Our young boys who are soon to go overseas must be
protected from their own innocent tendency to yield to the
attractions of vice.

GERTRUDE

Well, I'm just one of those women who aren't worth much in
respectable society, but I think it's less harm to a young boy to
let him hear some jazz and drink some liquor and laugh a
little, than to be sent to France to be killed by some Germans.

WOMAN

How dare you?

MAYOR

Ladies . . . .

As the women quarrel, the music comes in louder, etc.

MARBLE

We will return to Storyville later on, but first we have made
arrangements to go to Paris where Jazz arrived before the first
American troops. Come in, Ned Calmer, in Paris. Ned Calmer
in Paris. Are you there, Paris?

INT. FRENCH BAR AND CAFE

It is deserted except for a young Frenchman leaning against the bar
having a drink and autographing a pile of books, a smiling bartender
who can't stop gazing into the camera, and LOUIS MITCHELL, a
drummer. Behind them is the little bandstand, and centered there is an
amazing battery of percussion instruments.

CALMER

This is Ned Calmer in war time Paris, and we are in a small
cafe here between crowds. The young man to my right who is
autographing the books is Monsieur Goffin, a young Belgian
(MORE)

CALMER (CON'T)

poet and a great enthusiast of the new music introduced here
on the continent by Mr. Louis Mitchell, the American jazz
drummer on my left. There are more important things than
jazz in France, but few things about which the young are more
passionate. Monsieur Goffin, why has Paris become so
enthusiastic about American Jazz?

GOFFIN

Because Paris embraces art and jazz is the art of the twentieth
century.
                (pointing to Mitchell)
Louis here is a troubadour out of the new world and I
celebrate the new intoxication in my book of poems.

MITCHELL

Just a trap drummer, Robert.

CALMER

Do you think there is any relation between the excitement and
tension of the war and the new music?

GOFFIN

Not what you think. The war is something thrown on us by
the failure of the old, the generations of our fathers before us.
It is the proof that their culture and civilization amount to
nothing but one grand zero. So people here, the young, the
intellectuals, the artists, they seize upon jazz as a message from
the future. Goodbye to big orchestras, the harmonies, the
terrible banality of musical past, and welcome to that cocktail
of sound and color, improvised, polyphonic, American jazz.

He drinks to it.

CALMER

The Americans have hardly heard of it except in a few rather
obscure haunts of vice.

GOFFIN

The Americans don't want to hear it because it is the free
creation of the Negro people whom they still don't recognize
as free and equal. That is an irony, isn't it, that from the slaves
                                        (MORE)

GOFFIN (CON'T)
and the oppressed comes the only original contribution to art
made by the American nation. All else is imitation. How do
you like that, Louis?

Louis smiles.

CALMER
Where are you from, Mr. Mitchell?

LOUIS
Philly. I played around in most places, but I introduced jazz
into New York. Played at the Taverne Louis in the Flat Iron
Building in 1912.

CALMER
People in New York think the Original Dixieland Band are the
first.

LOUIS
Why, I played in Reisenweber's in 1914. That was in February
and my quintet was the best in America. Yes, sir, the best
ragtime in America.

CALMER
Monsieur Goffin, what makes you think that jazz is important?
Most people consider it just a lot of noise.

GOFFIN
It's noise, too. All music is noise. Louis, please, for me, a
demonstration on the drum.
(as Louis goes behind his outfit
of percussion)
It is important to remember that jazz is different because it is
improvised, free, because it is polyphonic like the great music
of the middle ages, because it is a liberation of music from the
chains of convention and snobbery. It comes from the human
heart, not from the academies. It is free. It is honest. It is art
the way art should be; all the rest, as our great poet Verlaine
has said, is merely literature.

He turns and gives Mitchell a signal, and the drums start. A solo that
gets louder and more frenetic.

CALMER
(above the jungle of sound)
Thank you Monsieur Goffin and Mr. Mitchell. We take you
back to the United States, to Reporter 2 in California. Come in,
Reporter 2 . . . .

INT. A SMALL ROOM — CALIFORNIA

In contrast to the racket and sound, we find ourselves in a small room
where a neat and delicate man sits at a piano and plays a graceful and
lyrical beat. This is MORTON.

REPORTER 2
This is Reporter 2 in California, and I am here with one of the
great innovators and composers of the new jazz music. His
name is Ferdinand Joseph Morton . . . .

MORTON
Call me "Jelly Roll." That's what they call me, that's how I'm
known.

He plays throughout, never stopping even when he speaks.

REPORTER 2
Mr. Jelly Roll Morton is known among the jazzmen of
Storyville, of Chicago and St. Louis, as one of the finest
inventors and players of this new kind of music.

MORTON
Thank you kindly, sir, for I have put my mark on the music
and when you hear it they are often playing my melodies.

REPORTER 2
He has been explaining and demonstrating just how this new
music comes about.

MORTON
And I will continue to elucidate and indicate to you how it all
happens. Jazz started in New Orleans and this "Tiger Rag" . . .
(plays the eight bar intro)
. . . happened to be transformed from an old quadrille that
(MORE)

was in many different tempos and rhythms, and I'll no doubt
give you an idea how it went. This was the introduction,
meaning that everyone was supposed to get their partners.
(calls out)
Get your partners, everybody get your partners . . . . And
people would be rushing around the hall getting their
partners. Maybe five minutes lapse between that time, and of
course, they'd start it over again and that was the first part of
it. And the next strain would be the waltz strain, I believe.
(plays)
That would be the waltz strain. And they had another strain
that comes right beside it. Mazooka time.
(plays Mazurka)
That was the third strain and, of course, they had another
strain and that was a different tempo.
(plays)
Of course, they had another one.
(plays)
I will show you how it was transformed. It happened to be
transformed by your performer at this particular time. "Tiger
Rag," for your approval. I also named it. It came from the way
I played it by making the tiger on my elbow. I also named it
. . . a person said once, "it sounds like a tiger hollerin'". I said,
"Fine." To myself I said, "Fine, that's the name." This is the
way things happen and jazz is born. It comes from hearing
your mother's voice when you're on her knee and hearing
there the voice of Africa and the drums and the people crying
when they were dragged out of their homes and brought here
to be slaves . . . and it comes from working in the fields and
talking up and singing against the hot sun and the pain and
not letting on to the master what you were saying, and the
river boat whistles and the locomotive trains . . . and the
marching songs and funerals, and always the blues, always the
slow drag, always searching for home and not finding it but
not stopping, always looking . . . and ending up like a man
does in Storyville, surrounded by sin and lights and liquor and
playing a piano and hearing it all and bringing it all together
. . . so I'll play it for you.

He plays "Tiger Rag."

REPORTER 2

Thank you, Mr. Morton.

MORTON

Why, call me Jelly Roll, the Winning Boy. That's what they
called me . . . Mister Jelly.

He moons over the piano, still playing.

REPORTER 2

We return you now to Storyville and Harry Marble.

INT. PETE LALA'S CABARET — STORYVILLE

The smoky low ceilinged hall, with shuttered windows and a door to the
street. Chairs and tables, a bar, a bandstand on which a group are
playing a blues. At a table near one of the windows sits KING OLIVER
Laughter and noise around and from the street, The shuffle of a crowd,
voices. Now and then snatches of other band music float in and fade.
High excitement. A couple of dancers.

MARBLE

This is Harry Marble and we are back in New Orleans but in
the section known as Storyville. This is Pete Lala's cabaret at
the corner of Marais and Iberville Streets and tonight is the last
night in which this region of vice and jazz will be permitted to
exist. Before us is Joseph Oliver, known as King Oliver, a
cornet player who is considered the best in the business.
Tonight is the final night on which he will be called king of the
Storyville jazz players for the kingdom is being destroyed, its
denizens scattered, its houses and gambling joints closed up,
and the word finis being written to the honky-tonk which has
been the home of the new music. How do you feel about the
end of Storyville, Joe?

OLIVER

I feel bad and I feel good. It was a living and the folks who
came liked what we played, but I feel good too because there
ain't no reason for this music to be all tied up with such goings
on. Maybe we'll all go out and play it somewhere else. I hear
they like it in Chicago and in New York and even far away in
gay Paree.

MARBLE
How did you get the name King Oliver, Joe?

OLIVER
(laughs)
Lost my head. Everybody was always talking about Bolden
and Perez, and Bunk Johnson, and Keppard and so one night
at Aberdeen Brothers where I was playing with a small band I
just marched out into the street with my horn and I blowed so
loud and so hot I dragged all the folks away. I pointed my
horn at the other places and I blew them out of the world and
when I marched back in still blowing they called me king, and
king I've been since.
(a burst of music comes in from
off)
They're riding tonight.

MARBLE
Everybody has to leave by midnight I'm told.

OLIVER
Yes, sir, the parade will form and march out to nowhere, and
this is the end.
(he looks around)
Funny, how you get to like something that's really rotten, but
you get to like it cause it feeds you. You like what you need to
like and you do what you need to do. I remember when they
used to make the colored players sit with their faces to the wall
and their backs to the folks outside and play that way, and
now the black and white are side by side sometimes.

MARBLE
Do you think any of the white jazz players really play the New
Orleans way?

OLIVER
They do and they don't. You play what you are and so it's
kind of mixed, I guess. But it's music . . . .

From off, someone with a band, as if a window were opened, has begun
a horn solo of the "Saints." Joe listens. His face lights.

OLIVER (CON'T)
Hear that . . . why that man next door he's opened the window
and he wishes to cut the king on the last night in Storyville.

He rises and flings open the windows. A glare of reflected light comes in
. . . and the music louder . . . . Joe puts his head out the window.

OLIVER (CON'T)
Blow, you loser, blow!

The horn blows. Joe runs to the bandstand and gets his horn. He waits
as his band stops playing. When the outside solo ends, Joe gives the beat
with his foot and the band starts on the tune. They beat it solid march
time . . . . and then Joe lifts his horn and blows out his solo . . . . When he
stops, applause . . . . And then from the outside, the other horn comes
back with his best answer. Joe listens and then he raises his horn and he
starts. He walks to the window and he sticks his horn out and he blasts
out. The music wells up magnificently. Off, a church bell begins to toll
twelve . . . .

VOICES
Closing time . . . . Closing time in Storyville.

Joe starts for the door, marching slowly, his horn blowing the great notes
of the melody while a line of customers form behind and they start
marching out. The place grows deserted. Other bands seem to fade in
but Joe's trumpet sounds above all as it goes off in the distance.

INT. CBS STUDIOS

CRONKITE
And so Storyville closed down on that night and Jazz moved
out with it, and the players black and white took their music
all over the world. The twenties arrived, and to it, Jazz gave its
name. The music caught on and Oliver went on to great
triumphs in Chicago. His place in New Orleans was taken by
a young lad named Louis Armstrong . . . .

In a way the Age of Jazz came and went before most
Americans really got to know the music. It merged with the
popular songs and ballads, what the musicians call sweet and
commercial. And yet basically the true jazz is still unknown,
(MORE)

CRONKITE (CON'T)
still hidden, still waiting to be brought into the open of
American life for what it is, a vital contribution and expression
of the American Negro past and an important part of the spirit
of the American future.

What sort of a day was it? A day like all days, filled with those
events that alter and illuminate our time . . . and YOU WERE
THERE!

FADE OUT.

THE TORMENT OF BEETHOVEN

Ranking as one of the greatest figures in the history of Western music, Ludwig van Beethoven (baptized 17 December 1770, Bonn, Germany—d. 26 March 1827, Vienna) dominates a period of musical history as no one else before or since. Rooted in the Classical traditions of Haydn and Mozart, his art reaches out to encompass the new spirit of humanism expressed in the works of Goethe and Schiller, his elder contemporaries in the world of literature, and above all in the ideals of the French Revolution, with its passionate concern for the freedom and dignity of the individual. He revealed more vividly than any of his predecessors the power of music to convey a philosophy of life without the aid of a spoken text; and in certain of his compositions is to be found the strongest assertion of the human will in all music, if not in all art. Though not himself a Romantic, he became the fountainhead of much that characterized the work of the Romantics who followed him. His personal life was marked by a heroic struggle against encroaching deafness, and some of his most important works were composed during the last ten years of his life when he was quite unable to hear. In an age that saw the decline of court and Church patronage, he not only maintained himself from the sale and publication of his works, but he was also the first musician to receive a salary with no other duties than to compose how and when he felt inclined.

The overview essay suggested that Polonsky's teleplays tended to be structured around a grid of recurring thematic oppositions. Here it is again:

INDIVIDUALISM v. CONFORMITY

INVENTION v. CONVENTION
(Innovation, Creativity)   (Formulaic Repetition)

FREEDOM v. CONSTRAINT
(Artistic, Religious, Political)   (Censorship)

This design structure is never more effectively utilized than in Polonsky's "The Torment of Beethoven." It is evident from Walter Cronkite's initial exposition. Note the italicized elements:

CRONKITE

October 6, 1802. There is an uneasiness in Europe today, a sense of change and disaster. The peace treaty between Austria and France, *between what some men call the past and the future,* has only emphasized this sense of foreboding. The *revolutionary* government of France with its new permanent first consul, young Napoleon Bonaparte, *threatens not only the political habits of the states around it, but also their social, intellectual and artistic life. Nothing is steady or certain any more. People feel as if a new breed of men as well as ideas are loose among the loved, familiar things.* And they resent it. They are attracted to it. They hate it, love it, fear it. . . . [We will] try to interview a musician whose strange career typifies in a most significant way *the emergence of the new with its arrogance, its hostility to the past, its sense of urgency and passion.* (pp. 261-262)

Music, in this episode, will metaphorically represent a wide range of social and political allusions in both historical and contemporary contexts—what Polonsky has discerned as "the liberty of the soul" in conflict with "the chains of convention and snobbery." The following is a character's personal narrative, but note the wider social implications:

COUNTESS DEYM

I recall when my sisters and myself were children and lived a life wild and unrestrained on our estate at Martonvasar. There in those great expanses, half marsh, half desert, we were free to be what our hearts made us. When we grew up . . . a husband was chosen for me, a life selected for me, a regimen prescribed for me. I lived, but as it were, on the surface. In this new music of this obscure stranger from Bonn, I feel again some of that liberty of the soul that made each day magical in my youth, and some of that depth and velvet quality that made each night a poem, some of that romantic turbulence, the breath of nature, of human nature, opposed to the sterile society in which we all live. It is as if in this man and his music, the energy, the wildness, the whole brooding future of this newborn nineteenth century comes alive. I welcome it. (p. 275)

These editorial notes have posited an approach toward Polonsky's work which might help define his philosophical orientation. Since "The Torment of Beethoven" may be the richest, most extended exploration of these ideas in the *You Are There* series, a few further comments might be useful.

The famous existentialist writer Albert Camus advances a theory of art in an appropriately titled book, *The Rebel [L'Homme revolte]*. In this work Camus argues that all artists in one way or another revolt against the natural formlessness of life and reconstruct the world according to their own plan. The artist, through the exercise of selectivity, creates out of the chaotic world known to us a world that is peopled by men and women who complete things which we in the real world cannot ever consummate. Through the isolation of the subject matter in time and space, the artist unifies and reconstructs the world according to a plan and can "stylize and imprison one significant expression" in order to illuminate one aspect of the "infinite variety of human attitudes." [Camus, *The Rebel* (Vintage Books, 1956), p. 256.]

Within this philosophy, man is called upon to recreate the world in spite of the inevitability of death; for it is only through the recognition of the power of the individual to effect a positive change in the values of the world that a person can hope for any degree of human happiness. These ideas help make comprehensible the fictional works of artists like Camus, Polonsky, and others which concern people's quest to find value in a world of constant change and endless contradiction. In a sense, the characters in these works know that they will never achieve final triumph in their struggle with the world; but they also know that for life to have any meaning, they must follow the only course open to them and create their own values within the limits imposed upon them by their own natures. They all echo the statement of Camus in *The Rebel* that "on my self alone rests the common dignity which I cannot allow to be debased either in myself or others." (Camus, *The Rebel*, p. 277.)

In "The Torment of Beethoven" Polonsky helps to establish these dark assumptions about the world—a raw, indifferent universe from which the artist must select his materials—through the words of noted composer Franz Joseph Hayden: "[Beethoven's] music cries out that those who are happy are falsely happy . . . that there is no rest and refreshment on this earth . . . that we are marked for doom and sorrow, and death is everywhere about us. He struggles with an underworld of phantoms and ghosts, monsters drawn from the deeps. . . . [Beethoven's music] belongs to this new age in which no man knows whether he will live or die from day to day."

For Beethoven, a prototype of the existential artist if ever there were such a thing, the potential for despair entered with his deafness. By 1802 he knew that his malady was both permanent and progressive. During a summer spent at the village of Heiligenstadt he wrote the "Heiligenstadt Testament," which puts the sense of Hayden's words into a painfully personal context. The document begins: "O ye men who think or say that I am malevolent, stubborn or misanthropic, how greatly do you wrong me. You do not know the cause of my seeming so. From childhood my heart and mind was disposed to the gentle feeling of good will. I was ever eager to accomplish great deeds, but reflect now that for six years I have been in a hopeless case, made worse by ignorant doctors, yearly betrayed in the hope of getting better, finally forced to face the prospect of a permanent malady whose cure will take years or even prove impossible."

He was tempted to take his own life. But what existential palliative prevented him? "Only Art held back; for, ah, it seemed unthinkable for me to leave the world forever before I had produced all that I felt called upon to produce." And it is indeed significant that Polonsky chooses to end his portrait of this challenged artist by selecting words from Beethoven's letter to his friend Franz Wegeler: "I am in exile . . . and yet *my conception of life is heroic, to struggle, to seize fate by the throat and strangle it.* . . . I cry out that I will not be defeated . . . and yet all the while I am defeated! (he starts to play) So I imagine . . . I call to mind, I reach into the unknown which surrounds us all to touch fate itself . . . with the hand and soul of the hero. And I see a step beyond which no man has gone. . .where I will go I say. . .which I must reach . . ." (p. 284)

The rhapsodic nature of Polonsky's writing—especially evidenced in Cronkite's tag at the end—offers strong linguistic documentation that, in Beethoven's torment and its attempted amelioration, Polonsky found a tragic, poetic, and noble subject who was in harmony with his own personal vision: "Deafness finally overcame Beethoven, but on that extraordinary night in Heiligenstadt he found the will to overcome his destiny. He found the courage to struggle and persist. The kings and aristocrats, their institutions and ideals, perished from the world, while Beethoven, the rebel, created a new universe of feeling and thought which is ours today. He was truly a *hero*." (p. 285)

❖❖❖

"Erich Leinsdorf was the guest conductor for the New York Philharmonic at the time so I," writes producer Charles Russell, "contacted him and sent him a script to read. He called me, almost immediately and demanded that he supervise the music on the show, supply the musicians required for the pre-recording session of the music indicated in the script—and he insisted that everyone be paid only scale. I accepted gratefully. The recording session included parts of a string quartet and a piano sonata—derived from his personal copy of an unpublished piano composition. Part of this was on camera, and the hands of Erich's pianist doubled for Lorne Greene's hands on a dummy keyboard. Lorne Greene [of *Bonanza* fame] was Beethoven. The rest of the music was used off-stage during on camera scenes.

"The script was excellent, the show was very good, and [production manager] Walter Blake did not have to ask me, 'Where did you find Leo Davis?'" [Davis was Polonsky's front.] (Russell, "In the Worst of Times," p. 142.)

Walter Blake was a close associate of Bill Dozier, and, of course, was not taken into Russell's confidence concerning the use of blacklisted writers. But this deep into the series, and in light of Dozier's comment regarding Polonsky's authorship of the "Jazz" show (see preface to "The Emergence of Jazz," p. 237), things were beginning to unravel. Thus, there were certain ominous overtones in Blake's earlier comments to Russell about "Kate Nickerson's" (Arnold Manoff's) script of "The Trial of Susan B. Anthony": "Kate Nickerson is a very good writer, where did you find her?" said Blake. "She's a short story writer," Russell replied, "and a friend of Paddy Cheyefsky. He introduced us and she had a good idea for a *Danger* show—and I think she likes me." Blake looked at Russell and said, "You sly fox."

There were many ways that Russell could interpret that remark: 1) Oh, you ladies man, you; 2) Blake and Dozier know that Russell is using some blacklisted writers; 3) Blake had guessed that Nickerson was the front for Manoff, whose nickname was the grey fox. How much did Dozier and Blake really know?

Leo Davis was now fronting for Polonsky on "The Torment of Beethoven." This time Russell did not fear a question regarding Davis's provenance. Leo Davis had been the associate producer on the final live shows of *You Are There* and had written several scripts for *Danger*; he was therefore a known presence.

But, as Walter Bernstein writes, no front was ever permanent: "Permanency was an illusion. There were too many reasons why people could not remain fronts. Fronting made impossible demands on the person. It was unnatural, a violation of the ego. You had constantly to pretend to be what you were not. Polonsky always thought the fronts were saving our lives while we were destroying theirs. I thought he exaggerated, but not by much. None of these high-minded thoughts kept us from using whoever was agreeable." (*Inside Out*, p. 239.)

Associate producer Bill Dozier had been lobbying to move the *You Are There* series to Hollywood, but Charles Russell thought of the problems involved if it did happen:

"Lumet, although he hadn't received any offers to work there, called Hollywood an industry town and was outspoken about never wanting to work there—he still feels the same way.

"My blacklisted writer friends were justifiably bitter about their Hollywood betrayal and I knew they would never consider going back there—but if the show did move it might be necessary, since the scripts required detailed discussion that couldn't be handled on the phone or in the mail. It wasn't that kind of series.

"I asked myself, 'What is the worst that can happen?' I had no answer. It was out of my control." (Russell, "In the Worst of Times," pp. 144-145.)

THE TORMENT OF BEETHOVEN
by Abraham Polonsky
(signed by Leo Davis)

Air Date:
January 2, 1955

YOU ARE THERE
October 6, 1802

FADE IN:

INT. CBS STUDIOS

CRONKITE
Walter Cronkite reporting. October 6, 1802. There is an uneasiness in Europe today, a sense of change and disaster. The peace treaty between Austria and France, between what some men call the past and the future, has only emphasized this sense of foreboding. The revolutionary government of France with its new permanent first consul, young Napoleon Bonaparte, threatens not only the political habits of the states around it, but also their social, intellectual and artistic life. Nothing is steady or certain any more. People feel as if a new breed of men as well as ideas are loose among the loved, familiar things. And they resent it. They are attracted to it. They hate it, love it, fear it.

In our attempt to present some of the main currents of this age of transition, we are going to take you to Vienna, capital of the Holy Roman Empire of Austria, Bohemia and Hungary . . . and there try to interview a musician whose strange career typifies
(MORE)

in a most significant way the emergence of the new with its
arrogance, its hostility to the past, its sense of urgency and
passion. That man is Ludwig van Beethoven.

This seems to be a time in which men erupt dramatically from
obscurity to seize the attention and sometimes the power in the
world. Nothing could be more remote from politics than
music, with its audience of aristocratic patrons, its salons, its
cheerful decent amusements, yet here, too, the dark, the
strange, the obscure has arrived in the person of young
Ludwig van Beethoven. And he has astounded Vienna, not so
much with his compositions, but with his demonic
improvisations on the piano, alienating and attracting in turn,
representing the *Sturm* and *Drang* of the time. What kind of
man he is, what he thinks he is doing, are questions he can
perhaps best answer himself. We take you to the suburbs of
Vienna. All things are as they were then, except . . . YOU ARE
THERE.

INT. PEASANT HOUSE — HEILIGENSTADT

It is dusk. We are in a corridor, or hallway. In the rear is a closed door
behind which can be heard piano music: soft brooding chords based on
the theme of the adagio of *The Third Symphony*. Very faint, as if the
keyboard is but touched. In the background, Beethoven's servant is
standing at the door listening. As the reporter talks, softly, quickly, the
camera moves in slowly upon servant and the closed door.

MARBLE
This is Harry Marble in Heiligenstadt, a small town near
Dobling, in the suburbs of imperial Vienna. We are in a
peasant house to which Herr van Beethoven has retreated for
peace and quiet. The man listening at the door is his servant
and we have asked permission to interview the famous
virtuoso pianist.

The camera has reached the servant and door. A brilliant chord strikes
within. Then the keyboard is smashed, a splatter of discord. Silence.
The servant turns into camera, shrugs his shoulders.

SERVANT
Perhaps later. Perhaps. But now, no.

MARBLE
If you would just ask him, please, perhaps . . . .

SERVANT
Impossible.

MARBLE
He doesn't seem to be playing at the moment . . . .

SERVANT
Impossible. Even his patrons, members of the aristocracy, the
Princes Lichnowsky, Lobkowitz, even Prince Kinsky, even . . .
        (he smirks)
. . . his female acquaintances, none would be admitted.
        (he moves slowly toward
        camera which retreats)
Herr van Beethoven has given me absolute instructions not to
be disturbed when he is working . . . .

MARBLE
And when he isn't working?

SERVANT
        (shrugs)
That's even worse.

A series of great pounding chords within in which the fate theme of the
opening of *The Fifth Symphony* can be heard. These are themes present in
his sketchbooks of the period. Then silence. The servant raises his right
forefinger and makes a screwing motion into his right temple to indicate
that Beethoven is crazy.

MARBLE
Is he ill or something, is that what you mean?

SERVANT
        (shrugs, smiles knowingly)
Yesterday he threw the soup in my face. I told him I was
leaving, that it was humiliating in this enlightened age to be
        (MORE)

SERVANT (CON'T)

treated in this way. He then took the hot tureen, handed it to
me, and directed me in the name of the French Revolution to
throw the contents at him.

MARBLE

And did you?

SERVANT

He would have killed me. He is a very powerful man. I
suppose he is a very great man. However, he has terrible
manners and a worse temper.

Front door opens and two young men enter. The younger, JOHANN,
tall, dashing . . . a dandy. The older, short, ugly, redheaded . . . CARL.
Servant bows low to them and they turn curiously to camera.

SERVANT

The brothers of Herr van Beethoven, Johann and Casper Carl
van Beethoven.

CARL

I am my brother's secretary and manager, and a notary in His
Majesty's national bank. At your service, sir.

JOHANN

And I, sir, am a licensed apothecary.

MARBLE

We would like to interview your brother.

CARL
(exchanging a conspiratorial
glance with brother)

That, sir, I think is impractical. My brother is a man who
avoids society and dislikes the presence of strangers.
However, any information which would add to his fame and
fortune, I would be glad to offer. I am, after all, somewhat of a
composer myself and I handle all of my poor brother's affairs.

MARBLE

It is said that you have tried to cut him off from his friends, to
isolate him . . . .

CARL
(angrily)
Not true.

JOHANN
(smoothly)
Only in the sense that we are buffers between my brother and all those who exploit his talents and use him for their own purposes.
(to servant arrogantly)
Tell my brother that we are here and wish to see him at once.

CARL
Ludwig is absentminded, of a sensitive and delicate nature. He leaves his compositions carelessly about to be stolen by others. He has no sense of the value of money and would be cheated right and left by the music publishers if it weren't for my care.

JOHANN
A whole tribe of leeches have gathered about him.

CARL
I do his negotiating, all his business . . . and when he is very busy, sometimes I do his musical arranging, and even, when in haste or carelessness he forgets to finish a section of work, why naturally I complete it for him . . . .

BEETHOVEN
(Beethoven's voice inside
yelling)
No, no . . . .
(as the door flies open and the
servant backs out)
Tell those two fraternal thieves that I have no more money for them to steal. Tell them to go back to the gutter out of which they came. I have nothing for them. I don't want to see them. They're not my brothers. They're highway robbers, beggars, cutpurses, filth, swine . . . .

The door slams shut. The brothers look uneasily at each other, embarrassed.

CARL
My brother, as you can see, is of a tempestuous and temperamental nature. But we understand . . . we comprehend the difficulties of genius.
>(from within a storm of piano
>music reflecting the mood)

Some other time, perhaps . . .

MARBLE
Thank you Carl and Johann van Beethoven. We'll return later to see if an interview is possible. Come in, Lou Cioffi, in Vienna.

[INT. HAYDEN'S HOME

HAYDEN is seventy, getting quite frail. His servant JOHANN ELLSLER, age thirty-three, will fuss about him, and serve him tea in the English fashion. Hayden is neat, contained, precise, with an air of serenity now being tainted with the melancholy of old age. Ellsler is putting a rug about Hayden's knees. The setting should be a corner of an eighteenth century drawing room, with a table full of object d'art. It is dusk.

CIOFFI
>(low voice, respectful, in the
>presence of a great old man)

This is Lou Cioffi on the west side of Vienna, number 19 Steingasse, the home of Franz Joseph Hayden, who is sitting here before us. As you all know, Herr Hayden, a native of Vienna, has dominated for more than thirty years the musical life of Europe.
>(as the servant moves aside)

Sir, we should like to ask you some questions about musical life in Vienna?

HAYDEN
>(pleasant, ironic)

And I would like to answer, if I can remember. Now it is that I sometimes find it a little difficult to recall things, but I will try.

CIOFFI

Who would you say, sir, of all the composers in the field has the greatest promise for the future?

HAYDEN

You mean, I presume, who will succeed me, now that I am almost dead?

CIOFFI

Why, no, sir.

HAYDEN

(smiling)

Why, yes, sir. Naturally . . . I have given it some thought, one does, without wanting to. With Mozart dead, there seems to be no one of great moment except the Grand Mogul, and Heaven knows just what it is he is promising.

CIOFFI

The Grand Mogul?

HAYDEN

(laughing)

I call him that, this wild Turk of music . . . the composer from Bonn, Ludwig Beethoven.

CIOFFI

He was a pupil of yours?

HAYDEN

(chuckling)

He studied counterpoint with me, but was displeased so he went to that old organ grinder, Schenck, and took lessons on the sly, all the while pretending he was studying with me. He is an original, sir, in this age of originals. Napoleon is an original. Beethoven, too, and he stalks Vienna like a little Napoleon, planning great campaigns to astonish and humble the musical world.

The servant comes in with tea, which Hayden takes and sips.

CIOFFI

Would you say you have influenced him?

HAYDEN

Indeed, but fundamentally, he is individual, different. If I
compose the music of daylight and the sun, then his is the
music of the night and the moon. I look around me. I see that
there are but few contented and happy men here below on
earth. Everywhere grief and care prevail. Perhaps my labors
in the field of music may one day be a source from which the
weary and the worn, or the men burdened with affairs, may
derive a few moments rest and refreshment. That is my
musical goal. But Beethoven seems to show a contrary strain, I
would say. His music cries out that those who are happy are
falsely happy . . . that there is no rest and refreshment on this
earth . . . that we are marked for doom and sorrow, and death
is everywhere about us. He struggles with an underworld of
phantoms and ghosts, monsters drawn from the deeps. That
may be music, sir—it is certainly a kind of genius, of energy—
but it is not my music nor my kind. It belongs to this new age
in which no man knows whether he will live or die from day
to day.

CIOFFI

Do you think young Beethoven will ever achieve your fame
and reputation?

HAYDEN

If his kind of world comes to birth then he will be its hero.

CIOFFI

As you have been in yours?

HAYDEN

Thank you, sir. Beethoven will be himself, whatever it is, for
good or evil, for greatness or disaster . . . if his talent comes to
flower . . . .

CIOFFI

Then you think it has not yet . . . matured?

HAYDEN

The real Beethoven comes to life only when he improvises, and
never, sir, in the history of music, has such a marvel come to
pass upon the keyboard. It is as if he, like the Faust of our

(MORE)

HAYDEN (CON'T)
great Goethe, had made a compact with a musical devil . . . for
hell itself comes forth from beneath his hands . . . and yet, of
such a sweetness and marvel of spontaneity that is beyond
description. In his composed works there are as yet only signs
of all this. He is a fine composer . . . a little odd . . . . This is
not yet the man whose breath we hear when lost at the
keyboard he lets his strange spirit brood upon its mysteries. If
that should ever come to birth in his works, then, sir, to the
names Bach, Hayden and Mozart, history will add that of
Beethoven.

CIOFFI
Thank you, Herr Hayden.

HAYDEN
It is a pleasure to wake briefly from this slumber of old age to
observe the world again.

CIOFFI
The composer of the *Creation* can only look forward to greater
triumphs . . . .

HAYDEN
In another world, sir, perhaps, but not in this one. It has
exhausted me.

CIOFFI
Thank you. Come in, Ned Calmer . . . .]

INT. PRINCE LICHNOWSKY'S

Should consist of an elegant salon and ante-room separated by doors. In
the salon are a bevy of handsome women, some men, etc. Four chairs
have been arranged about a piano for music, but are empty. The people
are being served with light refreshments. In the anteroom, or side room,
there is a table at which the servants replenish their supplies and there
with their quartet of instruments lounge four young men, the players. In
salon, behind half closed doors, Prince CARL LICHNOWSKY, a strong,
rather impressive man, is chatting with the ladies. Camera in anteroom
with general view of the scene. It is evening.

CALMER

This is Ned Calmer at the home of Prince Carl Lichnowsky, one of the patrons of Beethoven. There is going to be a musicale shortly and we will be able to interview the Prince as soon as he is free. You can see him in the salon there chatting with Countess Deym, the former Josephine Brunswik, one of three beautiful sisters with whose names that of Beethoven has been associated. The countess is a pupil of Beethoven's as is her young cousin, Giulietta Guicciardi, to whom Beethoven dedicated his now famous *Piano Sonata in C Sharp Minor*. While we are waiting for the Prince, we can talk with the musicians who spend their time with the other servants until they are needed.

Camera in on young musicians who are gorging themselves on food and fooling around with a pretty maidservant. She has a tray in her hand and is helpless. The leader of the four is a very fat young man, IGNAZ SCHUPPANZIGH. All are twenty or under.

CALMER (CON'T)

This is Ignaz Schuppanzigh, the leader of the quartet. He plays first violin.

The instruments are there, too, and KRAFT has one arm around the girl and other about his cello.

SCHUPPANZIGH
(with a mock bow of courtesy)
Or Herr Falstaff as the Herr van Beethoven calls me. And this is Sina, second violin . . . Weiss, viola . . . and Kraft . . .
(just about to let the girl go after
taking a kiss)
. . . who plays the cello and the chambermaids with equal dexterity.

Each young man bows in turn, with mockery and humor. They have a slapdash air, like most students.

CALMER

You head up this quartet which is supported by Prince Lichnowsky.

SCHUPPANZIGH

We belong to the prince who in turn has directed us to play for the Maestro at his beck and call. We are the first to play his string music.

CALMER

Perhaps you can account for his reputation as a strange man. Is that the way he seems to you?

SCHUPPANZIGH

To us he is a wonderful friend. He lends us money. He cooks up a meal for us . . . terrible, but with love. He sends us a note . . . come to my place and we arrive and all night we thump and bump and romp and play and sing and drink. We do not find him strange. But . . .
(with a jerk of his thumb to the
salon)
. . . in there, he is a little strange. He refuses to sit with the servants, as we do and must. He will not wait his turn, or be anything but the equal of the lords and ladies who pay for his compositions. He is proud and independent and to a prince, a count, a baron, this on the part of a mere musician is indeed strange.

CALMER

He sounds like one of those French revolutionists.

SCHUPPANZIGH

No one in Vienna, sir, is a revolutionist. We are too much in love with the emperor. But the Maestro admires men of energy like Napoleon.

CALMER

Are you going to play anything of Beethoven's at this musicale?

SCHUPPANZIGH

One of his trios.

CALMER

The one that caused all the comment?

SCHUPPANZIGH
The one that Hayden said was too far ahead of the public
. . . but, sir, how far ahead must a piece of music be to be
beyond a prince?

The young men laugh.

CALMER
What do you find remarkable in Beethoven's music?

SCHUPPANZIGH
The beginning of something new.

KRAFT
He writes for us the way Hayden wrote for our fathers.

At this moment the door opens and the prince appears together with the
COUNTESS DEYM. Graciously he motions to the musicians who at
once grow polite, deferential and take up their instruments and file in
between the prince and the countess.

PRINCE
Thank you, gentlemen . . . .

He is somewhat ironic. During part of the conversation we will hear the
instruments being tuned.

PRINCE (CON'T)
(to camera as it closes in on him
and countess)
I have given thought to your request, sir, and asked the
Countess Deym to be here with me. She was and is a friend of
the composer in question . . .

COUNTESS
And have been a pupil, along with my sisters.

ZMESKALL shoulders his way out of the salon and closes the door
behind him. He is a man of forty.

PRINCE

And this is Count Nicolaus Zmeskall von Domanovecz, an
official of the Royal Hungarian Chancellory, a close friend of
the composer and himself an incomparable cellist and
composer of music.

ZMESKALL

(bowing to prince)

Thank you, Prince, but to my friend, Beethoven, I am other
things besides.

(he takes two notes from his
pocket)

I save his notes, realizing full well that my only fame in life
will be to have known him.

(to camera)

An if you are interested in his character and philosophy there
is a passage here that might illuminate both . . . .

(reads)

My dearest Baron Muckcartdriver . . .

COUNTESS

(laughing)

He seems to resent your rank.

ZMESKALL

And yours, too, Pepi, but since you are beautiful and so
simpatica, and I am neither, he puts up with your hauteur as
he would not do with mine.

PRINCE.

You should be prouder, Count.

ZMESKALL

I am only a count by sufferance, not like your rank, sir, which
is hereditary.

PRINCE

I grant you that even to me he shows a little less than the
ordinary courtesy, thinking nothing of walking out of my
house at the least sign of discourtesy on the part of a servant or
a lord.

His bad manners seem to be in part shyness and in part a
philosophy. Listen . . . .
    (reading)
I forbid you henceforth to rob me of the good humor into
which I occasionally fall, for yesterday your Zmeskall-
Damonovitzian chatter made me melancholy. The devil take
you. I want none of your moral precepts for power is the
morality of men who loom above the others, as it is also
mine . . . .
    (looking up)
You note that.

COUNTESS

Sometimes I think he is utterly mad. He brings a new sonata
to my house and I play it. Then he starts to shout . . . not
pianissimo, fortissimo . . . and I am playing fortissimo all the
time.

PRINCE

That is his absentmindedness which increases from day to day.
It makes him act like one of these mad followers of the French,
without regard for anything in the past, people, ideas,
customs.]

The door behind is opened by a servant and attracts the attention of the
prince. A pale and lovely woman appears there. The prince bows to her
and then into camera.

PRINCE (CON'T)

The princess is impatient. You will excuse us, sir, for I am to
play the piano and Zmeskall the cello parts of one of the
Beethoven Trios.

Both men bow to the countess and go within. The door is closed in part.

CALMER

Thank you Prince Lichnowsky and Count von Zmeskall.
Countess Deym, what is your particular interest in Herr van
Beethoven?

COUNTESS

You mean, I presume, in his music?

CALMER
In that, too.

COUNTESS
(as the *Trio in C Minor* begins
within)
Both he and his music, sir, give one a profound sense of one's
own value, the value of one's individual life, and this, sir, is
something that even a countess infrequently feels in her circle
of life.
(she half turns to the closed
door)
Infrequently.
(then back again)
I recall when my sisters and myself were children and lived a
life wild and unrestrained on our estate at Martonvasar. There
in those great expanses, half marsh, half desert, we were free
to be what our hearts made us. When we grew up, we were
brought here. A husband was chosen for me, a life selected for
me, a regimen prescribed for me. I lived, but as it were, on the
surface. In this new music of this obscure stranger from Bonn,
I feel again some of that liberty of the soul that made each day
magical in my youth, and some of that depth and velvet
quality that made each night a poem, some of that romantic
turbulence, the breath of nature, of human nature, opposed to
the sterile society in which we all live. It is as if in this man
and his music, the energy, the wildness, the whole brooding
future of this newborn nineteenth century comes alive. I
welcome it.

She quickly turns and enters the salon.

CALMER
We now take you back to the home of Beethoven. Come in,
Harry Marble

EXT. PEASANT HOUSE — HEILIGENSTADT

A door in the dusk, and a lighter window.

MARBLE

This is Harry Marble again, just outside of Beethoven's house
in Heiligenstadt. We are waiting for the return of the great
virtuoso who is expected back momentarily. Two visitors are
waiting for him, one of whom Vienna gossips call La Belle
Guicciardi, a young girl whose name has been romantically
linked with Beethoven's. With her is Count Gallenberg.
Beethoven comes stalking out of the night into the house.

MARBLE (CON'T)

Giulietta Guicciardi is a pupil of the composer. Here he is
now.
                    (a moment later Ries follows . . .
                    he stops at the camera)
Ferdinand Ries, a protégé of Beethoven's.

RIES
                    (who seems distraught and
                    worried)
There won't be any chance. I've asked him. He absolutely
refuses. Absolutely. My own feeling is, sir, that he is unwell at
the moment and incapable of being interviewed calmly and
intelligently.

MARBLE

We're sorry to hear that.
                    (Ries starts to move away,
                    pauses)
Ferdinand Ries is one of the most brilliant of the younger
pianists in Vienna today.

RIES
                    (absently)
Thank you.
                    (he hesitates)
I had the most extraordinary experience today. It seems
incredible and yet it happened.
                    (he is quite shaken)
I went for my usual walk with Beethoven. We walked over to
that valley just between here and that long vista to the
Carpathians. It's a favorite spot of the Maestro's . . . .
                                                    (MORE)

RIES (CON'T)
(he stops)
The thing is, von Bruening, he's one of the Maestro's oldest
friends, remarked on this fact last winter. It's unbelievable.

MARBLE

What fact, sir?

RIES
(he walks so that the window is
behind him)
I believe . . . I'm sure Dr. Schmidt suspects it . . . and this is
why he ordered the Maestro to this quiet countryplace.

MARBLE

Yes?

RIES
(losing his voice)
We were walking along and suddenly from the woods I heard
a shepherd piping quite agreeably on a flute made of elder. It
was a charming and melancholy folk tune such as the Maestro
loves, and I stopped. He saw me halt and paused also, looking
about him with interest while I listened a few minutes. I then
remarked how beautifully the shepherd was playing . . . and
he looked at me . . . and asked . . .
(he pauses)
. . . What shepherd, where? And then as I pointed to the
woods and he looked . . . suddenly he turned back, a tragic
and surprised expression on his face. I could still hear that
clear and pleasant piping. And he said . . ."Where . . . in what
direction . . . ?" [I pointed and he began to walk toward it,
cocking his head forward, listening intently . . . and then
wandered off, going away from the music. I took his arm . . .
and he shook it off and cursed me for an idiot and began to
laugh boisterously, crying out it was a joke against me.
(he looks about incredulously)
Von Bruening said he thought the Maestro's hearing was not
good. Today it was bad . . . and] I wonder with horror if it is
not possible that he is growing deaf?

MARBLE

Do you think it's possible?

RIES

I don't know. It would be a tragedy beyond description.

BEETHOVEN
(calling from within)
Ries, you devil, where are you?

RIES

Excuse me.

He hurries to the front door. The camera moves slowly to the window and then just seems to tip toe in.

INT. BEETHOVEN'S STUDY

Beethoven has opened the inner door and is calling to Ries. The girl and the young man seem to be nervously waiting, side by side, as Ries comes in.

BEETHOVEN
We're waiting for you. You know my fair pupil, the lovely Giulietta, and that is Count Gallenberg who has come to show us a little bagatelle of his.

GIULIETTA
It is more than that.

BEETHOVEN
With most composers, my dear, it is usually less. I have written bagatelles which were not fit to be seen, but my rascally brother Carl stole them and sold them to some mad publisher. I regret them . . . . But come, Count, let us unbag this bagatelle of yours, and play loudly, sir, for I have a humming in my ears such as birds make when they fly to die in a hunter's gun.

As GALLENBERG goes to piano and sets up his music quite nervously, Beethoven comes and takes the girl's hand, kisses it.

BEETHOVEN (CON'T)
It was charming of you to make this excuse for seeing me.

GIULIETTA

It's no excuse. I wanted you to meet the young count who, despite his rank, is also a composer like yourself. I thought it would please you.

The music starts. It is a mechanical little thing with a pleasant melody which tinkles on. Beethoven slowly comes to the piano. He leans over, listening, and his face gets angrier and angrier. Suddenly he grabs the music from the piano.

BEETHOVEN

Enough. Too much. Extraordinary. You come all the way from Vienna to play something for me that was already second hand fifty years ago when some dunce made it up to please some chambermaid?

He pushes the count away from the piano.

COUNT

She wanted me to play it for you, sir.

BEETHOVEN
(laughing, a little wildly)

To make fun of you. This is a joke, my dear Count. My charming little pupil knows enough to realize that this is nonsense. But look, if I turn it upside down, and fling some ink on it . . .
> (he suits his words, sprinkling
> the page with inkblobs)

. . . and if I play the melody, playing all the ink marks as well as flies and scratches on it . . . upside down and backwards . . . then it makes a little theme . . . .
> (playing with one finger)

. . . and then if to the theme I add the fire and passion of music . . . something comes.

He improvises brilliantly and briefly. He stops with a thump and rips up the music.

BEETHOVEN (CON'T)

Back to your hunting and salons, dear Count, and leave the music to Beethoven.

Coming up to the girl and leaving the humiliated young man standing there.

                    BEETHOVEN (CON'T)
You mustn't play such tricks on these poor youths who like myself love you too much, Giulietta . . .

She goes to the count and takes his hand.

                    GIULIETTA
It was no trick. I wanted you to see that I respect you enough to fall in love with someone of my own rank who is also a musician. We will be married within the year and I wanted you to hear it from me.

They stand hand in hand and Beethoven is crestfallen.

                    BEETHOVEN
Another joke?
                    (he cries out)
I'm the only one who makes jokes around here. What do you mean?

                    GIULIETTA
I mean, sir, what I said. That Count Gallenberg is my betrothed. And Pepi said that I should tell you myself before you heard it through others.

                    BEETHOVEN
                    (sarcastically)
Let me congratulate you, Count. You have evidently given her better lessons than I, and had I known, I would have dedicated my sonata to both of you, to remind you of how music should be written and your betrothed of how much I misunderstood her many kindnesses to me. Goodnight.

He turns his back on them.

                    COUNT
I only wish to say, sir . . .

                    BEETHOVEN
Goodnight.

Ries closes the door behind them.

BEETHOVEN (CON'T)
(with savage humor)
She came here to crush me, but I think they'll remember me
longer than I remember them.

RIES
(trying to lighten it all)
The ladies often mistake their love of music for the music
maker, as I have seen and you know, Maestro.

BEETHOVEN
(interrupting him gloomily)
Come here, Ries.

As Ries comes over, Beethoven puts his hands on his shoulders.

BEETHOVEN (CON'T)
You know . . . .

RIES
(playing it innocently)
What do I know, Maestro?

BEETHOVEN
Don't play the dunce, Ries. You know . . . you know I am
growing deaf. I've hidden it for two years. Who else knows?

RIES
No one. It's only temporary, a condition that comes from your
colic.

BEETHOVEN
(doggedly ignoring him)
It is not temporary. It is permanent and every day it grows
worse. Who else knows?

RIES
Stephen von Bruening . . . he suspects . . . .

BEETHOVEN
Who else?

RIES

No one, Maestro . . . .

[BEETHOVEN

I wrote to Amenda and Wegler. They know. But no one else
must, you understand . . . no whisperings, no suspicious
talking, nothing, you hear me.
(savagely)
Think how it would look to my rivals here, a deaf musician. It
is as idiotic as a blind painter, a speechless orator.]

RIES

It can be something that comes and goes . . . .

Beethoven picks up a tuning fork from the piano. He strikes it and holds
it at arms length.

BEETHOVEN

Can you hear it?

RIES

Yes.

BEETHOVEN

Out there I cannot. The buzzing in my ears drowns it out.

He paces the room in silence and Ries watches not knowing what to say,
how to comfort him. Suddenly Beethoven breaks out in the great cry of
the Heiligenstadt document.

BEETHOVEN (CON'T)

Men declare that I am malevolent, stubborn, misanthropic.
How greatly they wrong me, who do not know the secret
cause behind the appearance. All my life, from childhood
even, I longed to do great deeds, heroic ones. My secret dream
was the dream of the hero, the human hero striding through
the world, defying fate and eternity. And yet, for six long
years this secret affliction has crept up upon me until it has
become an incurable affliction. I, whose temperament is fiery,
impulsive, passionate. I, who love the distractions of society
people, gaiety, life and the world. I am slowly being doomed
like a wild beast to solitude, to silence, to the prison of despair.

RIES
(gently)
Let your friends who love you, let them know, and they will be
the world around you.

BEETHOVEN
(in despair)
How can I? [When I venture near some social gathering I am
seized with burning terror, the fear that I may be found out.
How can I possibly admit that I am defective in the one sense
which in me should be more highly developed than in all men,
a sense which I once possessed in its perfect form, a form as
perfect as few in my profession surely know or have known in
the past.] I shrink back. I cannot mingle. I think I hear them
whispering around me . . . . Beethoven is deaf . . . he is deaf . . .
deaf.

He bangs the piano with his fists once. The great jangle of the chord.

BEETHOVEN (CON'T)
I fear the day when even this will be silent. I fear as I sit
playing that no sound comes forth. I tremble . . . and all the
while I hear the humming and buzzing, the ringing of dreadful
sounds in my head that no one hears in the world, and
meanwhile, the birds are silent, the shepherd's song, the
whisper of voices, a woman's laugh, the child's cry.
Everything human is lost and only the inner cacophony goes
on. I am being drowned in my own noises. At such moments
I am driven to the verge of despair and today I contemplate
with hope the very thought of ending my own life. I tell you,
Ries, only one thing held me back, one thing. Art. It seemed
impossible. I defied that fate which would drive me from life
before I had produced all that I felt capable of producing.

He takes his conversation book which lies on the piano and holds it
before Ries.

BEETHOVEN (CON'T)
You know this book. Here I sketched the ideas, the dreams,
the visions of sound which are the very language of my inmost
thoughts. These I hear in all the buzzing and all the silence.
I told myself to be patient. Be patient and it will pass. But the
deafness will not pass, the suffering does not pass . . . and
everything I am passes into the silence . . .
(almost in a whisper)
. . . the utter silence . . . .

Ries comes to the piano and opens the sketchbook. He looks at it and at
Beethoven, and then to distract him.

RIES
What are these themes for . . . for what do you intend them?

BEETHOVEN
For a music that has never been heard before. But I have heard
it. I hear it now, under the noise in my head. I hear it welling,
this ineffable language that speaks to me. I stand over it like a
man who looks into a bottomless crevice. I hear it beneath the
last sounds that come to me from the world outside, hidden
beneath the things of life, of nature. I am a man who wonders
about his fate, who cannot forget the terrible poverty of
childhood, of my poor father reeling and broken with
drunkenness and my mother who died to escape the burden of
living. I cannot forget my poor bothers whom I love and the
love that I will never have because I am what I am. I am an
exile . . . and yet, my conception of life is heroic . . . to struggle,
to seize fate by the throat and strangle it. I cry out that I will
not be defeated . . . and yet, all the while, I am defeated!
(he starts to play)
So I imagine . . . I call to mind, I reach into the unknown which
surrounds us all to touch fate itself . . . with the hand and soul
of the hero. And I see a step beyond which no man has gone
. . . where I will go, I say . . . which I must reach . . .

He improvises from the famous notebook on the great themes of *Eroica*
and he is transported out of his state of despair while Ries retreats to
door.

INT. CBS STUDIOS

CRONKITE

It was on this night at Heiligenstadt that Beethoven, all alone with his own destiny, wrote that famous testament in which his spirit reached into death and then with utmost energy returned. And it was just after this night that he launched upon his new career and created his third symphony, the *Eroica*. Deafness finally overcame Beethoven, but on that extraordinary night in Heiligenstadt he found the will to overcome his destiny. He found the courage to struggle and persist. The kings and aristocrats, their institutions and ideals, perished from the world, while Beethoven, the rebel, created a new universe of feeling and thought which is ours today. He was truly a hero.

What sort of a day was it? A day like all days, filled with those events that alter and illuminate our time . . . and YOU WERE THERE.

FADE OUT.

THE TRAGEDY OF JOHN MILTON

John Milton (b. 9 December 1608, London—d. 8 November 1674, Chalfont St. Giles, Buckinghamshire) stands next to Shakespeare among English poets; his writings and his influence are a very important part of the history of English literature, culture, and libertarian thought. He is best known for his long epic poem *Paradise Lost* (1667), in which his "grand style" is used with superb power; its characterization of Satan is one of the supreme achievements of world literature. Milton's prose works, however, are also important as a valuable interpretation of the Puritan revolution, and they have their place in modern histories of political and religious thought.

It was pointed out in the prefatory notes to "Cortes Conquers Mexico" (p. 40) how these 1950s *You Are There* episodes took for granted an intelligent viewership, an audience which either possessed the requisite knowledge of an individual show's historical context, or the willingness, once stimulated by the dramatization, to pursue additional information on the subject. Polonsky's script for "John Milton" assumes audience knowledge of: the so-called "Eleven Years' Tyranny" of Charles I (1629-1640), the British Civil War (1640-1649), Oliver Cromwell and the Interregnum (Commonwealth Period, 1649-1660), and the Restoration of Charles II.

In order to appreciate Polonsky's nuanced manipulation of the political and intellectual freedom issues of 1660 as a mechanism to comment on those same issues in a 1950s context—the reader and/or viewer needs to be able to understand those scrutinized values as they are associated with Cromwell's Commonweath and as they are in conflict with the "Eleven Years' Tyranny" and the Restoration.

Here is historian Maurice Ashley on Oliver Cromwell: "In all his political compromises and even during the period of Puritan military dictatorship which he imposed, Oliver Cromwell never departed from the principle that he held dear, that of 'liberty of conscience.' This principle was ingrained within him. Cromwell in his heart believed in what most of us mean by freedom of the spirit. He maintained that it was 'an unjust and unwise jealously to deprive a man of his natural liberty upon a supposition that he may abuse it: when he doth abuse it,' he added, 'then judge.' Cromwell believed that the mind was the man.

He thought we all have a right within limits to seek truth in our own fashion. These political and economic freedoms which came down to us with the spirit of nonconformity we owe in no small measure to the precepts of Oliver Cromwell. And the ferment of ideas that arose during the Interregnum was finally absorbed into English history." [*England In the Seventeenth Century, 1603-1714* (Penguin Books, 1958), pp. 103-104, 118.]

Clearly, Polonsky and his blacklisted colleagues had found their counterparts in the seventeenth-century personages of Oliver Cromwell and John Milton.

The years 1641-1660 Milton gave almost wholly to pamphleteering in the cause of religious and civil liberty. His best known pamphlets (at any rate for modern readers) were published in 1644. *Of Education* advocates the molding of an enlightened, cultivated, responsible citizenry. Its basis would be the study of the ancient classics, in due subordination to the Bible and Christian teaching. But he also gave notable emphasis to science. In *Areopagitica*, on the freedom of the press, he writes as a scholar and poet and lover of books and reasserts above all his belief in the power of truth to win its way through free inquiry and discussion.

On 13 February 1649, two weeks after the execution of Charles I, Milton's first political tract, *The Tenure of Kings and Magistrates*, appeared. In it he expounds the doctrine that power resides always in the people, who delegate it to a sovereign but may, if it is abused, resume it and depose or even execute the tyrant: "All men naturally were born free. . . . The power of Kings and Magistrates is nothing else but what is only derivative, transferr'd and committed to them in trust from the People, to the common good of them all, in whom the power yet remaines fundamentally, and cannot be taken from them without a violation of their natural birthright."

Milton's last political pamphlet, *The Readie and Easie Way to Establish a Free Commonwealth* (March 1660), was a courageous but futile act, since machinery was moving to bring back Charles II to power. Milton's essay is a cry of incredulity and despair from the last champion of "the good Old Cause." The glories of the Commonwealth, to which he himself had given 20 years and his eyesight, are being swept away by a nation of slaves "now choosing them a captain back from Egypt." The Restoration was the last and heaviest of Milton's many disillusionments.

Again there is the nobility of struggle in a losing cause. But the cause is what Milton calls "the great issue of our time: liberty . . . of conscience, of thought, of worship, of action." It is the great issue of every time and every age, but it is the issue which demands, in Polonsky's text, an active, ethical (existential) engagement, not passivity:

MILTON
I cannot praise a fugitive and cloistered virtue, unexercised and unbreathed, that never sallies out to see her adversary. . . . *That which purifies our natures is trial, and trial is by what is contrary. Only after a lifetime of struggle, of making the choice, doth a man live to die in innocence and virtue.*

❖❖❖

The memoirs of Charles Russell conclude with a sour betrayal and a poignant benediction: "On the last day Bill Dozier and I screened some dailies. We left the projection room and on the way to the elevator he said, 'There's no need for you to go to the cutting room tomorrow, the editor will handle it.' We stopped at the elevator doors and he pushed the down button, then said, '*You Are There* is going to be done in Hollywood from now on and I will be producing it. Also, your services are no longer required by CBS.' The elevator doors opened and he got on, while I just stood there and let him go down."

Russell maintains in his manuscript that Dozier told CBS that "he had *recently* [emphasis added] learned about Russell's subversive activities, including using blacklisted writers on the program—which could mean only one thing—and if that information was revealed it would seriously jeopardize the image of The Prudential Insurance Company" [the show's sponsor]. Thus, Russell and his blacklisted-writer colleagues would have to go.

As only one indication of Dozier's purported duplicitous motives, note the following:

• Dozier had made his earlier comment to Russell about Polonsky's writing—"Tell Abe I think it's a good script"—in connection with "The Emergence of Jazz" episode, which was broadcast on 5 September 1954.

• Russell's firing, precipitated by Dozier's "recent" knowledge of the blacklisted writers, occurred during post-production on "The Triumph of Alexander the Great," which was broadcast on 27 March 1955. The discrepancy in the dates seems to do some injury to the notion that the firings were driven by a *recent* revelation of facts or by ideological outrage.

Russell: "We all knew that Bill Dozier didn't care who wrote the shows as long as they were good and he gained the recognition. He reminded me of the man who sells his soul to the devil in exchange for knowledge and power—but Bill wanted it both ways: he didn't want to make the actual deal. Eternal damnation made him uncomfortable." A fascinating cultural and political phenomenon had ended.

As Walter Bernstein remembers: "Russell and Lumet and the three of us had been lucky to have found one another at a particular time and now that time was over. There was no doubt that Lumet's talent would be rewarded with success, and we three believed that by now, by virtue of our group, we also would somehow survive. . . . But Russell had stuck his neck out when he had everything to lose. He had done it for himself, for his self-respect and for what he felt was right, but he had also done it for us. There was no way we could thank him enough or pay him back. All we could do was worry about him, about his future." (*Inside Out*, p. 235.)

Charles Russell, fittingly, continues and concludes the narrative: "When I told my friends what had happened to *You Are There*, they were mostly concerned about what would happen to me. We talked about that for awhile, but somehow in the end it was the show itself that became suddenly a symbol of all I had lived through and what they had shared with me in the years of its success. It had become a voice of reason in an age of wild alarms. We began to remember and we began to laugh.

"It was like a wake, sad, and then, suddenly, laughter as the living goes on.

"We started to talk about other shows, other possibilities; we talked about everything, and in the end we knew, as friends, that we had been there in the worst of times and I knew that for me at least I would remember *You Are There* and my new friends as the best of times in my life." (Russell, "In the Worst of Times," pp. 149-152.)

THE TRAGEDY OF JOHN MILTON

by Abraham Polonsky

(signed by Jeremy Daniel)

Air Date:

January 30, 1955

YOU ARE THERE

August 13, 1660

FADE IN:

INT. CBS STUDIOS

> ### CRONKITE
> Walter Cronkite reporting. August 13, 1660. The restoration of
> Charles II to the throne of England continues smoothly as
> royalist politicians replace republican ones in all public offices,
> and former high church officials once again dominate the
> spiritual councils of the nation. In general, the people seem
> happy and attend in great numbers the fetes and festivals
> which have been arranged to mark the end of the 12 year old
> Commonwealth founded by the Puritan army under the
> leadership of Oliver Cromwell. Nevertheless, there have been
> a number of anxious inquiries from abroad about the fate of
> some distinguished republican Roundheads, notably the blind
> poet, John Milton.
>
> Each day as Parliament adds and subtracts names from the
> official list of those to be punished by death, imprisonment or
> other civil disabilities, new Puritan leaders have been arrested.
> The most notable of these are being held in the Tower of
> London. Others are being sought for throughout the land.
>
> (MORE)

CRONKITE (CON'T)
Among the latter are John Milton who disappeared from his home three months ago and has not been seen or heard of since. The fact that Milton is blind makes it difficult for him to travel and it is believed he is in hiding in London.

We take you to London where Parliament is in session . . . . All things are as they were then, except . . . YOU ARE THERE.

INT. PARLIAMENT

A corridor or foyer. A certain movement there, little knots of men.

MARBLE
This is Harry Marble and we are in the corridors outside the great room of the House. Inside they are still debating the names and fate of many Roundheads. There, to our left, talking to a few of his followers, is William Prynne, member for Newport in Cornwall. He is a leader of those who would extend the execution list widely.
> (Prynne wears a cowl and a
> muffled face)

And over there is Andrew Marvell who heads up a very small group of men who have resisted every attempt to extend the list of those to be punished.

MARBLE
Mr. Prynne?

PRYNNE
Sir?

MARBLE
What is the status of the Bill of Exceptions?

PRYNNE
Both houses are in consultation but we cannot as yet agree on the final names of those to be executed capitally.

MARBLE
We are informed, sir, that the delay is caused because of your constant addition of new names.

PRYNNE
That sounds like the criticism of Mr. Marvell.

MARBLE
You do add names each day, don't you?

PRYNNE
I do, and shall.

MARBLE
What is your reason?

PRYNNE
Because, while the House cannot punish all of these
Roundheads, I can draw attention to these vermin and keep
their names and crimes before the members and the people. In
this way they will suffer the pains of notoriety and the
punishment of their neighbors until such time as the anger and
hate of all the people rise and they force the king and the
parliament to go beyond this small list of regicides.

MARBLE
Do you think John Milton is an important republican criminal?

PRYNNE
He is the chief of the literary regicides.

MARVELL is moving up past Prynne and stops to listen, a smile of
contempt on his face.

MARBLE
It is said that you have personal reasons for disliking John
Milton.

MARVELL
(stepping in)
Indeed, Prynne has, for he has been worsted more than once in
a controversy with him.

PRYNNE
(viciously)
Mr. Marvell, I should advise you that being a member of
Parliament does not exempt you from charges which have led
to the punishment of others even more highly placed.

MARVELL

Mr. Prynne, your hate will not be satisfied until half the
kingdom is dead. Take off your cowl and show your cropped
ears and slit nose. Did John Milton do that or was it your love,
the late king's father, when he had you before the Star
Chamber? And yet you crawl now before the son and curse
those who would have saved your ears and nose. You are a
fanatic, sir, hot for blood, your soul twisted, playing on the
whims and fears of lords and commons.

PRYNNE
(with slow violence)

Sir, you were John Milton's assistant in his secretaryship. You
yourself may yet adorn this list of regicides.

MARVELL

No man is safe from you if he defies you. Your politics are
born of your lust for power, your religion of your hate for
mankind, not love. But I defy you, Prynne. Do what you can.

PRYNNE
(to camera)

The king has ordered today the seizure of the books of John
Milton and commanded they be burnt by the public hangman.
The writer will be so treated later.

MARVELL

And you are proud of that, Prynne?

PRYNNE

I would be prouder if Milton's head were pickled and stuck on
the pikes at Tyburn.

Prynne walks off.

MARVELL

Prynne is a madman.

MARBLE

Do you realize the grave risk you run, sir, in opposing these
popular measures for revenge?

MARVELL

I am not like those in the land, who, having shared the life of the republic, would now find safety by being first to cry down their own companions. I am not eager, sir, that my tombstone should read: "Here lies a man who survived despite all." He who dies after his principles have died, sir, has died too late.

MARBLE

Do you have any news of the whereabouts of John Milton?

MARVELL

I am not likely to have such news.

MARBLE

Have you heard anything at all about him?

MARVELL

You must pardon me, sir. I am needed in the House.

Marvell goes off.

MARBLE

Thank you, Andrew Marvell. We now take you to Herringman's, a popular London bookshop and stationer's, to interview the new poet-laureate of England. Come in, Lou Cioffi.

INT. HERRINGMAN'S — THE FAMOUS LONDON STATIONER'S ON THE NEW EXCHANGE

DAVENANT is posed and attentive against piled books. Beside him is HERRINGMAN, the publisher and bookseller.

CIOFFI

This is Lou Cioffi. We are in Herringman's shop at the sign of the Blue Anchor in the Lower Walk of the New Exchange, and here to our left is Mr. Herringman . . . .

HERRINGMAN
(nodding)
At your service, sir.

CIOFFI

And the other gentleman is Sir William Davenant, the new poet-laureate, and president, so to speak, of the world of letters under Charles II. There is an order issued by His Majesty today, commanding that the books of John Milton be collected and burnt by the public hangman.

(the two men look at each
other)

Mr. Herringman, you are a publisher and bookseller. Will you turn over any copies you have of John Milton's works to be burned?

HERRINGMAN

I have seen no such order.

CIOFFI

It has been publicly read in the Exchange, sir.

DAVENANT

I think it is a mere matter of form, to satisfy Prynne and those like him.

CIOFFI

As leader so to speak of the literary men, Sir Davenant, do you think they will protest this censorship of the press and this act against John Milton whose reputation is worldwide?

DAVENANT

I think not, sir. Most of these writers are turncoats. Having praised Cromwell to the skies and taken his money, they have now wheeled about and spat on the Protector while honey drips from their lips in praise of the king. Such men, sir, are not likely to risk their necks or fortunes in defense of principle.

As they speak a Quaker enters, a young man wearing the distinctive drab garb of that sect. He looks around and then as Herringman comes up to him . . .

HERRINGMAN

Can I aid you, sir?

ELLWOOD

I wonder if you have here any works by the poet, John Milton?

Herringman and Davenant exchange looks.

> HERRINGMAN
> We have just been informed that his work is to be burned
> publicly by the common hangman.

> ELLWOOD
> I heard the announcement in the Strand and hurried here to
> find examples of his work before they were all destroyed. I am
> a great admirer, sir, of that man and his work.

> HERRINGMAN
> Both the man and his work are now forbidden.

> ELLWOOD
> So is my faith, sir, but I have it, and so will his work exist, sir,
> whatever they say or do.

> HERRINGMAN
> (taking two books from the
> shelves)
> Here I have a copy of his tract on the liberty of the press called
> *Areopagitica* and a book of his poetry. You may have them free
> for they are only going to be burned.

> ELLWOOD
> God bless you.

He stands there and opens the book as the door flings open and two
young men come in. They are dressed in the most swashbuckling style
of the restoration, in their twenties, and very gay and laughing.

> SEDLEY
> How now, Herringman, what plots are you hatching against
> the poets.

> HERRINGMAN
> (bowing)
> Sir Charles Sedley . . . .

> SEDLEY
> I just met Dryden in the street with a face as long as Sir
> William's nose is short . . . .

He laughs.

> DAVENANT
> You are a wit, sir, and a courtier, and you call yourself a poet,
> but my nose is not apt matter for the length of your tongue.

> SEDLEY
> My pardon, sir, but we all know your nose is short and
> Dryden's face is long, for he cried out that John Milton's works
> are to be burned by the hangman, I suppose, since they cannot
> catch the blind old Roundhead.

He turns, sees Ellwood who is making for the door.

> SEDLEY (CON'T)
> S'faith, what have we here, a dogface, a drab, as sure as I am a
> man, a Quaker. Catch him, Wycherley, before he escapes.

WYCHERLEY blocks Ellwood who stands there solemnly.

> SEDLEY
> Are you a Quaker, sir?

> ELLWOOD
> I am.

> SEDLEY
> Then quake, sir, for I have heard that when you quake you see
> the Lord and I would see you quake the Lord into this shop.

> ELLWOOD
> It will be a long time, sir, before you see the Lord either here or
> in heaven.

> SEDLEY
> The Quaker has a tongue.
>   (drawing his rapier)
> We will split it for him as they do ravens and teach him to
> speak more sweetly to his betters.

Sedley slices at Ellwood and cuts his hat from his head.

SEDLEY (CON'T)
See, he doffs his Quaker hat and learns at once the first step in gentility. Down, sir, to the knee.

Wycherley pushes from behind, forcing Ellwood down.

SEDLEY (CON'T)
We will teach you, sir, to pray correctly in the true religion of His Majesty and the times.
(grabbing the books from
Ellwood's hands)
What holy text do we have here . . . . Milton . . . . Milton on liberty . . . and Milton on this and that. Do not you know, sir, that to read Milton is to insult His Majesty. You would insult our king and yours?

ELLWOOD
My King is in heaven.

SEDLEY
(putting the point to his
breast)
Then off you go to join him . . . .

DAVENANT
(springing forward)
Sedley, you're mad. You will kill the man.

SEDLEY
(ignoring Davenant)
Then recant, Quaker . . . recant . . . what is your name?

ELLWOOD
Thomas Ellwood.

SEDLEY
Ellwood, thou art an ell from hell. Would you go there?

HERRINGMAN
Sir Charles, I beseech you.

DAVENANT
Pray, Sir Charles . . .

SEDLEY

All beg but this beggar on his knees. Recant, Quaker.

ELLWOOD

If I say the truth is no truth, it is still the truth. And if every
man say it is no truth, it remains a truth. And if every man is
killed who declares the truth, then the man born will see it, so
why should I recant?

SEDLEY
(laughing)

To save your life!

Ellwood seizes the books as Sedley moves back.

ELLWOOD

Would you kill me, Sedley?

SEDLEY

No, I would see you quake, Quaker.

ELLWOOD

I cannot quake, for we Quakers cannot be destroyed. We can
meet in ruins, together or alone, for the truth is in our hearts.
And there no man can get even though he kill us. So what
would you do?

He leaves the shop.

DAVENANT

I do not like this order against Milton's books. It is a step
against his life.

All start to leave.

CIOFFI

We take you now to Ned Calmer for a special report. Come in,
Ned Calmer.

INT. BARTHOLOMEW CLOSE

An old row of tenements. Somewhere an arch in the background. The
whole, dingy and ramshackle.

CALMER

This is Ned Calmer here, and it looks like we may have an opportunity to see John Milton who has been hiding these past three months to escape arrest for treason.

A corridor.

[CALMER (CON'T)

We're in a corridor of an old tenement in Bartholomew Close, here in London. Many years ago, Dr. Caius, founder of Caius College, Cambridge, lived here, and it was somewhere in this warren of tiny rooms that Hubert Le Soeur modeled the statue of Charles I which was recently set up in Charing Cross.]

A young boy appears about the corner of the turn in the corridor. He is small, unkempt. He beckons. The camera slowly follows, takes the turn, and faces a door. The boy knocks and then turns and runs. The door is opened by a stalwart young man. He smiles into the camera and holds the door wide. Camera into a room. The door closes behind and we find ourselves in a poverty stricken chamber where Andrew Marvell waits and another young man armed with a musket.

MARVELL
(into camera)

Sir, I suggest you keep your talk short, for we must move Mr. Milton elsewhere to safer quarters.
(nodding to the lad with the
musket ironically)
You will excuse the martial air, sir, but these followers of the New Model Army have not yet forgot their ancient habits.

DR. PAGET comes out of an inner room.

PAGET

Nor you, Mr. Marvell, your skill to dissemble.

MARVELL

This is Dr. Paget, Mr. Milton's friend and physician. I am, as you know, Andrew Marvell, and these lads are Ned and Tom. This way, sir.

He opens the door to the inner room. It is darkened, the one window curtained. On the table a lamp burns in the midst of dozens of books large and small, and a pile of manuscript, a quill and ink, etc. Milton sits there in the light, his eyes closed, or when they are open, stare sightlessly.

MARVELL (CON'T)
Mr. Milton has been at work, at his great work, I may say, dictating to Ned.

CALMER
I would like to ask you a few questions, sir.

MILTON
I have a few lines to finish that run in my head, if I may. Ned? Where are you, Ned?

NED
Here, sir.

He sits down at the table

MILTON
Where were we?

They all cluster around the table, listening intently, while the blind man thinks out his work and goes on.

NED
(matter of factly)
. . . thus with the year
Seasons return . . .

[MILTON
(throwing back his head
and staring sightlessly to
the ceiling)
To go back a line or two, was it, indeed . . . the bird . . . I said:
. . . as the wakeful bird
Sings darkling . . .

He pauses.

NED
(continues for him)
. . . and, in shadiest covert hit,
Tunes her nocturnal note. Thus with the year
Seasons return . . .]

MILTON
(taking it up)
Seasons return; but not to me returns
Day, or the sweet approach of even or morn,
Or sight of vernal bloom, or summer's rose,
Or flocks, or herds, or human face divine:
                    (the listeners exchange
                    glances as the meaning
                    touches them deeply)
But cloud instead and ever-during dark
Surrounds me, from the cheerful ways of men
Cut off, and, for the book of knowledge fair,
Presented with a universal blank
Of nature's works, to me expunged and razed,
And wisdom at one entrance quite shut out.
So much the rather thou, Celestial light,
Shine inward, and the mind through all her powers
Irradiate; there plant eyes; all mist from thence
Purge and disperge, that I may see and tell
Of things invisible to mortal sight . . . .

He pauses. They all wait in silence.

MILTON (CON'T)
(softly)
God willing . . . .
                    (he rises)
Thank you, Ned. And sir, your questions. Do we have time,
Andrew?

MARVELL
Hardly, but your opinions should be heard. Before you are
hid.

While speaking one of the young men will be dressing Milton in the
clothes of an artisan or workman.

CALMER

What is your opinion, sir, of the restoration of Charles II to the throne?

MILTON

Being exiled in my own country and a fugitive from his officers, I cannot have a very high opinion.
(interrupts himself)
In what disguise will I be taken through the streets?

NED

A workman, sir, an artisan of jewels and silver.

MILTON

I must speak then of opals and rubies instead of the stocks and stones that are in my heart.
(facing the camera vaguely)
Truly, sir, we are drowned here in England in a second flood. How foolish men are to expect the son of Charles to be a different king than the father of Charles.

CALMER

Most people say that the present restoration is an improvement on the Commonwealth.

MILTON

These same optimists will be forced to fight over again all we have fought, and spend over again all we have spent when the novelty is over and they realize the depth of the depravity fallen on them, which they share, sir, which they share.

CALMER

The king has been welcomed back into England.

MILTON

Because men are weary of the task of liberty. Let us have it as it was, they cry out. Let us worship the golden calf and forget the pure image of God. They flinch from the labors, and run full stream and willfully into the old bondage, making vain and viler than dirt the blood of so many thousand faithful and valiant Englishmen who left us this liberty bought with their lives.

CALMER

Do you think Parliament will put your name of the final list of regicides?

MILTON

So it seems.

MARVELL

They may not, sir, for we have used much influence to keep it off, and were it not for William Prynne I would vouch for your clemency.

MILTON
(with a smile)
Poor Prynne. He could not have the best of his argument with me, so he wants my head.

CALMER

How do you explain the actions of this present parliament?

MILTON

It seems odd, does it not, that a body of men, a free government, should call King Stork back into the pond to rule them? How strange it is, sir, how passing strange, that this parliament which owes its freedom and power to the very men it hunts and kills, forgets that its independence was won by those it condemns. Men do not easily learn from history, but must, like sad dogs, be beaten more than once to learn the simplest rule of liberty.

CALMER

What is that rule, sir?

MILTON

Not to forsake it.

CALMER

You think you would be pardoned if you came forward and asked for it?

NED
(astonished)
You ask him to recant?

MILTON
(taking his arm affectionately)
Quiet, Ned. What pardon, sir . . . that I have seen the truth and
uttered it? For this I need no pardon.

PAGET
It might preserve your liberty and life and enable you by the
mere words of yielding to finish this great work.

He holds up the manuscript.

MILTON
Dear Dr. Paget, what is my work? Why, my life is my work,
and what I write merely the form my life takes. I will finish
this work, for I have here in my darkness and this black hour,
friends like summer suns, both young and old, and they will
guard and guide me so long as they have strength. If they fail,
I fail, and we fail together, and that, sir, is our victory—that we
did not separate and flee, each to die or survive alone.

CALMER
Have you been told of the king's order today for your books to
be burned by the common hangman?

MILTON
It is another deception of tyrants that they can destroy the
truth they dislike by burning books, but each book they burn
makes the others more precious, more deeply read. Even in
the Commonwealth, this disease of censorship raised its head
and I opposed it in a work you may know of—*The Areopagitica*.

MARVELL
But John, governments must protect themselves from attack,
and attack by books is still attack, even as the Commonwealth
knew and practiced.

MILTON
And was wrong, doubly wrong. It is wrong for books to be
censored and banned, and it is doubly wrong for a free nation
to practice it. When a king forbids books and free thought, it is
his nature; but when a free government does so, that teaches
men to hate such governments as if they were hating tyrants.
(MORE)

MILTON (CON'T)
The great issue of our time is liberty, of conscience, of thought, of worship, of action. Tell me, any of you, do you know of one honest government that has fallen because its people were free to write, to speak, to think, to worship as their consciences bade them?

PAGET
I am a doctor, your physician, and well I know that there are good drugs and evil ones. Should I not forbid the evil ones to come into the hands of men? So there are good books and evil ones, and some books can poison men's minds as bad drugs poison their bodies.

MILTON
That is often said. But books are as meat and viands are —some of good and some of evil substance. [Yet God in his unapocryphal vision said, without exception, "Rise, Peter, kill and eat."] I cannot praise a fugitive and cloistered virtue, unexercised and unbreathed, that never sallies out to see her adversary.

NED
But what of the effect of evil books on the minds of the innocent who are not trained to perceive the difference between good and evil?

MILTON
(smiling)
Say on you, Ned, is that what you mean? But assuredly, we bring not innocence into the world, we bring impurity much rather. That which purifies our natures is trial, and trial is by what is contrary. Only after a lifetime of struggle, of making the choice, doth a man live to die in innocence and virtue. What the censors call innocence is rather ignorance, and it is the ignorance of the young they would cherish rather than their innocence.

NED
I am not so innocent as that.

MILTON
Nor so ignorant.

By this time they have moved into the other room.

TOM
The carriage is here, below and ready.

MILTON
We will come . . . .
                      (holding their attention with
                      uplifted hand)
Who kills a man kills a reasonable creature, God's image; but
he who destroys a good book kills reason itself, kills the image
of God as it were in the eye. Many a man lives a burden to the
earth, but a good book is the precious lifeblood of a master
spirit embalmed and treasured upon a purpose to a life
beyond life.

MARVELL
But if books lead to sects and controversy and quarrels and
positions hostile to the government?

MILTON
The more freedom should be granted, because it is more
freedom that cures evils rather than less freedom. Where there
is much desire to learn, there of necessity will be much
arguing, much writing, many opinions . . . for opinion in good
men is but knowledge in the making. What is the best treasure
of old age? . . . The honest liberty of free speech in our youth.

PAGET
Well, sir, your love of free speech in your youth is bringing
you to prison and perhaps death in your middle age.

MILTON
That is perhaps true. Here I live in eternal darkness, blacker
than any hours I have ever known in sleep, and Ned tells me
that the room I hide in, even with eyes to see, is dark and small
and narrow . . . .

He walks around as he speaks, feeling the walls as a blind man will.

MILTON (CON'T)

I can feel the walls, the cracks therein, the dirt of this tenement.
I can measure the ambit of my life with these walls and it is
small. Here I never feel the sun for I must not be in the
daylight for fear of the government and its spies. Thus I sit in
my darkness and listen—and outside I hear the shouts of the
people as they welcome tyranny in the name of the new
freedom. I hear their shouts as they sing and dance to the new
king, and I ask, "who is in darkness?" I, who stand here in my
darkness, or they in their sight who see not the evil they
welcome? Yes, here I sit and meditate the hours recalling with
my mind's eye those lovely flowers I have known . . . and
known and loved . . . so many . . .

His voice dies away for a moment in memory and Marvell murmurs
softly.

MARVELL

Throw hither all your quaint enameled eyes,
That on the green turf suck the honeyed showers,
And purple all the ground with vernal flowers.

Milton begins to smile in memory and keeps the cadence as his friend
goes on.

MILTON
(taking it on)

Bring the rathe primrose that forsaken dies,
The tufted crow-tow, the pale jessamine,
The white pink, and the pansy freaked with jet,
The glowing violet,
The musk-rose, and the well attired woodbine . . .
With cowslips wan that hang the pensive head,
And every flower that sad embroidery wears . . .

I wrote those verses so many years ago—almost gone beyond
recalling . . . but now I think I see more richly the true flowers
that adorn our mortal lives, the flowers of the human spirit,
the flowers of life, the flower of reason, of thought, of love, and
that greatest blossom and crowning wreathe upon the head of
(MORE)

MILTON (CON'T)
man, the love of liberty. Tell me, sir, who is more blind, I in
my darkness of these stricken eyes, or they in the blindness of
their souls?

Outside there are shouts and calls. All listen.

NED
I think we had best go now whilst the crowd is in the streets
. . . and we can pass in the multitude.

He takes Milton's arm. The others gather around.

MARVELL
You go first, Tom, and see if the way is clear for us.

Tom goes. They all start out. The camera begins to follow, but Ned
stands across the door , blocking it.

NED
There is no need to see him leave, for his life depends on his
secrecy.

The others are gone. Ned stands there, young, strong, blocking the door.

INT. CBS STUDIOS

CRONKITE
And so John Milton was led off, changing his place of hiding
again and again, until the day came when his friends told him
it was safe to come out.

Nevertheless, he was arrested, spent some time in prison and
was finally released to create, in the years that followed, the
greatest epic poem in our language, *Paradise Lost* . . . .

John Milton in his blindness saw better than many with their
eyes, for the English people and their Parliament were both
stripped of liberty by the new king, and twenty-eight years
later had once again to revolt for their rights. But Milton
himself never swerved from the great task which he had
(MORE)

CRONKITE (CON'T)
chosen for himself, to justify the ways of God to man, and so
he did—proving by his works, his conscience and his conduct
the maxim of Aristotle, that "the good life is thought in action."

What sort of a day was it? A day like all days, filled with those
events that alter and illuminate our time . . . and YOU WERE
THERE.

FADE OUT.

APPENDIX I

Danger: The Blacklisted Writers and Their Fronts

Danger was a CBS network television series (1950-1954) whose narrative strategy was designed to focus on individuals at moments of physical or psychological jeopardy. The producer was Charles W. Russell, and most of the episodes were directed by Sidney Lumet. It was on this series that Russell gave the Walter Bernstein-Arnold Manoff-Abraham Polonsky trio their first jobs during the blacklist. Manoff and Polonsky entered the series, having already been blacklisted, by virtue of their friendship with Bernstein who provided the contact to Russell. It is interesting to note that Bernstein, who was a regular writer of *Danger* teleplays under his own name, became unemployable when he signed his name to a statement in *The New York Times* protesting the blacklist. Thus, on "The Paper Box Kid" (air date: 3 July 1951) Bernstein's real name appears as writer in the credits; but five weeks later, on "Goodbye Hannah" (air date: 7 August 1951), the nom de guerre, "Paul Bauman" (a name picked at random from the telephone book), is required to front Bernstein's authorship of the script.

The following *Danger* credit attributions are based on producer Charles Russell's personal annotations to the script list, his manuscript "In the Worst of Times It Was the Best of Times," and interviews with Abraham Polonsky (6 August 1992, 15 July 1989). [Housed in the Abraham Polonsky Collection, California State University, Northridge.]

Title /Air Date	Author	Front
"Goodbye Hannah" —7 Aug 51	Walter Bernstein	"Paul Bauman"
"Madman of Middletown" —28 Aug 51	Walter Bernstein	"Paul Bauman"
"Death Among the Relics" —4 Sep 51	Walter Bernstein	"Paul Bauman"
"Love Comes to Miss Lucy" —25 Sep 51	Walter Bernstein	"Paul Bauman"
"Deadline" —30 Oct 51	Walter Bernstein	"Paul Bauman"
"Deathbeat" —13 Nov 51	Walter Bernstein	"Elliot West"
"High Wire: High Steel" —6 Nov 51	Walter Bernstein	"Paul Bauman"
"The Killer Instinct" —20 Nov 51	Walter Bernstein	"Paul Bauman"
"The Friend Who Killed" —27 Nov 51	Arnold Manoff	"Joel Carpenter"

Title /Air Date	Author	Front
"The Face of Fear" —11 Dec 51	Abraham Polonsky	"George Marrow"
"Passage for Christman" —25 Dec 51	Walter Bernstein	"Paul Bauman"
"Prelude to Death" —5 Feb 52	Abraham Polonsky	"George Marrow"
"Hands of the Enemy" —12 Feb 52	Walter Bernstein	"Paul Bauman"
"Primary Decision" —9 Feb 52	Arnold Manoff	"Joel Carpenter"
"Benefit Performance" —4 Mar 52	Abraham Polonsky	"George Marrow"
"Border Incident" —29 Apr 52	Abraham Polonsky	"George Marrow"
"Dark As Night" —6 May 52	Arnold Manoff	"Joel Carpenter"
"The Double Deal" —1 Jul 52	Arnold Manoff	"Joel Carpenter"
"Date at Midnight" —29 Jul 52	Abraham Polonsky	"George Marrow"
"Murder Takes the 'A' Train" —5 Aug 52	Walter Bernstein	"Leo Davis"
"Flowers of Death" —12 Aug 52	Arnold Manoff	"Joel Carpenter"
"Death Signs An Autograph" —16 Sep 52	Walter Bernstein	"Eliot Asinof"
"A Thread of Scarlet" —7 Oct 52	Abraham Polonsky	"George Marrow"
"A Shawl for Sylvia" —13 Jan 53	Arnold Manoff	"Kate Nickerson"
"The Second Cup" —10 Feb 53	Arnold Manoff	"Kate Nickerson"
"Carpool" —24 Mar 53	Abraham Polonsky	"Jeremy Daniel"

Title /Air Date	Author	Front
"Sing For Your Life" —28 Apr 53	Arnold Manoff	"Kate Nickerson"
"Subpoena" —26 May 53	Abraham Polonsky	"Jeremy Daniel"
"Prodigal Returns" —14 Jul 53	Abraham Polonsky	"Jeremy Daniel"
"Sudden Shock" —12 Jan 54	Arnold Manoff	"Kate Nickerson"
"Return to Fear" —19 Jan 54	Abraham Polonsky	"Jeremy Daniel"

APPENDIX II

You Are There:
The Blacklisted Writers and Their Fronts

The following is a listing of writer attributions for those specific episodes of *You Are There* which can be verified by producer Charles Russell's script records and annotations. There are several titles from the complete series (which circumstantial evidence suggests may have been authored by the blacklisted trio) for which documentation is sketchy or non-existent, and these have *not* been included.

Title /Air Date	Author	Front
"The Landing of the Hindenburg" —1 Feb 53	Abraham Polonsky	"Jeremy Daniel"
"The Death of Jesse James" —8 Feb 53	Walter Bernstein	"Leslie Slote"
"The Capture of John Dillinger" —22 Feb 53	Walter Bernstein	"Leslie Slote"
"The Execution of Joan of Arc" —1 Mar 53	Abraham Polonsky	"Jeremy Daniel"
"The Hamilton-Burr Duel" —15 Mar 53	Walter Bernstein	"Leslie Slote"
"The Discovery of Anesthesia" —22 Mar 53	Arnold Manoff	"Kate Nickerson"
"The Witch Trial at Salem" —29 Mar 53	Arnold Manoff	"Kate Nickerson"
"The Conquest of Mexico by Cortes" —5 Apr 53	Abraham Polonsky	"Jeremy Daniel"
"The Impeachment of Andrew Johnson" —12 Apr 53	Walter Bernstein	"Leslie Slote"
"The Crisis of Galileo" —19 Apr 53	Abraham Polonsky	"Jeremy Daniel"
"The Death of Socrates" —3 May 53	Arnold Manoff	"Kate Nickerson"

Title /Air Date	Author	Front
"The Dreyfus Case" —31 May 53	Walter Bernstein	"Leslie Slote"
"The Signing of the Magna Carta" —7 Jun 53	Abraham Polonsky	"Jeremy Daniel"
"The Flight of Rudolph Hess" —14 Jun 53	Abraham Polonsky	"Jeremy Daniel"
"The Treason of Benedict Arnold" —21 Jun 53	Arnold Manoff	"Kate Nickerson"
"The Fate of Nathan Hale" —30 Aug 53	Abraham Polonsky	"Jeremy Daniel"
"The Capture of John Wilkes Booth" —6 Sep 53	Walter Bernstein	"Leslie Slote"
"The Louisiana Purchase" —13 Sep 53	Arnold Manoff	"Kate Nickerson"
"The Birth of a National Anthem" —27 Sep 53	Arnold Manoff	"Kate Nickerson"
"The Secret of Sigmund Freud" —4 Oct 53	Abraham Polonsky	"Jeremy Daniel"
"The Death of Cleopatra" —18 Oct 53	Walter Bernstein	"Leslie Slote"
"Grant and Lee at Appomattox" —1 Nov 53	Walter Bernstein	"Leslie Slote"
"The Recognition of Michelangelo" —15 Nov 53	Abraham Polonsky	"Jeremy Daniel"
"The Sailing of the Mayflower" —22 Nov 53	Arnold Manoff	"Kate Nickerson"
"The Gettysburg Address" —29 Nov 53	Walter Bernstein	"Leslie Slote"
"The Crisis at Valley Forge" —6 Dec 53	Abraham Polonsky	"Jeremy Daniel"

Title /Air Date	Author	Front
"The Vindication of Savonarola" —13 Dec 53	Abraham Polonsky	"Jeremy Daniel"
"The Fall of Troy" —20 Dec 53	Walter Bernstein	"Leslie Slote"
"Mallory's Tragedy on Mt. Everest" —3 Jan 54	Abraham Polonsky	"Jeremy Daniel"
"The Resolve of Patrick Henry" —17 Jan 54	Arnold Manoff	"Kate Nickerson"
"The Last Moment of Marie Antoinette" —31 Jan 54	Arnold Manoff	"Kate Nickerson"
"The Ordeal of Tom Paine" —7 Feb 54	Arnold Manoff	"Kate Nickerson"
"The First Command Performance of Romeo and Juliet" —21 Feb 54	Abraham Polonsky	"Jeremy Daniel"
"The Trial of John Peter Zenger" —7 Mar 54	Arnold Manoff	"Kate Nickerson"
"The Surrender of Burgoyne at Saratoga" —21 Mar 54	Abraham Polonsky	"Jeremy Daniel"
"The Conspiracy of Catherine the Great" —28 Mar 54	Arnold Manoff	"Kate Nickerson"
"The Death of Rasputin" —2 May 54	Walter Bernstein	"Alex Furth"
"The Court-Martial of Mata Hari" —9 May 54	Arnold Manoff	"Kate Nickerson"
"The Scopes Trial" —16 May 54	Abraham Polonsky	"Jeremy Daniel"
"The Decision of Robert E. Lee" —6 Jun 54	Walter Bernstein	"Leslie Slote"

Title /Air Date	Author	Front
"The Vote That Made Jefferson President" —27 Jun 54	Walter Bernstein	"Leslie Slote"
"The Emergence of Jazz" —5 Sep 54	Abraham Polonsky	"Jeremy Daniel"
"The Return of Ulysses" —26 Sep 54	Abraham Polonsky	"Jeremy Daniel"
"The Great Adventure of Marco Polo" —10 Oct 54	Abraham Polonsky	"Jeremy Daniel"
"The Burning of Rome" —24 Oct 54	Arnold Manoff	"Kate Nickerson"
"Lafitte and Jackson at New Orleans" —19 Dec 54	Walter Bernstein	"Howard Rodman"
"The Passage of the Bill of Rights" —26 Dec 54	Arnold Manoff	"Kate Nickerson"
"The Torment of Beethoven" —2 Jan 55	Abraham Polonsky	"Leo Davis"
"The First Flight of the Wright Brothers" —16 Jan 55	Abraham Polonsky	"Dunn Barrie"
"The Trial of Susan B. Anthony" —23 Jan 55	Arnold Manoff	"Kate Nickerson"
"The Tragedy of John Milton" —30 Jan 55	Abraham Polonsky	"Jeremy Daniel"
"The Tragic Hour of Dr. Semmelweis" —13 Feb 55	Walter Bernstein	"Howard Rodman"
"The Liberation of Paris" —20 Feb 55	Abraham Polonsky	"Leo Davis"
"The Hatfield-McCoy Feud" —20 Mar 55	Abraham Polonsky	"Jeremy Daniel"
"The Triumph of Alexander the Great" —27 Mar 55	Abraham Polonsky	"Jeremy Daniel"

APPENDIX III

Tales from the Blacklist

The following anecdotes, taken from Charles Russell's memoir, "In the Worst of Times It Was the Best of Times," seem to possess the heady mixture of ego, arrogance, irony, and human frailty so characteristic of the blacklist era.

1. Leslie Slote had been fronting for Walter Bernstein since 7 April 1953, for an episode in the old *Danger* series. After the completion of the *You Are There* episode, "The Fall of Troy" (20 December 1953), for which Slote had fronted for Bernstein, Slote called Russell at home one night and said, "Charles, I have to resign. I'm becoming too important."

So Bernstein began searching for fronts, and, as Russell writes, "even when he was at the bottom of the barrel he somehow managed to come up with someone. It was a tribute to the regard in which he was held and to his battling character. At one point he had so many fronts it was utterly confusing. I remember in 1959 when I was producing the first season of *The Untouchables*, Quinn Martin, the executive producer of the series, asked me if I knew a lady writer whose name escapes me now." [Russell is probably being protective here (in the manner of Abraham Polonsky's attitude toward his fronts) of those courageous people who risked a lot by lending their names as fronts, by not disclosing the true identity of any front unless they approve of it, or unless the name by some other process has been revealed.] "I told him I didn't know her. He said, 'She wrote this wonderful show for Susskind, *The Prince and the Pauper*. I thought it was so great I brought her out to Hollywood to write the opening show on the *Desilu Playhouse*. She wrote a terrible script. It was a dog.'

"I told him she was Walter Bernstein's front."

(Russell, "In the Worst of Times," pp. 105-106.)

2. The scripts [such as "The Abdication of Napoleon" (air date: 8 November 1953) and "William Pitt's Last Speech to Parliament" (air date: 19 September 1954)] by another blacklisted writer on the *You Are There* series, Saul Levitt, were fronted by a man named Maury Stern. Russell writes: "I had met Maury Stern several times through Saul but that was the extent of our relationship. On air days of shows bearing his credit he would appear in the studio to see how 'his' baby was delivered. After a few compliments from actors on the quality of 'his' script he would expand with a sense of importance, offering me advice on the direction, the performances, and the production.

"After one of these exchanges Lumet called me aside and whispered, 'Is he for real or is he a front?' I indicated the latter and Sidney said, 'Whoever it is I wish him luck.' It would have been difficult to ask Stern to leave the studio because of Saul's involvement. So we had to live with another irritant, a disease of another kind.

"But 'William Pitt's Last Speech to Parliament' was to be the last script of Levitt's under Stern's name. When Saul dropped off the script, he said, 'Hey, Charlie, it looks like it's finally over. It looks like I'm going to be cleared— and that means no more Maury Stern!' He was so excited he didn't bother to explain the developments and I barely had time to tell him, 'That's great, Saul,' before he left.

"Maury Stern appeared in Studio 41 on Sunday at the usual time with his usual comments. I didn't know if Saul had advised Stern of the clearing of his name, so I treated his suggestions in the usual manner. It didn't seem as if Stern were acquainted with Saul's good fortune."

[Saul Levitt would author a future episode of the You Are There series, "D Day" (air date: 6 March 1955), and receive credit under his own name.]

FLASH FORWARD

"I received a phone call from Saul in the summer of 1965 when I was in Hollywood working on a TV series pilot called *Selena*. The call was incredible. 'Could you come back to New York for about a week,' he said, 'I need your help.'

"Saul's play, *The Andersonville Trial*, had enjoyed a successful run on Broadway. Saul and I had discussed the idea when I produced, for a brief period, *The Alcoa Theatre* TV series in 1957. It seems that Maury Stern had filed suit against Saul for all money earned on the play, since Stern claimed to be the actual author. According to Saul a sizable amount of money was involved, and Stern actually thought he had written the play! He wanted compensation.

"I agreed to testify at a preliminary hearing, and I flew to New York. Since Stern claimed he had written all of Saul's television work as well, several days were spent going over facts, dates, details, anything relevant to his defense.

"Saul, his attorney, and I stood around in a steaming hot courtroom in downtown New York waiting for Stern to appear. The hearing was to determine if and when the suit would go to trial. Three hours later the plaintiff failed to appear and the judge dismissed the case.

"Stern failed to appear at his last stand."

(Russell, "In the Worst of Times," pp. 92, 131-133.)

Sidney Lumet   Charles Russell

POSTSCRIPT

by

Abraham Polonsky

[Mr. Polonsky has dedicated this volume to Charles W. Russell. The following is a benediction that Polonsky wrote for Russell and *You Are There* that was to accompany Russell's published memoir, "In the Worst of Times It Was the Best of Times." Charles Russell died 18 January 1985.]

Charles Russell has no sense of being brave, bold, or daring as a man. What he did on television in *You Are There* was all three of these. He chose his writer friends because he thought they had been treated meanly by the government and the industry, but he found their peculiarities not political but personal. And they were.

So there in the midst of the greatest social fright since the Palmer raids, he went about the business of trying to put on the best historical series possible. He did this over the malevolent stupidity of his executive producer, the cries of censors, the watchdogs of blacklisting in CBS, and the lack of sufficient money and time. He found talent everywhere, ingenuity, intelligence among directors, actors, designers, and so on. He made it work, and millions of people watched; schools used the shows as documents in history to intrigue the young in a time when every bit of history was defiled by fear and censorship, when the great trembled before McCarthy, generals quailed, and the usual boobies among the liberals ran for cover shouting I'm no Communist.

Charlie had no politics in that sense. He believed in actual free speech, actual civil liberties, actual freedoms about which others merely conversed. But it was an atmosphere in his life, an ambiance. Mainly, he wanted to make good shows, with character as in *Danger*, with truth as in *You Are There*, and with style as in everything he did. He was driven to small perfections. He was daring enough to go with the best he could do. But mainly, now that I think back over those days, he provided, of course with us as his friends, a world of rational life in a time of hysterical nonsense, danger, and personal timidity.

Of course, we took terrible advantage of him, and in fact, against our will, seduced strangers and friends into lives that were Jekylls and Hydes. I hope they forgive us. Among all our fronts one stands out as a man who enjoyed the wild race of Who did What. Leslie Slote had no envy, he had no desire to make anything out of it for himself, he didn't do it out of pity or pride. He did it because he liked the wild world of rapids and believed in the world of political individuality and personal freedom. He was and is a brave man, charming and gifted himself.

Other people had other experiences during the blacklist, funny, sad, tragic. These we shared.

For me, despite its terrible drawbacks and what it did to my career as a screenwriter and director, it provided friendship and a chance to be heard. Arnold Manoff is dead. Saul Levitt is dead. Leo Davis is dead. But Walter Bernstein, Leslie Slote, Sidney Lumet are alive.

This is a good time for Charles Russell to remember out loud. Naturally, I don't agree with everything he remembers. I only agree with what I will never forget.